TOR

A PREHISTORIC ODYSSEY

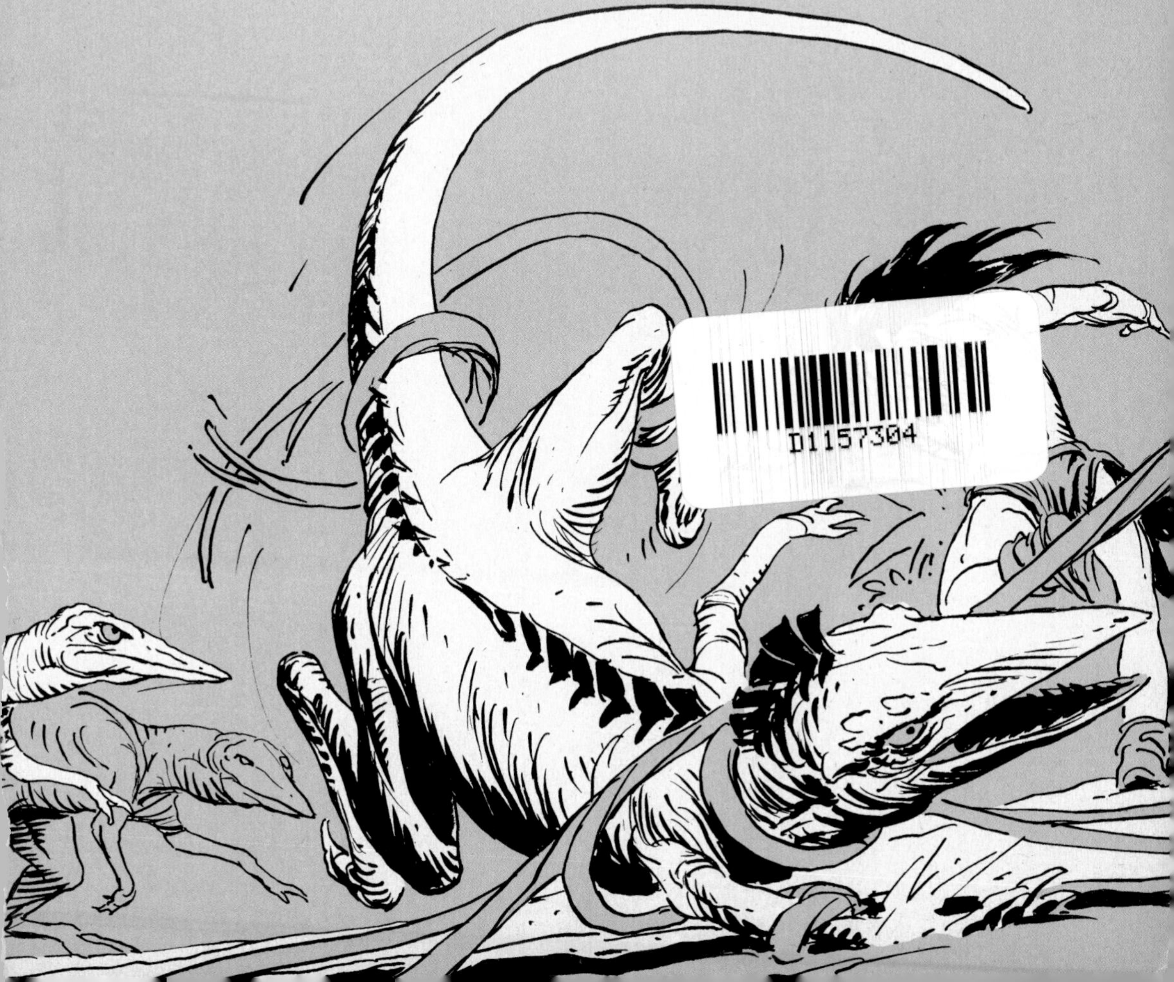

Cover art by Joe Kubert

Publication design by Amelia Grohman

TOR: A PREHISTORIC ODYSSEY

Published by DC Comics. Cover and compilation

Copyright © 2009 Tell-A-Graphics, Inc.

All Rights Reserved.

DC Comics, 1700 Broadway, New York, NY 10019

A Warner Bros. Entertainment Company

Printed in USA. First Printing.

HC ISBN 13: 978-1-4012-2148-5

SC ISBN 13: 978-1-4012-2149-2

TOR

A PREHISTORIC ODYSSEY

By Joe Kubert

Joe Kubert with Pete Carlsson: colors

Introduction by Roy Thomas

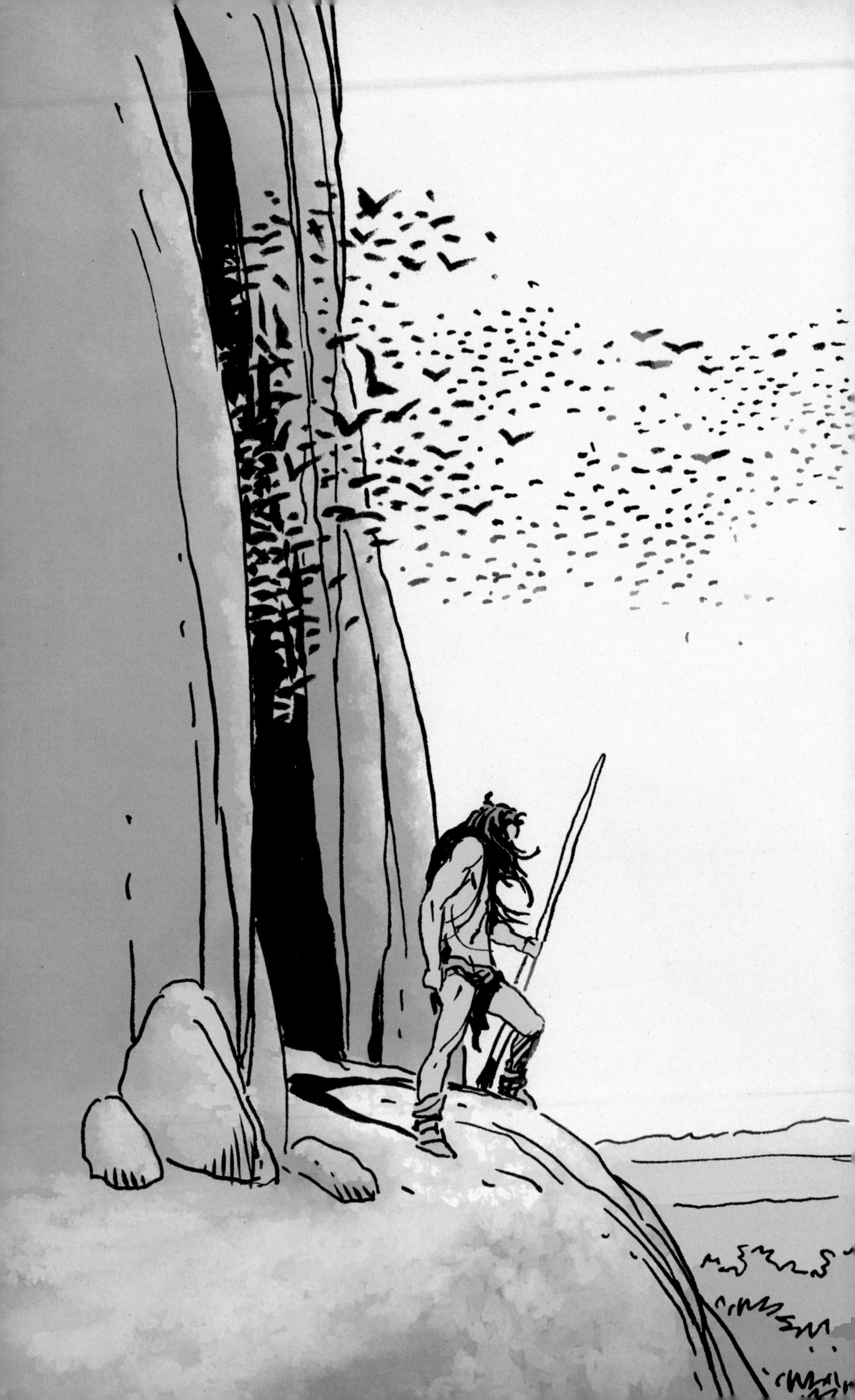

INTRODUCTION BY ROY THOMAS

ALL HIS LIFE, Joe Kubert has refused to be typecast by editors — or even by those of us, his worshipful fans, who might unconsciously want to do so.

In the early to mid-1940s he was a promising young super-hero artist, starting out on minor features at Harvey and working his way up to Hawkman and the Flash at DC. But by the end of the decade and the beginning of the next, he was forever striving to stretch himself, by taking on work in new genres such as crime, Western, horror, war — even romance.

And when 1953 came along and he got his shot at being artist *and* writer *and* editor at St. John Publishing, he virtually invented a *new* genre, so far as comic books were concerned. *Tor*, a.k.a. *One Million Years Ago*, was the only "caveman comic" in sight — although, even if there'd been others, Tor would doubtless have been the best of the lot. His dark-maned hero was noble and handsome without being a pretty-boy to the extent that most comic book super-heroes and detectives were... his dinosaurs were the equivalent of the Willis O'Brien *King Kong* species that still loomed large in America's visual landscape... *and* his stories were both potent morality tales and heady action fare. Not only that, but I'd rate his proto-monkey pal Chee Chee as one of the best of either simians or side-kicks in the history of the medium.

At the age of 12-13, I devoured each of those half dozen issues, and I was genuinely sad when I realized there would be no more.

Only there *would* be.

In the early 1970s, after nearly a decade's preparation, came the single promising issue of Joe's multi-creator publication *Sojourn*, and those of us who'd been patiently waiting got a few more pages of *Tor* to marvel at.

A couple of years later, Joe arranged for DC to reprint the '50s *Tor* material, with new covers and even one mostly-new story. Every year or so, also, a new drawing of Tor would pop up in a fanzine (like my own *Alter Ego*) or in the program book for the San Diego Comic-Con, just to keep us salivating for more.

Then, in 1993, we rejoiced when he wrote and drew a new four-issue *Tor* series — for Marvel, this time. But, following up on what had only been hinted at in the *Sojourn* material, Joe reinvented his hero — and, to a certain extent, himself — by limiting Tor's world in some ways, and enlarging it in others.

First, there was a new *realism* in the tales — and not only in Joe's art, where the romanticism of the '40s and '50s had been replaced by something a wee bit closer to nitty-gritty reality, no doubt as a result of his having drawn a zillion World War II stories during the interim. Gone was the world of the St. John stories, in which humans and dinosaurs coexisted and interacted upon an earth of "one million years ago"... an era probably several hundred thousand years too early for anthropologically certified humans, and millions of years too late for the giant saurians. Oh, there were a few oversize reptilians in evidence in '90s *Tor*, but these were obviously mere survivals — the last of their breed. From a personal standpoint, I was sorry to see the T. rexes and their scaly ilk gone down the road to extinction — and I missed Chee Chee! — but I understood, I think, Joe's viewpoint. He was no longer the same romantic young guy he'd been (or at least had seemed to us, from a distance) in the '40s and early '50s, and so his primeval world had had to come down to earth.

At the same time, Joe introduced something in last decade's *Tor* which we likewise hadn't seen in the '50s — an openness to the *fantastic*. In the St. John adventures, except for one Goliath-issue "Giant-One" just a foot or three beyond the physiologically possible in height —

and of course not counting all those anachronistic dinosaurs — there had never been any super-normal foes for Tor to battle. It had been only prehistoric beasts and primitive men — and, yes, himself — with which Tor the Hunter had had to contend.

To this was added, in '93, a new species of humankind — one with overtones of the ape with maybe just a little bit of the lizard — to give the hero something new to react to. And then there was that pair of quasi-reptiles, the female possessed of ample green mammaries, in the final of the four issues. And the huge worm-thing, that seemed to have slithered in from some heroic fantasy written by Robert E. Howard, creator of Conan the Cimmerian. Again, though, all these creatures seemed less like true rivals of mankind for eventual mastery of the world than like survivals — remnants of some vanished time — hanging on to sheer existence by fingernails or talons or slime-stickiness. By the end of the series, only the ape-men still lived, and they seemed somehow doomed to early extinction.

Cut to 2008.

For the first time, Joe creates a new *Tor* story arc for DC.

And, because he's Joe Kubert, *and* because he gets bored easily, *and* because Tor is almost certainly an axe-wielding stand-in for Joe himself and thus always needs new and untried challenges, suddenly the archetypal caveman is knee-deep in situations that go those extra few steps beyond what Joe has done before. There is another and different type of human/simian race — but this one lives amid the ruins of a higher civilization than was ever envisaged in previous incarnations of the world of "one million years ago." A towering four-armed mutation (though not called such) stalks terrifyingly out of the forest — only to begin, a few pages later, to cry. He turns out to be the protector of a group of children, each of them also "different" in his way from the primeval norm. There's even a pale, subterranean race of nearly blind humanoids — an octopoidal monstrosity that could've eaten the 1993 worm-thing for breakfast — and a Yeti.

Somehow, through it all, the (more or less) realism of the 1990s *Tor* remains — but the world of a thousand millennia ago has expanded to allow in various types of creatures and survivals in which some folks believe as fervently as scientists do in dinosaurs. The fantasies of

the early 20th century, after all, are filled with subterranean races, often the descendants of humans or near-humans who fled underground to escape their enemies and evolved further there on their own. The ape-men are an extension of the old myths about the Neanderthal — or, to go even further back, the "missing link" for which scientists have long hunted. And what is the Yeti or Abominable Snowman or Bigfoot, in the eyes of many, but some ancient species that even now refuses to die, and must surely have been around when dinosaurs (or at least mastodons) ruled the earth.

And then, as if just to remind us what caused us all to fall in love with *Tor* in the first place, ringmaster Joe snaps his whip — and in charges a pack of raptors and, a bit later, a huge carnosaur. It's not a real *Tor* series without a *few* dinosaurs, after all! You can't forget the basics.

Joe has tossed them all — dinosaurs and lost species — into a fervent mixmaster of a series, and topped it all off with a young ape-boy who is perhaps his 21st-century version of the innocent, wide-eyed Chee Chee of 1953.

Like a number of other faithful fans who've followed Joe and Tor around for more than half a century, I'm just glad to be along for the ride. Like more recent enthusiasts who were grabbed by the 1970s *Tor* reprints at DC, or only a decade and a half ago by the series published by Marvel, I revel in seeing all six 2008 issues re-presented in this hardcover volume.

But you know what? I can't wait to see what Joe dreams up *next* for his primeval hero.

The only thing I'm sure of is that, if — no, *when* — that series arrives, it'll carry Tor yet another giant step forward on his journey into both the past and future of humankind.

I'm with Joe every step of the way — except that, in closing, I do have one abject confession I just have to make:

I still miss Chee Chee!

ROY THOMAS

Roy Thomas has written and edited comic books, mostly for DC and Marvel, since 1965, and freely admits that Joe Kubert's 1950s Tor was always a powerful influence on the way he thought about Conan the Barbarian when he introduced that character into Marvel comics in the 1970s. Roy continues to script comics, and also edits the comics-history magazine Alter Ego.

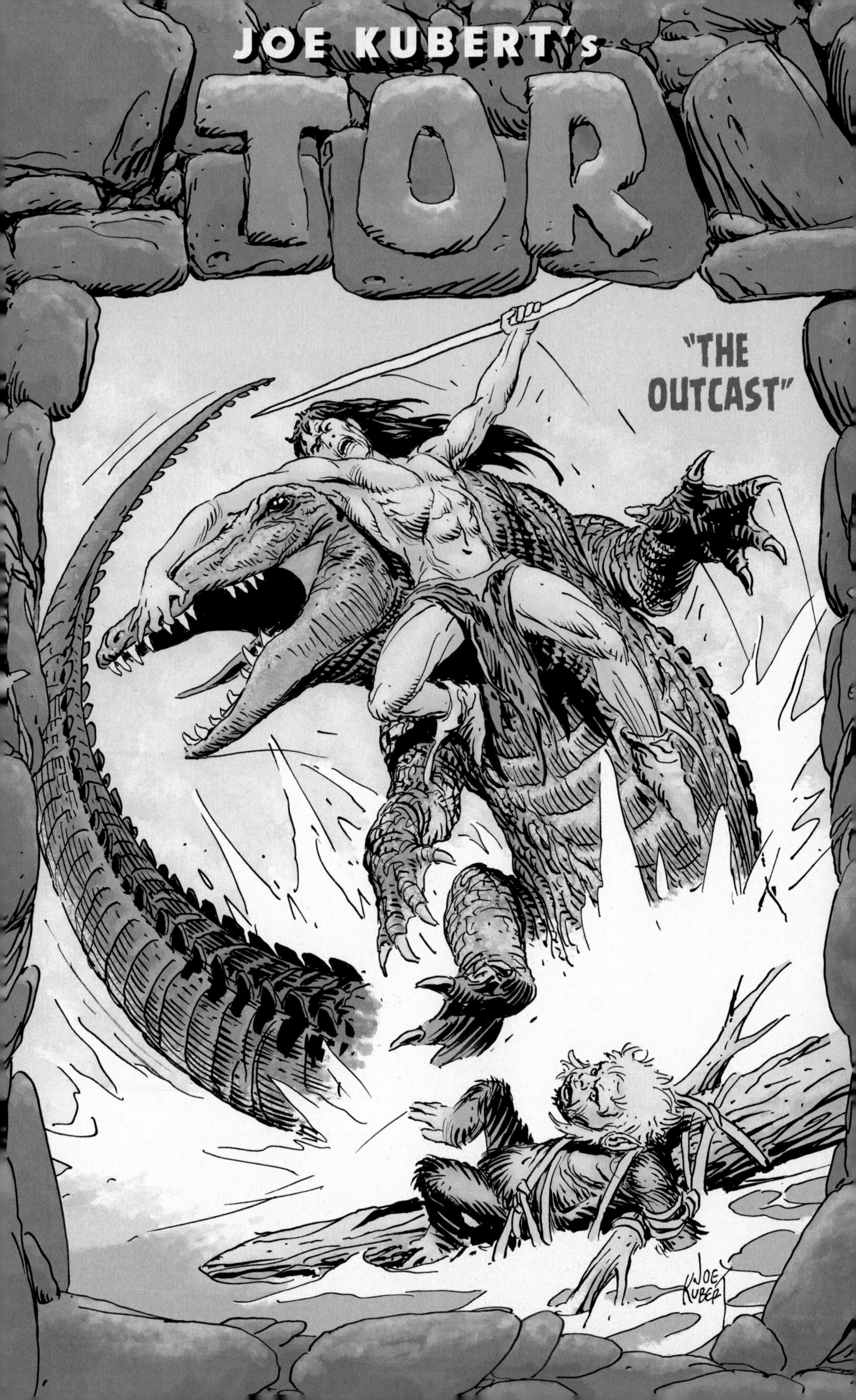
JOE KUBERT's
TOR
"THE OUTCAST"
JOE KUBERT

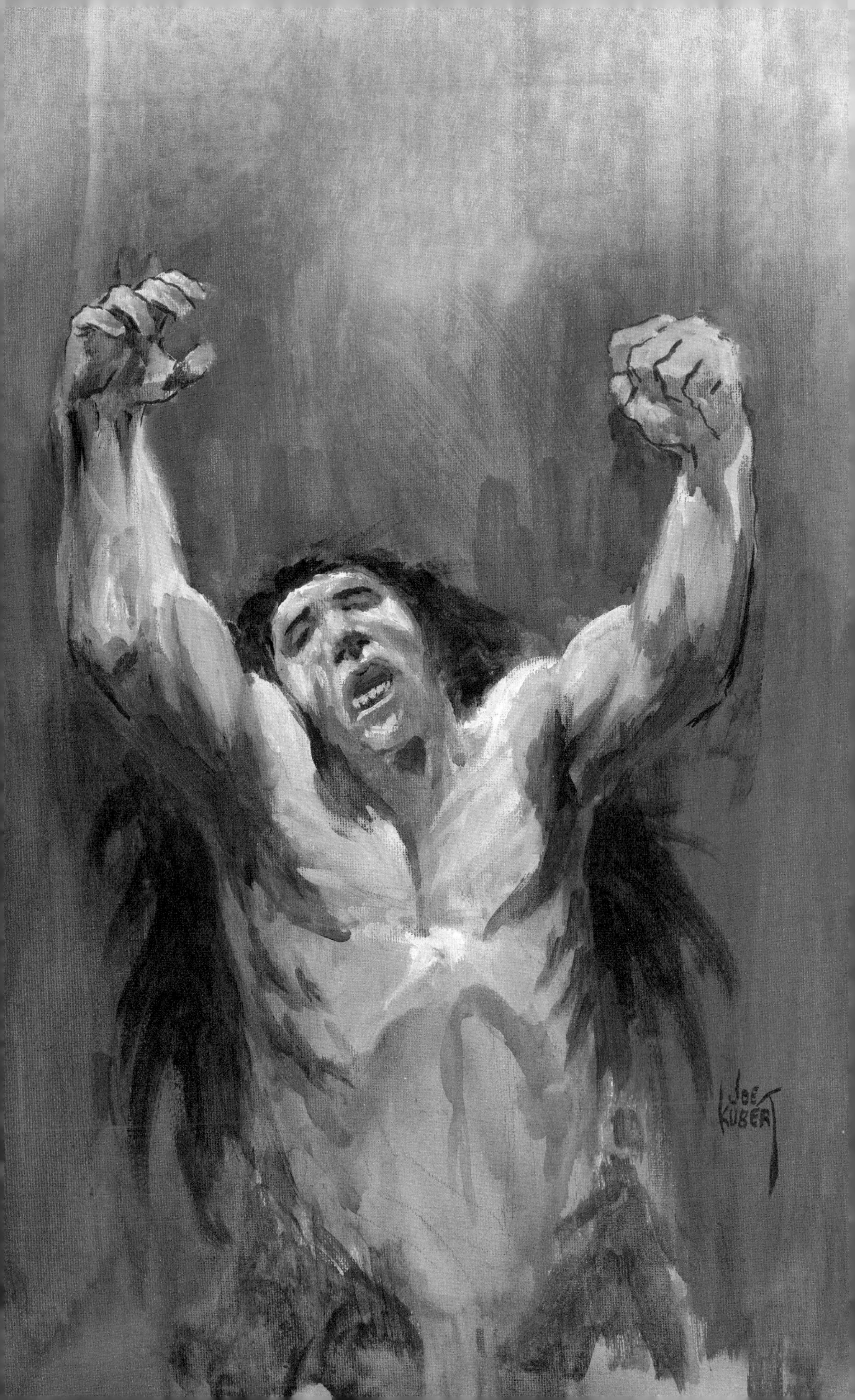
JOE KUBERT

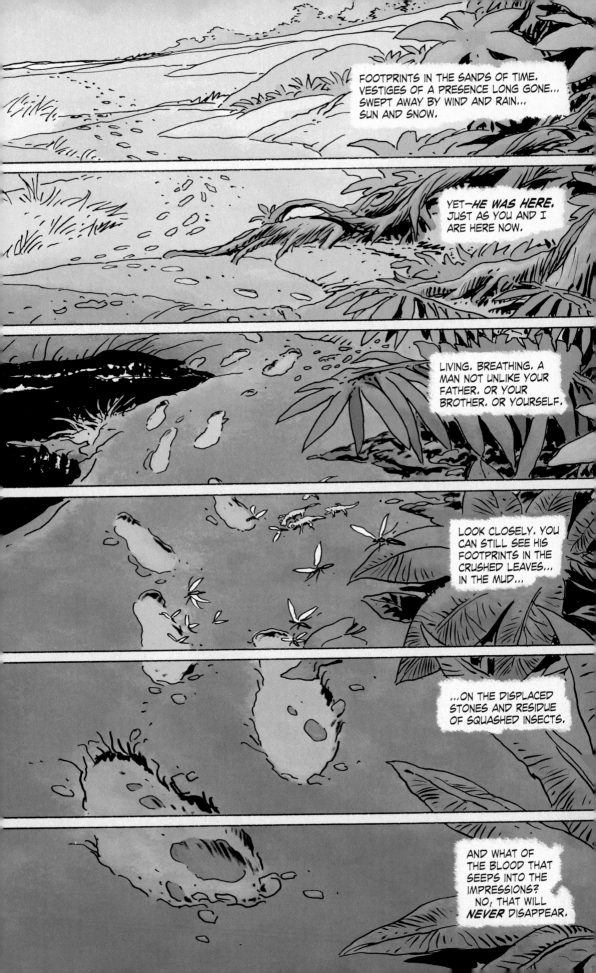

FOOTPRINTS IN THE SANDS OF TIME. VESTIGES OF A PRESENCE LONG GONE... SWEPT AWAY BY WIND AND RAIN... SUN AND SNOW.

YET—*HE WAS HERE.* JUST AS YOU AND I ARE HERE NOW.

LIVING. BREATHING. A MAN NOT UNLIKE YOUR FATHER. OR YOUR BROTHER. OR YOURSELF.

LOOK CLOSELY. YOU CAN STILL SEE HIS FOOTPRINTS IN THE CRUSHED LEAVES... IN THE MUD...

...ON THE DISPLACED STONES AND RESIDUE OF SQUASHED INSECTS.

AND WHAT OF THE BLOOD THAT SEEPS INTO THE IMPRESSIONS? NO, THAT WILL *NEVER* DISAPPEAR.

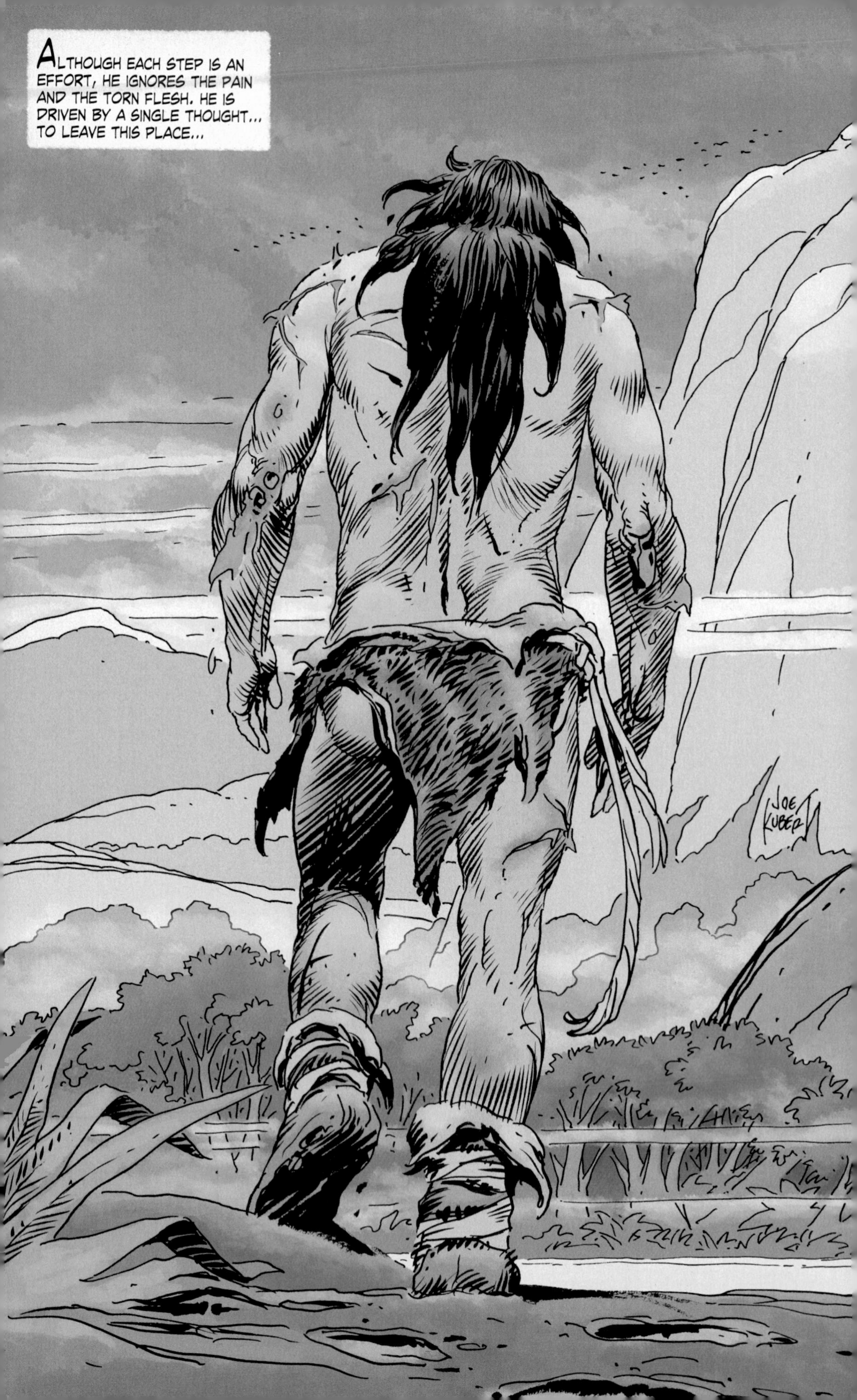
ALTHOUGH EACH STEP IS AN EFFORT, HE IGNORES THE PAIN AND THE TORN FLESH. HE IS DRIVEN BY A SINGLE THOUGHT... TO LEAVE THIS PLACE...
JOE KUBERT

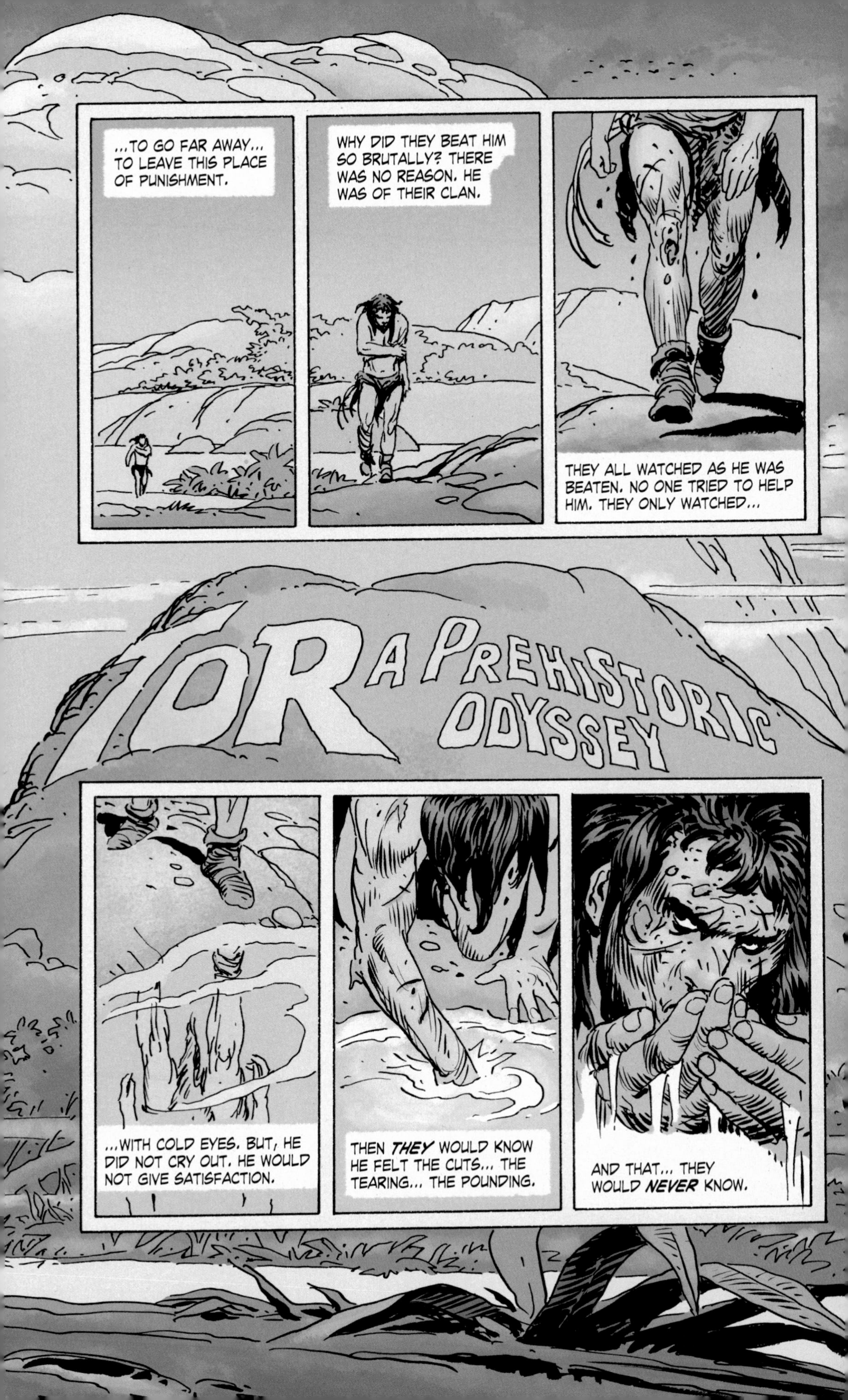
...TO GO FAR AWAY... TO LEAVE THIS PLACE OF PUNISHMENT.
WHY DID THEY BEAT HIM SO BRUTALLY? THERE WAS NO REASON. HE WAS OF THEIR CLAN.
THEY ALL WATCHED AS HE WAS BEATEN. NO ONE TRIED TO HELP HIM. THEY ONLY WATCHED...
TOR
A PREHISTORIC ODYSSEY
...WITH COLD EYES. BUT, HE DID NOT CRY OUT. HE WOULD NOT GIVE SATISFACTION.
THEN THEY WOULD KNOW HE FELT THE CUTS... THE TEARING... THE POUNDING.
AND THAT... THEY WOULD NEVER KNOW.

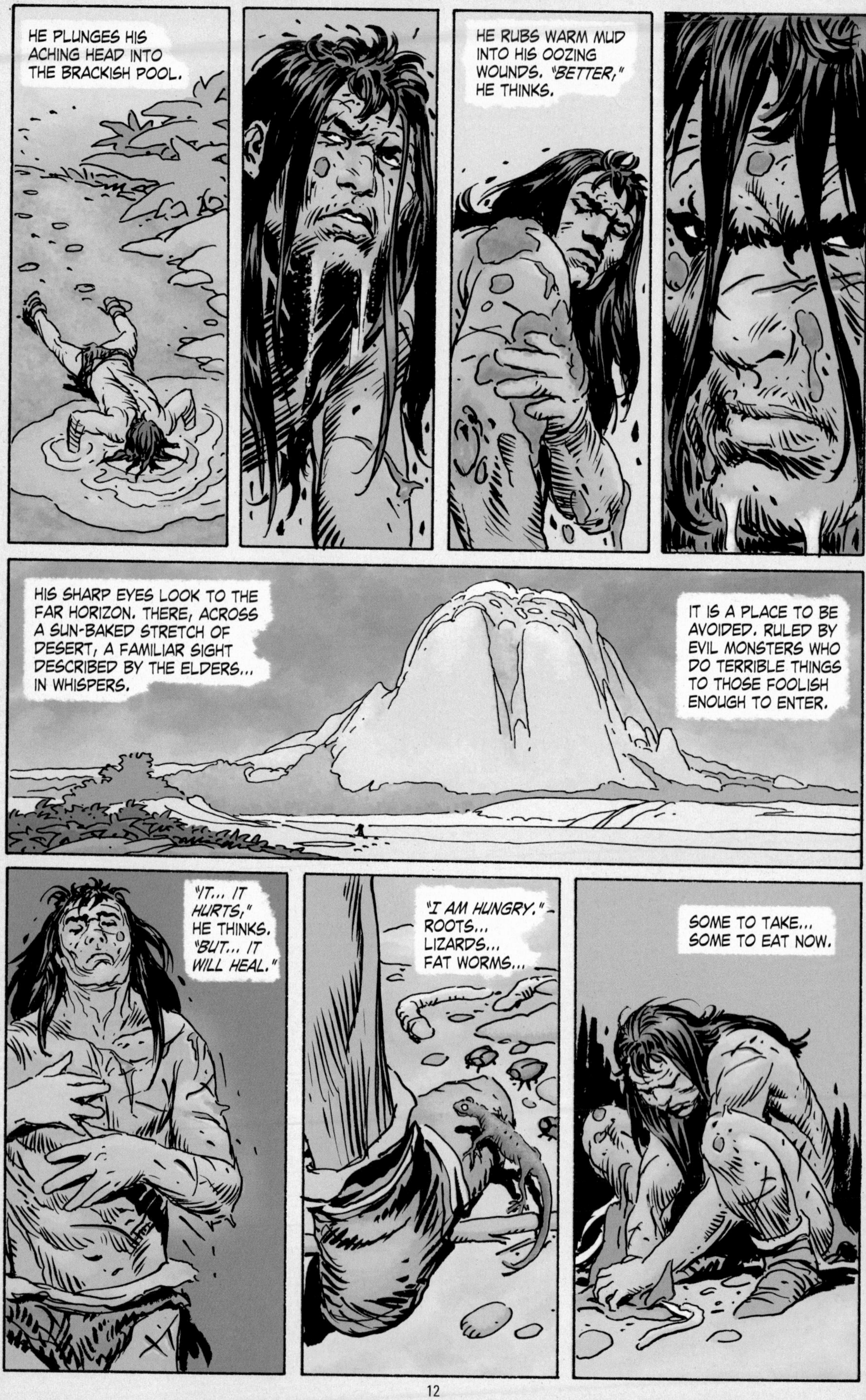
HE PLUNGES HIS ACHING HEAD INTO THE BRACKISH POOL.
HE RUBS WARM MUD INTO HIS OOZING WOUNDS. "BETTER," HE THINKS.
HIS SHARP EYES LOOK TO THE FAR HORIZON. THERE, ACROSS A SUN-BAKED STRETCH OF DESERT, A FAMILIAR SIGHT DESCRIBED BY THE ELDERS... IN WHISPERS.
IT IS A PLACE TO BE AVOIDED. RULED BY EVIL MONSTERS WHO DO TERRIBLE THINGS TO THOSE FOOLISH ENOUGH TO ENTER.
"IT... IT HURTS," HE THINKS. "BUT... IT WILL HEAL."
"I AM HUNGRY." ROOTS... LIZARDS... FAT WORMS...
SOME TO TAKE... SOME TO EAT NOW.

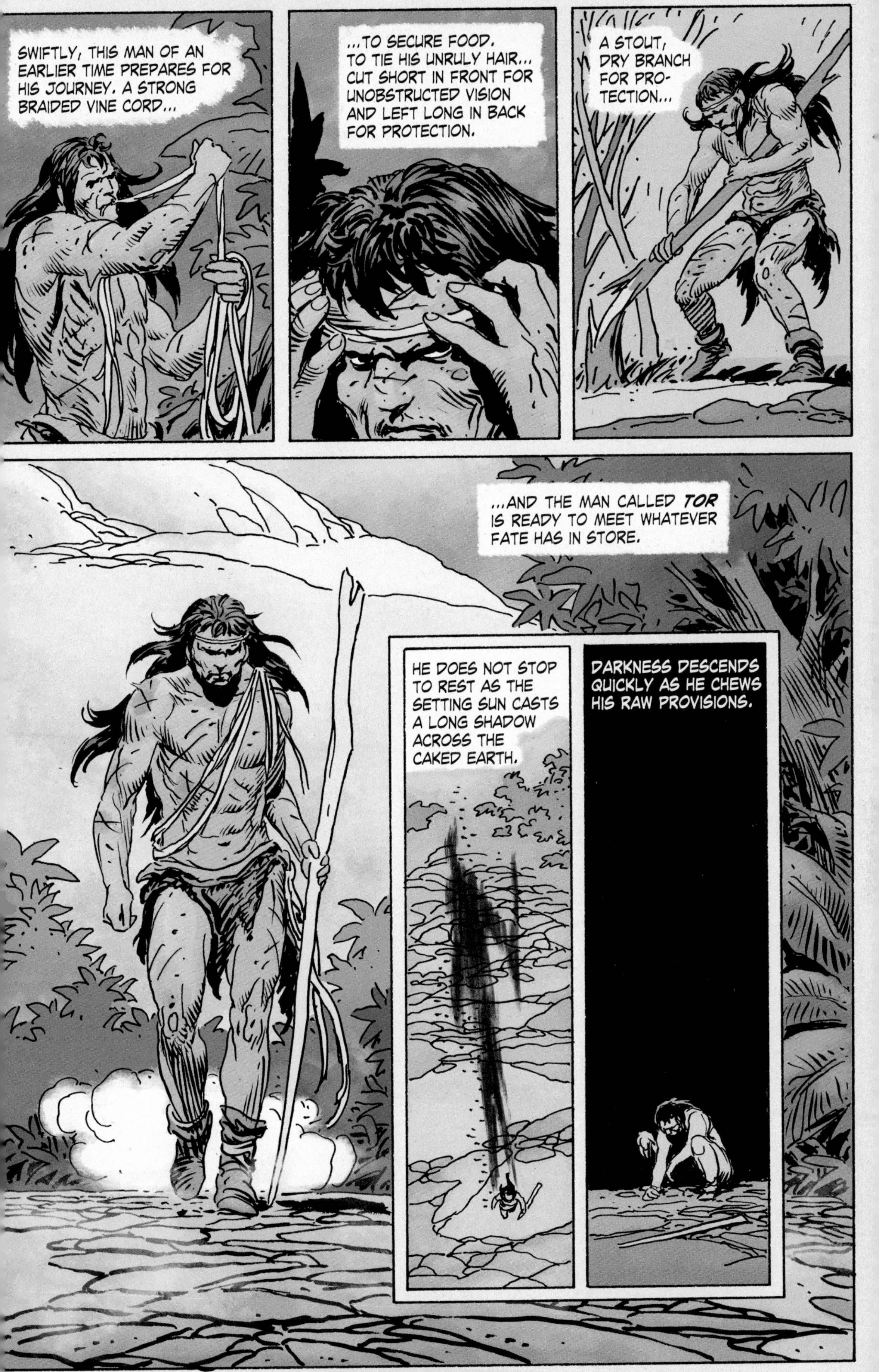
SWIFTLY, THIS MAN OF AN EARLIER TIME PREPARES FOR HIS JOURNEY. A STRONG BRAIDED VINE CORD...
...TO SECURE FOOD. TO TIE HIS UNRULY HAIR... CUT SHORT IN FRONT FOR UNOBSTRUCTED VISION AND LEFT LONG IN BACK FOR PROTECTION.
A STOUT, DRY BRANCH FOR PRO-TECTION...
...AND THE MAN CALLED TOR IS READY TO MEET WHATEVER FATE HAS IN STORE.
HE DOES NOT STOP TO REST AS THE SETTING SUN CASTS A LONG SHADOW ACROSS THE CAKED EARTH.
DARKNESS DESCENDS QUICKLY AS HE CHEWS HIS RAW PROVISIONS.

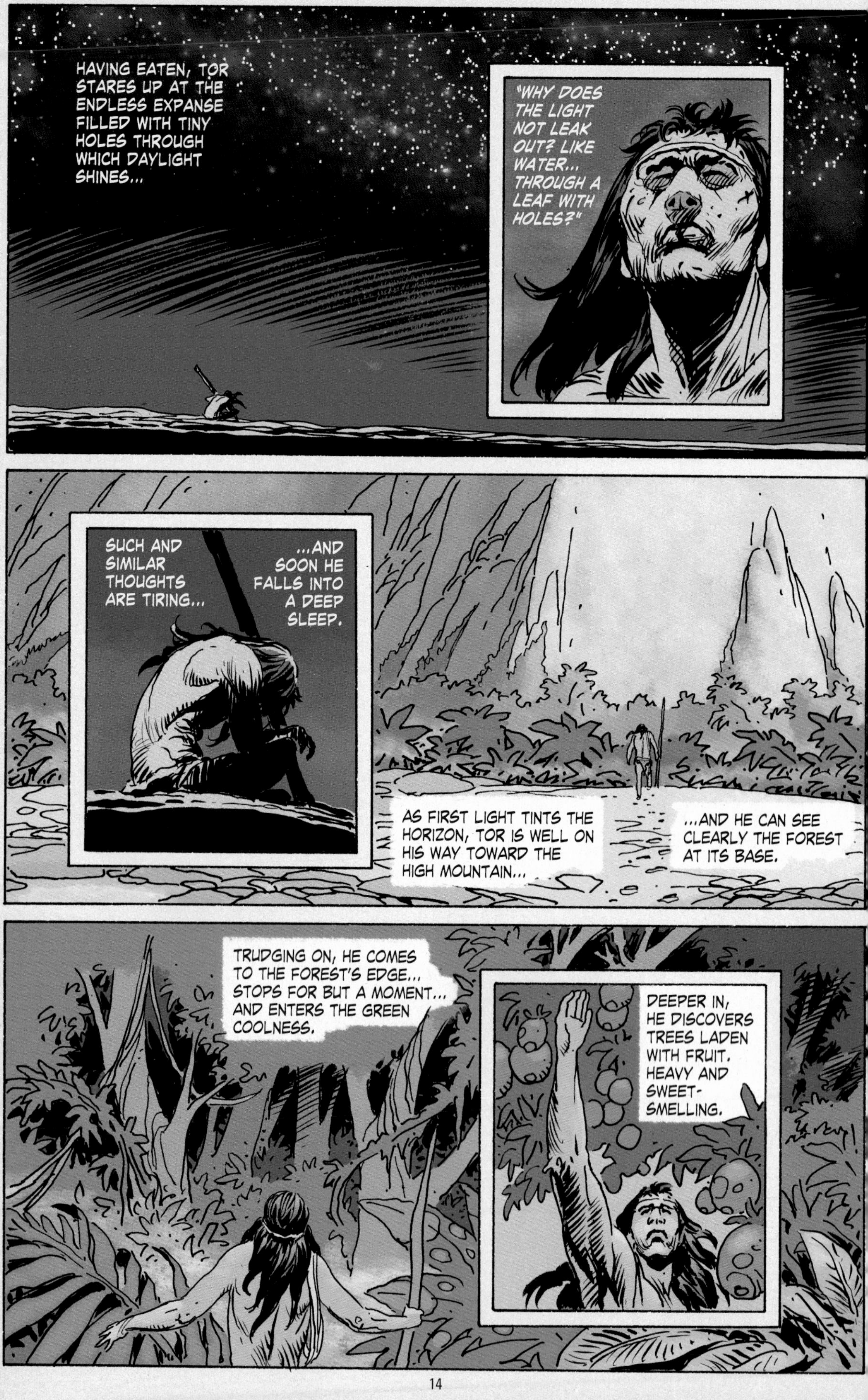
HAVING EATEN, TOR STARES UP AT THE ENDLESS EXPANSE FILLED WITH TINY HOLES THROUGH WHICH DAYLIGHT SHINES...
"WHY DOES THE LIGHT NOT LEAK OUT? LIKE WATER... THROUGH A LEAF WITH HOLES?"
SUCH AND SIMILAR THOUGHTS ARE TIRING...
...AND SOON HE FALLS INTO A DEEP SLEEP.
AS FIRST LIGHT TINTS THE HORIZON, TOR IS WELL ON HIS WAY TOWARD THE HIGH MOUNTAIN...
...AND HE CAN SEE CLEARLY THE FOREST AT ITS BASE.
TRUDGING ON, HE COMES TO THE FOREST'S EDGE... STOPS FOR BUT A MOMENT... AND ENTERS THE GREEN COOLNESS.
DEEPER IN, HE DISCOVERS TREES LADEN WITH FRUIT. HEAVY AND SWEET-SMELLING.

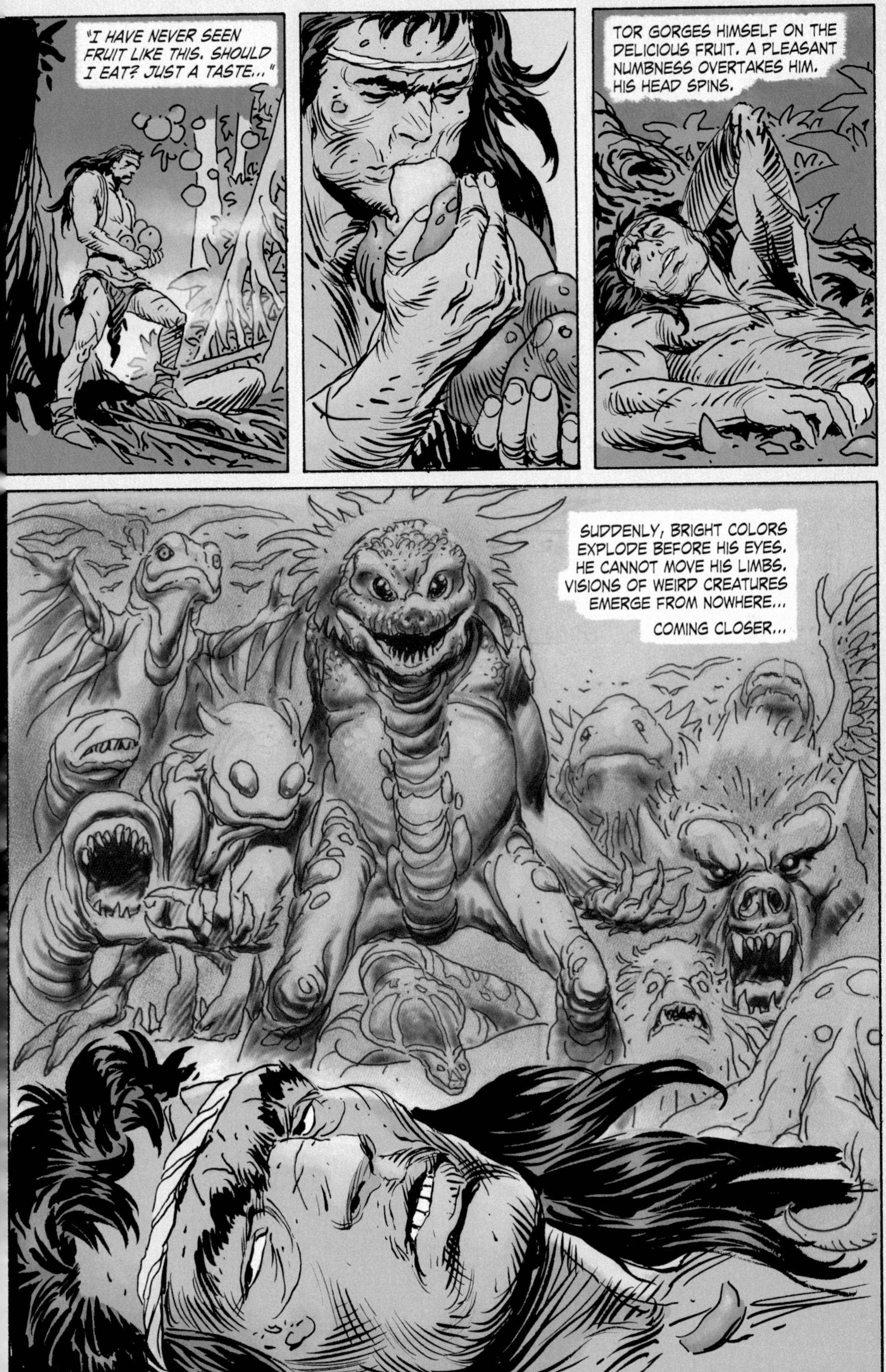
"I HAVE NEVER SEEN FRUIT LIKE THIS. SHOULD I EAT? JUST A TASTE..."
TOR GORGES HIMSELF ON THE DELICIOUS FRUIT. A PLEASANT NUMBNESS OVERTAKES HIM. HIS HEAD SPINS.
SUDDENLY, BRIGHT COLORS EXPLODE BEFORE HIS EYES. HE CANNOT MOVE HIS LIMBS. VISIONS OF WEIRD CREATURES EMERGE FROM NOWHERE...
COMING CLOSER...

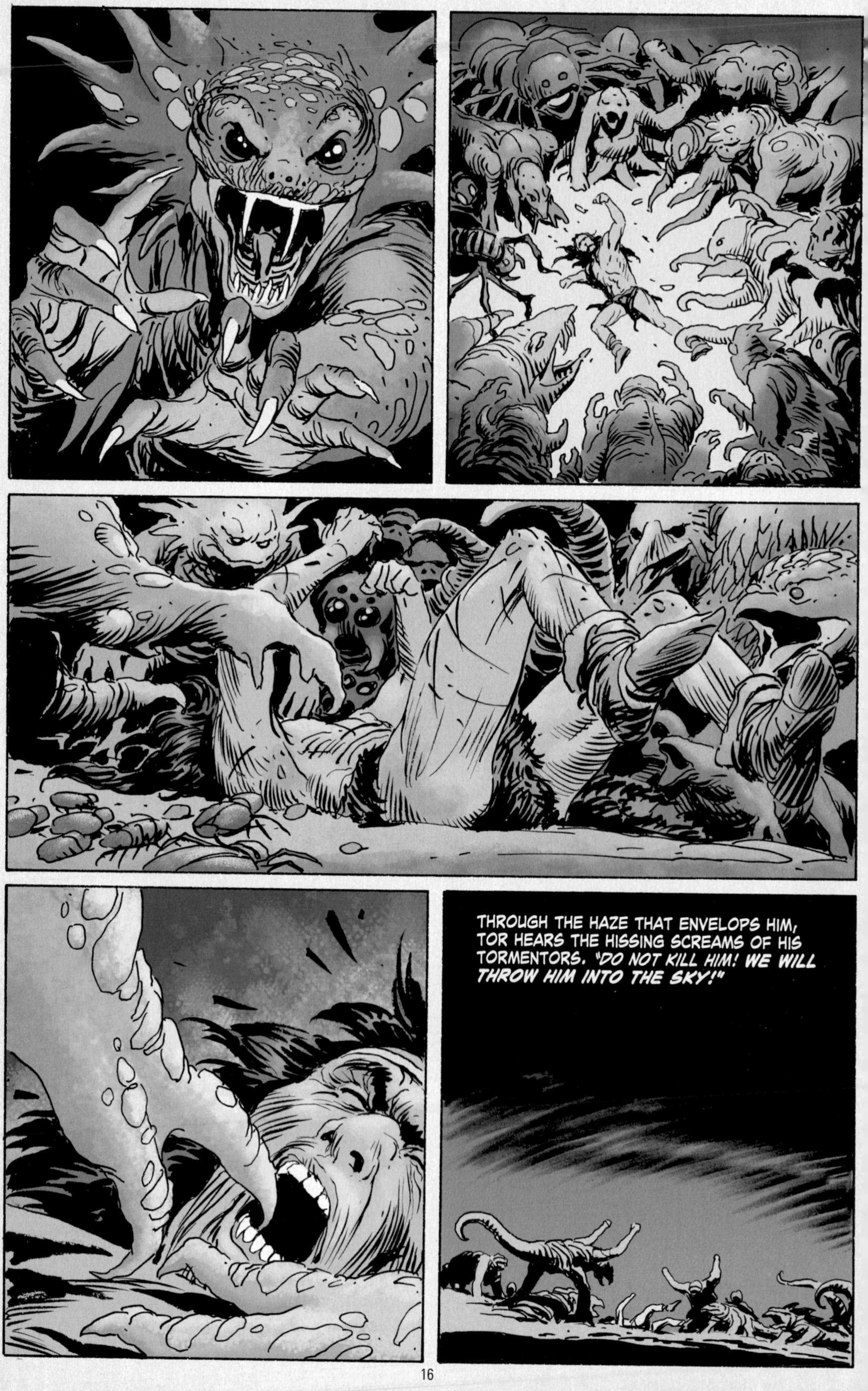
THROUGH THE HAZE THAT ENVELOPS HIM, TOR HEARS THE HISSING SCREAMS OF HIS TORMENTORS. "DO NOT KILL HIM! WE WILL THROW HIM INTO THE SKY!"

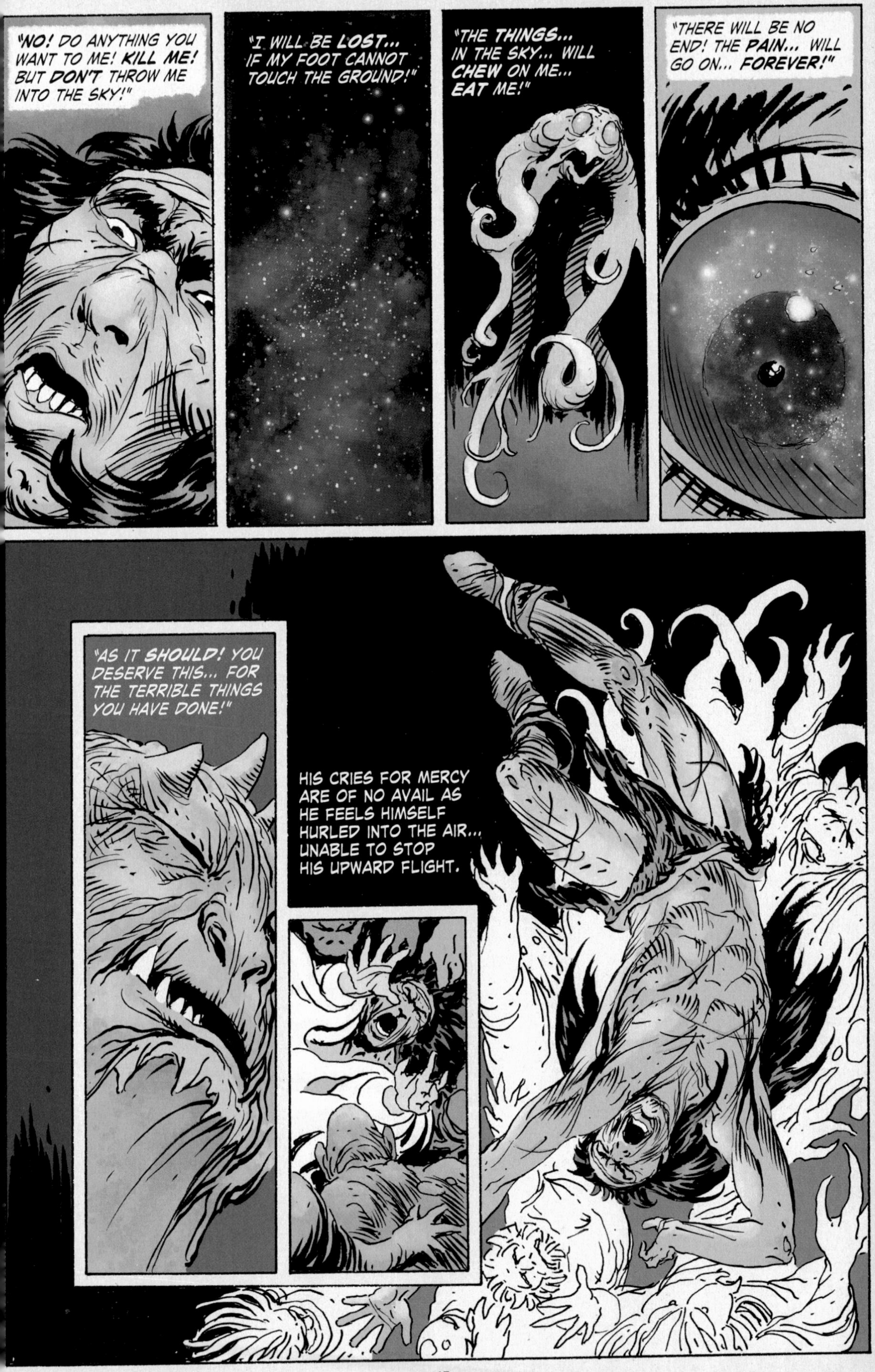
"NO! DO ANYTHING YOU WANT TO ME! KILL ME! BUT DON'T THROW ME INTO THE SKY!"
"I WILL BE LOST... IF MY FOOT CANNOT TOUCH THE GROUND!"
"THE THINGS... IN THE SKY... WILL CHEW ON ME... EAT ME!"
"THERE WILL BE NO END! THE PAIN... WILL GO ON... FOREVER!"
"AS IT SHOULD! YOU DESERVE THIS... FOR THE TERRIBLE THINGS YOU HAVE DONE!"
HIS CRIES FOR MERCY ARE OF NO AVAIL AS HE FEELS HIMSELF HURLED INTO THE AIR... UNABLE TO STOP HIS UPWARD FLIGHT.

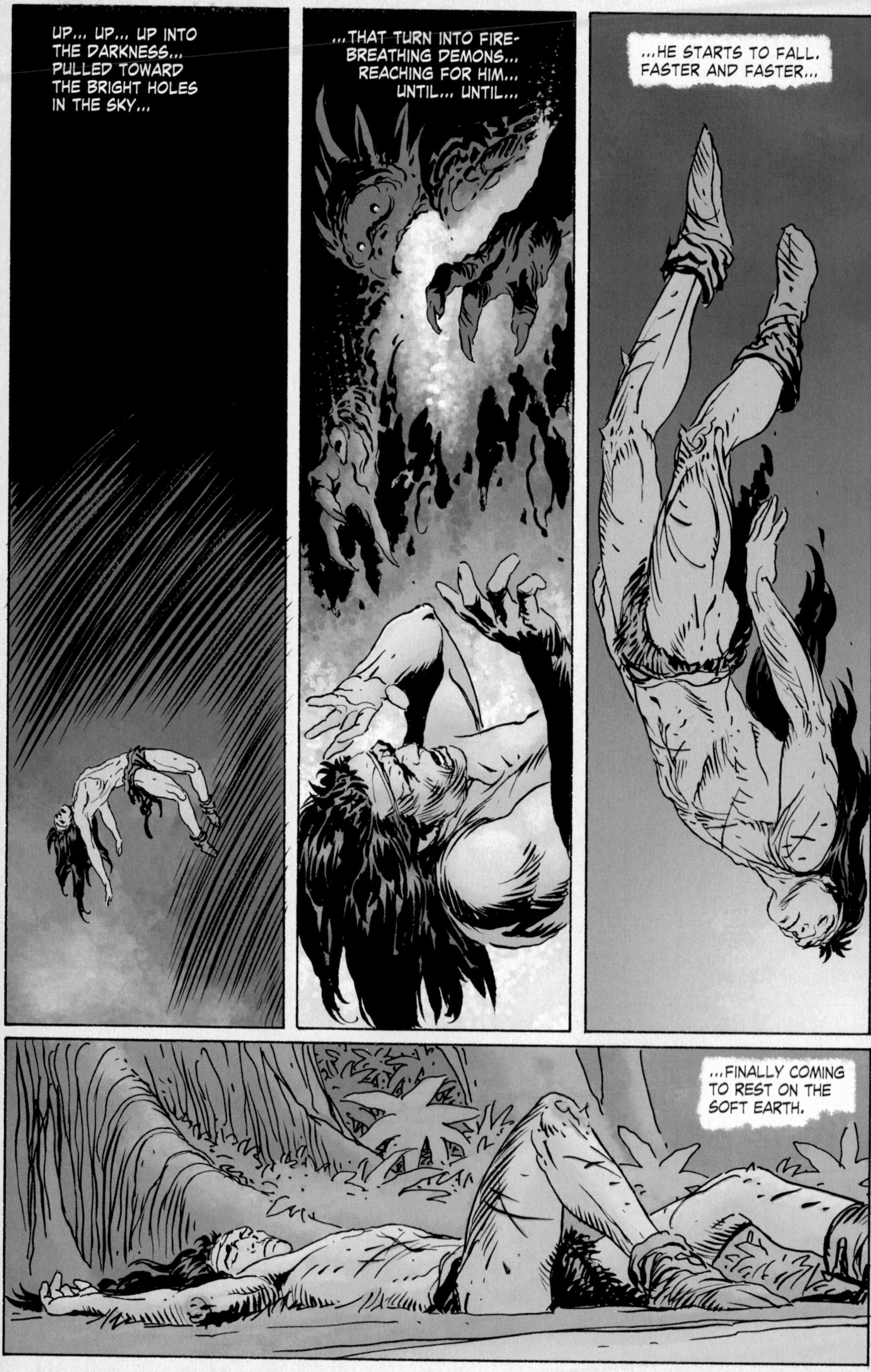
UP... UP... UP INTO THE DARKNESS... PULLED TOWARD THE BRIGHT HOLES IN THE SKY...
...THAT TURN INTO FIRE-BREATHING DEMONS... REACHING FOR HIM... UNTIL... UNTIL...
...HE STARTS TO FALL. FASTER AND FASTER...
...FINALLY COMING TO REST ON THE SOFT EARTH.

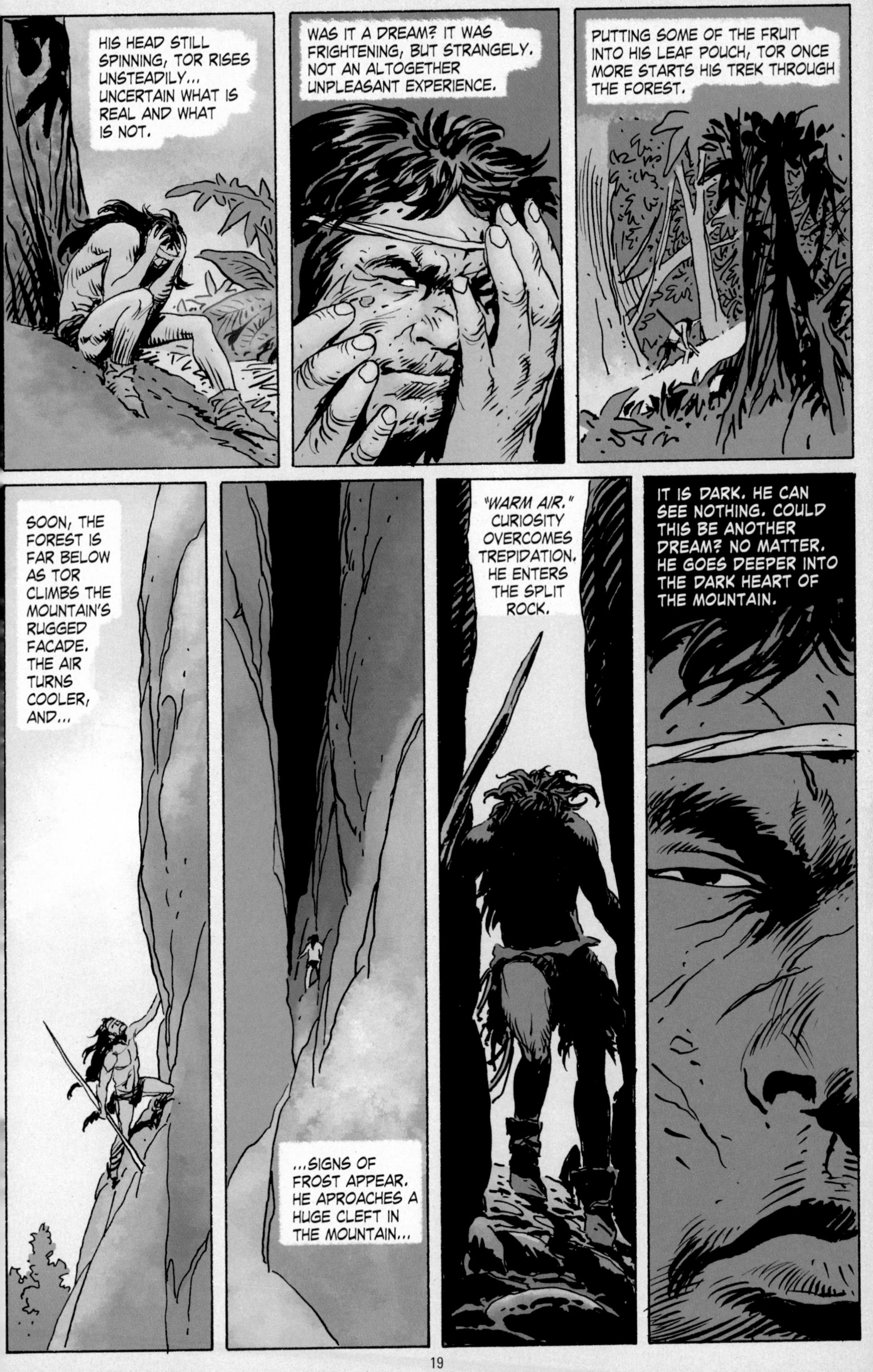
HIS HEAD STILL SPINNING, TOR RISES UNSTEADILY... UNCERTAIN WHAT IS REAL AND WHAT IS NOT.
WAS IT A DREAM? IT WAS FRIGHTENING, BUT STRANGELY. NOT AN ALTOGETHER UNPLEASANT EXPERIENCE.
PUTTING SOME OF THE FRUIT INTO HIS LEAF POUCH, TOR ONCE MORE STARTS HIS TREK THROUGH THE FOREST.
SOON, THE FOREST IS FAR BELOW AS TOR CLIMBS THE MOUNTAIN'S RUGGED FACADE. THE AIR TURNS COOLER, AND...
...SIGNS OF FROST APPEAR. HE APROACHES A HUGE CLEFT IN THE MOUNTAIN...
"WARM AIR." CURIOSITY OVERCOMES TREPIDATION. HE ENTERS THE SPLIT ROCK.
IT IS DARK. HE CAN SEE NOTHING. COULD THIS BE ANOTHER DREAM? NO MATTER. HE GOES DEEPER INTO THE DARK HEART OF THE MOUNTAIN.

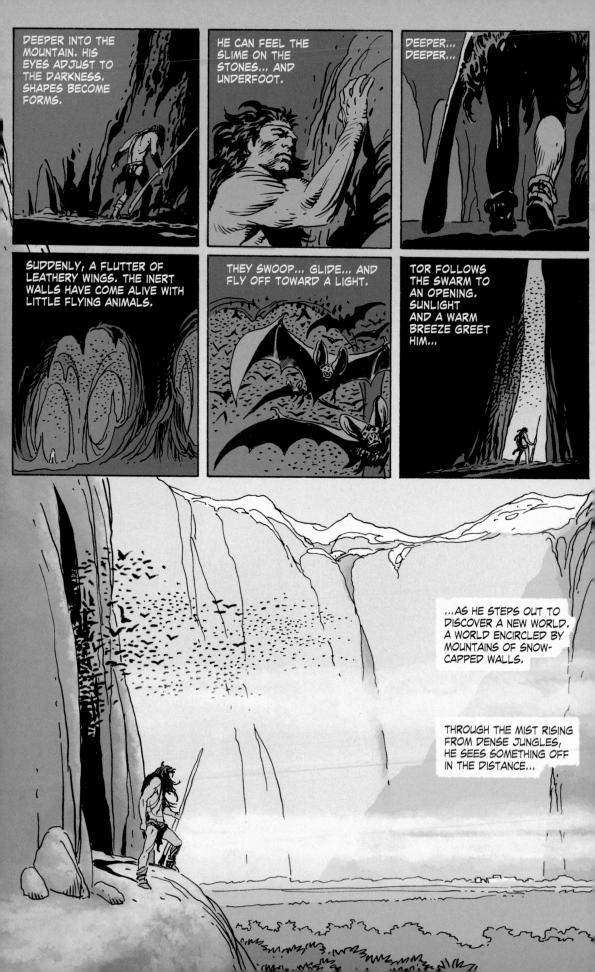

DEEPER INTO THE MOUNTAIN. HIS EYES ADJUST TO THE DARKNESS. SHAPES BECOME FORMS.

HE CAN FEEL THE SLIME ON THE STONES... AND UNDERFOOT.

DEEPER... DEEPER...

SUDDENLY, A FLUTTER OF LEATHERY WINGS. THE INERT WALLS HAVE COME ALIVE WITH LITTLE FLYING ANIMALS.

THEY SWOOP... GLIDE... AND FLY OFF TOWARD A LIGHT.

TOR FOLLOWS THE SWARM TO AN OPENING. SUNLIGHT AND A WARM BREEZE GREET HIM...

...AS HE STEPS OUT TO DISCOVER A NEW WORLD. A WORLD ENCIRCLED BY MOUNTAINS OF SNOW-CAPPED WALLS.

THROUGH THE MIST RISING FROM DENSE JUNGLES, HE SEES SOMETHING OFF IN THE DISTANCE...

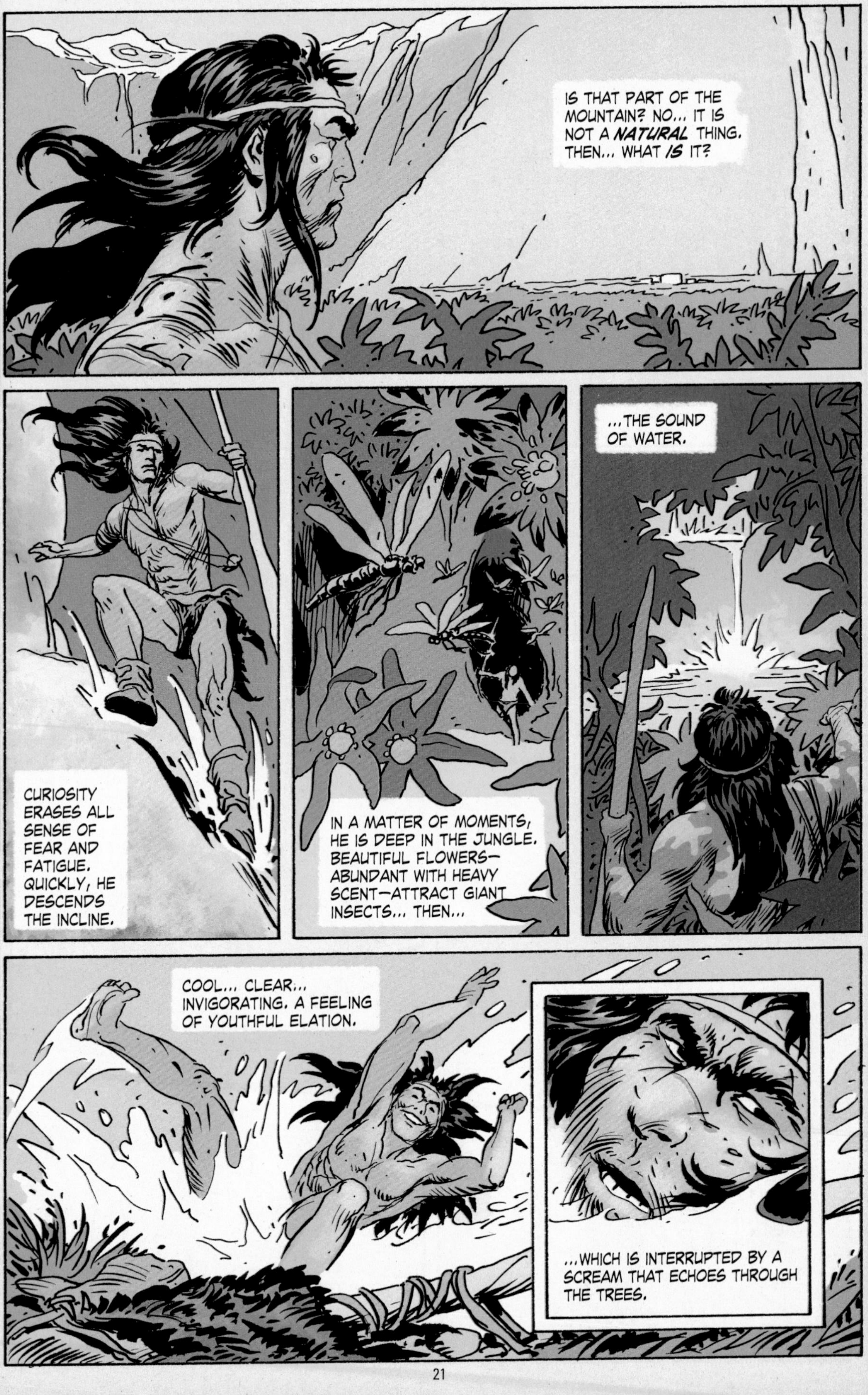
IS THAT PART OF THE MOUNTAIN? NO... IT IS NOT A NATURAL THING. THEN... WHAT IS IT?
CURIOSITY ERASES ALL SENSE OF FEAR AND FATIGUE. QUICKLY, HE DESCENDS THE INCLINE.
IN A MATTER OF MOMENTS, HE IS DEEP IN THE JUNGLE. BEAUTIFUL FLOWERS—ABUNDANT WITH HEAVY SCENT—ATTRACT GIANT INSECTS... THEN...
...THE SOUND OF WATER.
COOL... CLEAR... INVIGORATING. A FEELING OF YOUTHFUL ELATION.
...WHICH IS INTERRUPTED BY A SCREAM THAT ECHOES THROUGH THE TREES.

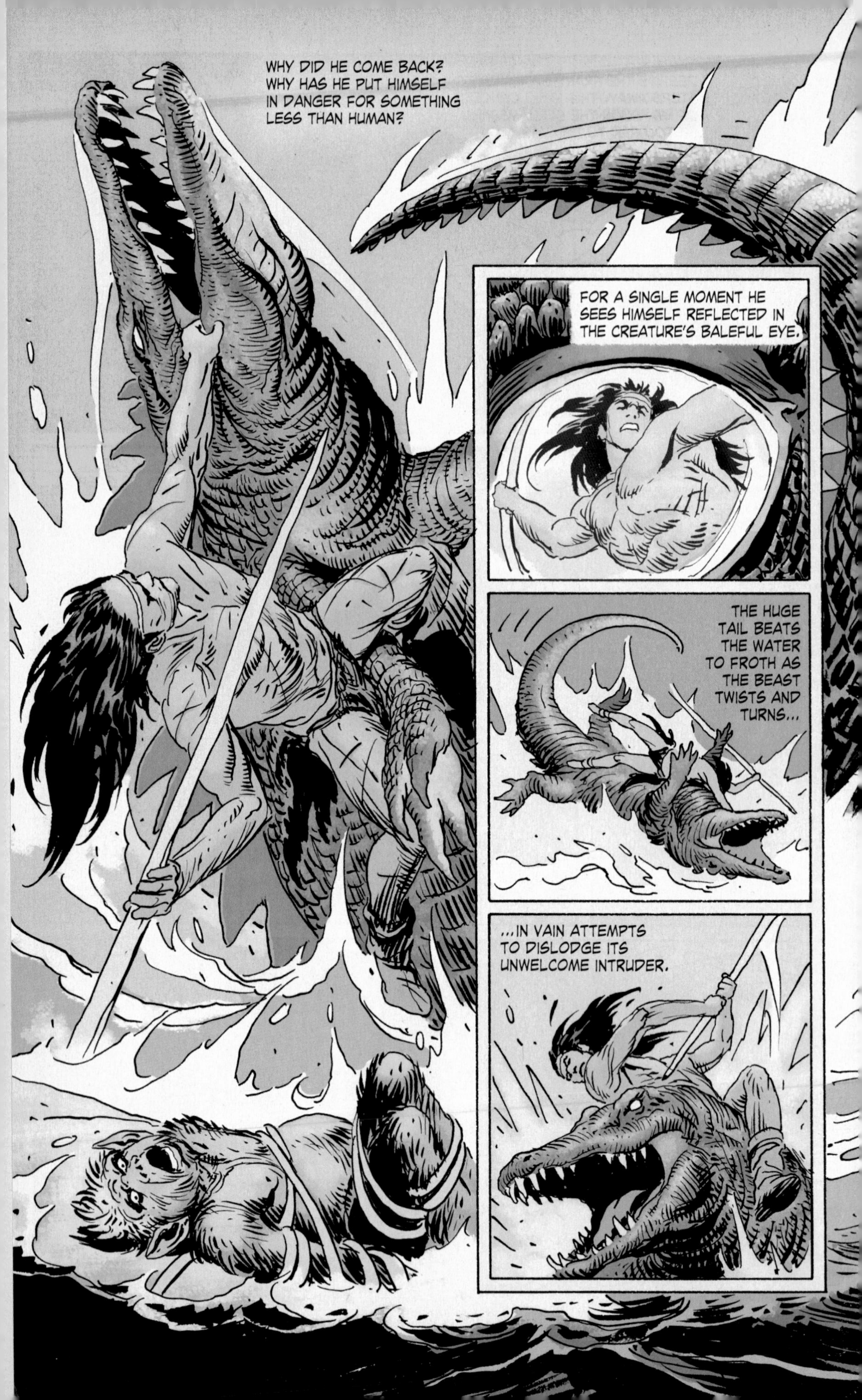
WHY DID HE COME BACK? WHY HAS HE PUT HIMSELF IN DANGER FOR SOMETHING LESS THAN HUMAN?
FOR A SINGLE MOMENT HE SEES HIMSELF REFLECTED IN THE CREATURE'S BALEFUL EYE.
THE HUGE TAIL BEATS THE WATER TO FROTH AS THE BEAST TWISTS AND TURNS...
...IN VAIN ATTEMPTS TO DISLODGE ITS UNWELCOME INTRUDER.

SUMMONING ALL HIS STRENGTH... MUSCLES CONTRACTING LIKE THICK ROPE CORDS... HE PLUNGES THE WOODEN STAFF INTO THE SAUROPOD'S EYE...

...WITH DEVASTATING EFFECT. NOW THE WHITE FROTH TURNS RED IN DEATH'S AGONY.

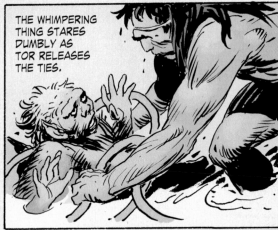

THE WHIMPERING THING STARES DUMBLY AS TOR RELEASES THE TIES.

ONCE FREE, IT CLINGS TIGHTLY TO THE MAN'S LEG. TOR GRUNTS HIS DISPLEASURE.

FOR THE FIRST TIME TOR REALIZES, "IT'S A HAIRY CHILD."

AS HE CONSIDERS HOW TO RID HIMSELF OF THIS UNWELCOME BURDEN...

...UNKNOWN TO TOR, THE ENCOUNTER HAS BEEN WITNESSED FROM THE JUNGLE'S SHADOWY FOLIAGE.

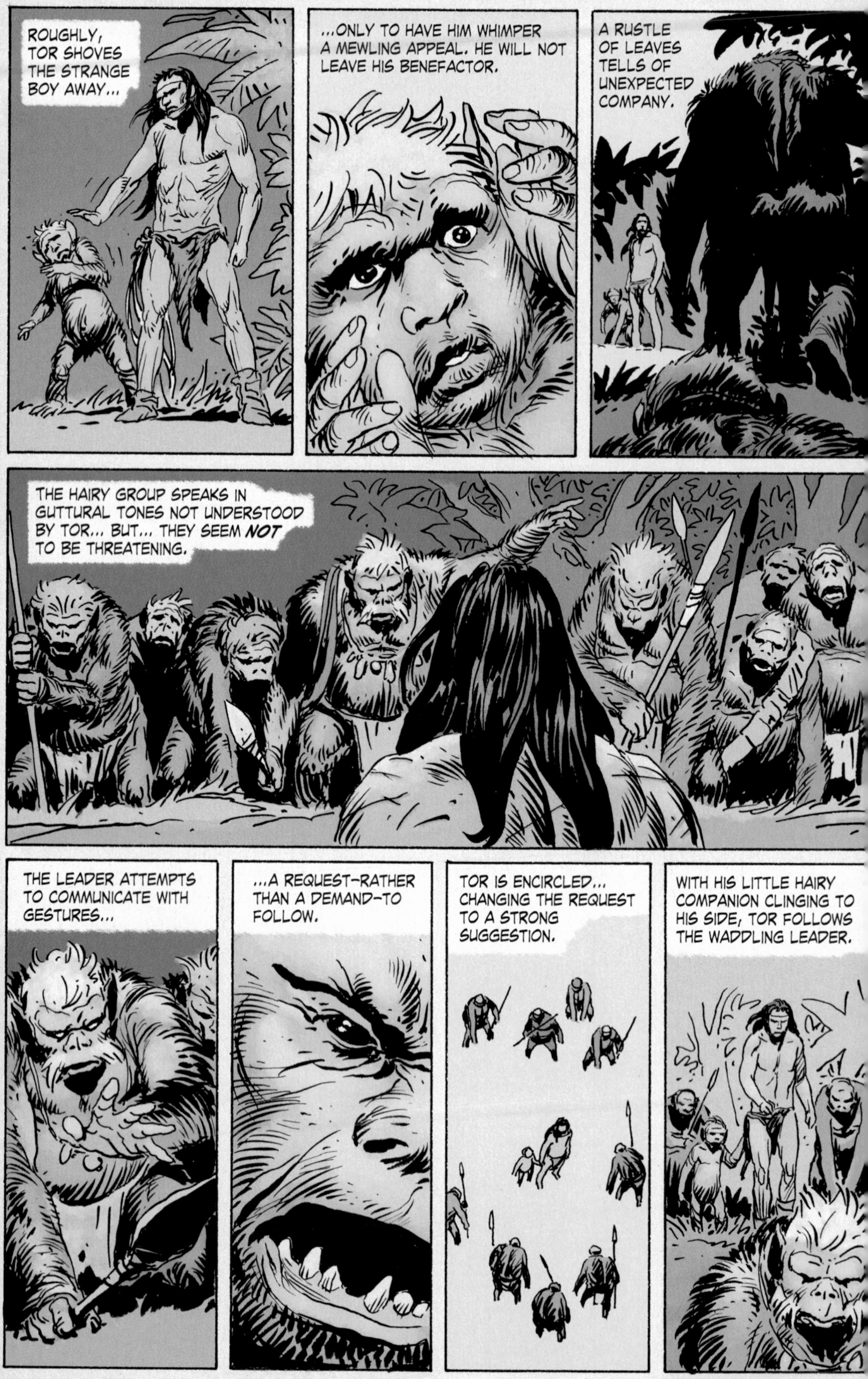
ROUGHLY, TOR SHOVES THE STRANGE BOY AWAY...
...ONLY TO HAVE HIM WHIMPER A MEWLING APPEAL. HE WILL NOT LEAVE HIS BENEFACTOR.
A RUSTLE OF LEAVES TELLS OF UNEXPECTED COMPANY.
THE HAIRY GROUP SPEAKS IN GUTTURAL TONES NOT UNDERSTOOD BY TOR... BUT... THEY SEEM *NOT* TO BE THREATENING.
THE LEADER ATTEMPTS TO COMMUNICATE WITH GESTURES...
...A REQUEST-RATHER THAN A DEMAND-TO FOLLOW.
TOR IS ENCIRCLED... CHANGING THE REQUEST TO A STRONG SUGGESTION.
WITH HIS LITTLE HAIRY COMPANION CLINGING TO HIS SIDE, TOR FOLLOWS THE WADDLING LEADER.

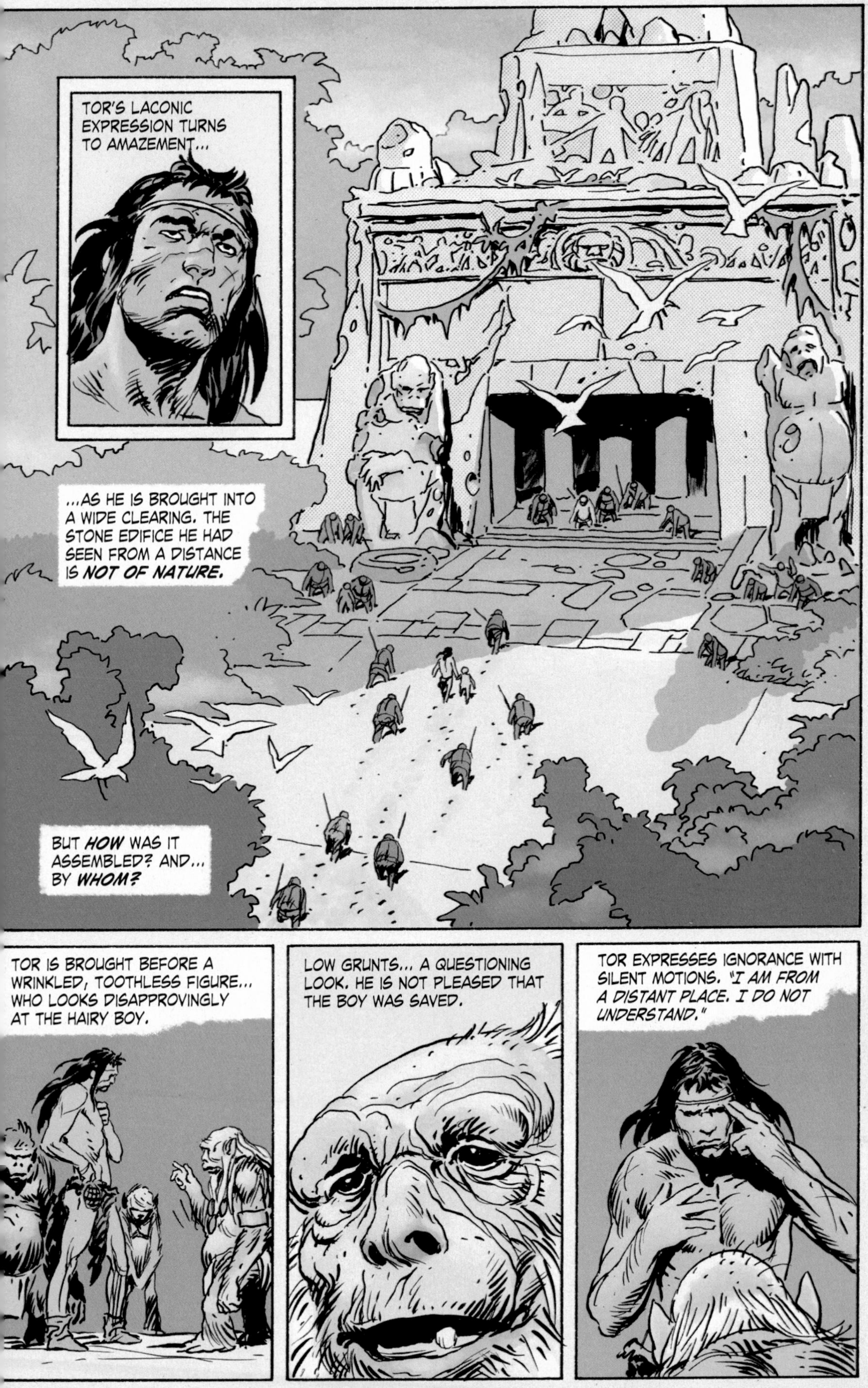
TOR'S LACONIC EXPRESSION TURNS TO AMAZEMENT...
...AS HE IS BROUGHT INTO A WIDE CLEARING. THE STONE EDIFICE HE HAD SEEN FROM A DISTANCE IS NOT OF NATURE.
BUT HOW WAS IT ASSEMBLED? AND... BY WHOM?
TOR IS BROUGHT BEFORE A WRINKLED, TOOTHLESS FIGURE... WHO LOOKS DISAPPROVINGLY AT THE HAIRY BOY.
LOW GRUNTS... A QUESTIONING LOOK. HE IS NOT PLEASED THAT THE BOY WAS SAVED.
TOR EXPRESSES IGNORANCE WITH SILENT MOTIONS. "I AM FROM A DISTANT PLACE. I DO NOT UNDERSTAND."

AS TOR WATCHES, THE OLD MAN PICKS UP A SHARP STICK...

...AND STARTS TO SCRATCH LINES INTO THE EARTH.

TOR THINKS, "THE BOY. HE MAKES THE BOY."

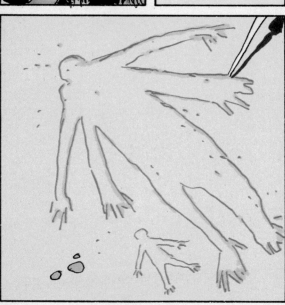

"WHAT IS *THAT?* A MAN... A *BIG* MAN WITH MANY ARMS?"

TOR WATCHES IN SILENCE AS THE TELLING PROCEEDS.

"THE BOY... IS GONE. THE BIG MAN WITH MANY ARMS... REMAINS."

SLOWLY, TOR UNDERSTANDS. THE BOY WAS A *GIFT* TO THE BIG MAN.

28

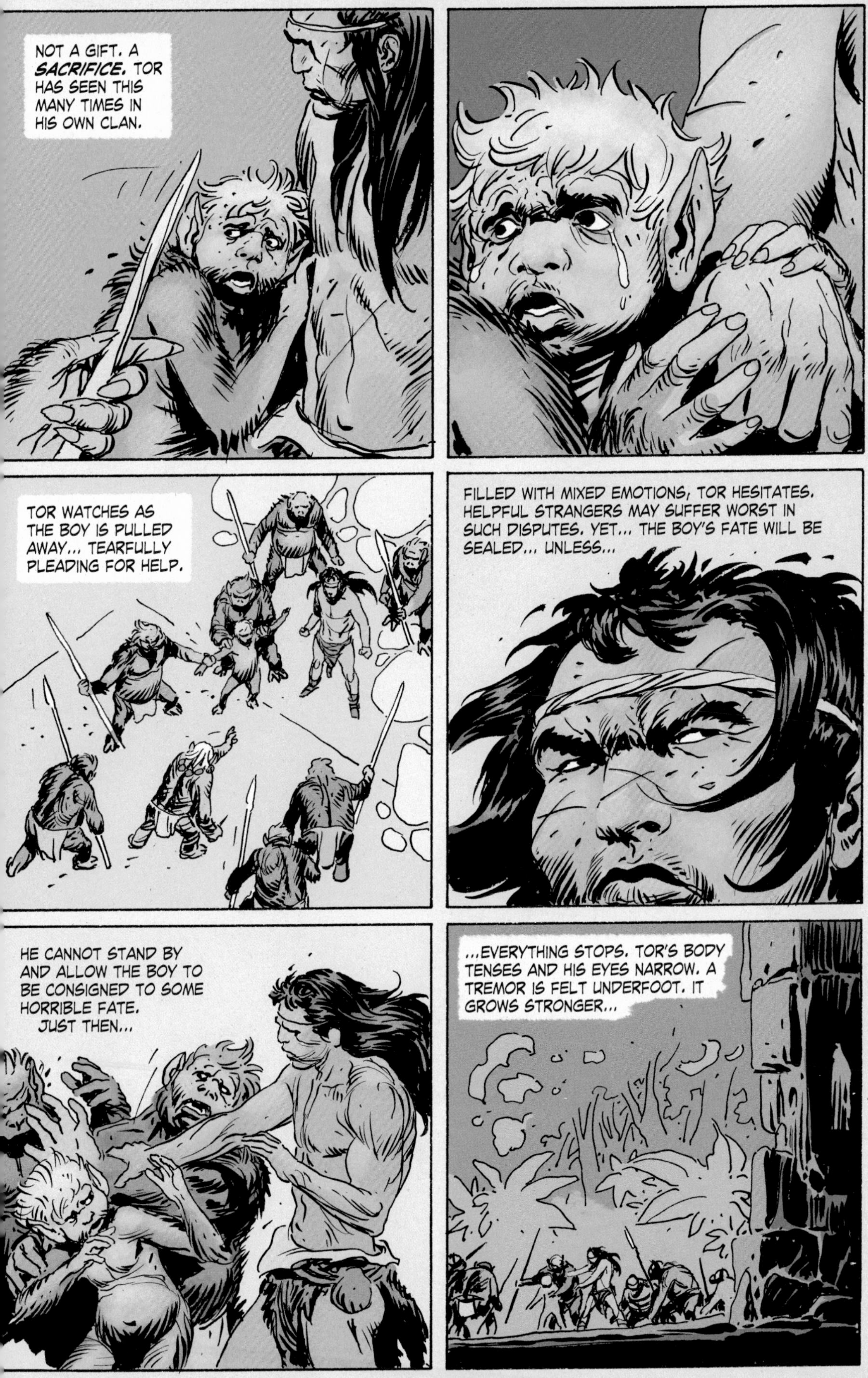
NOT A GIFT. A *SACRIFICE.* TOR HAS SEEN THIS MANY TIMES IN HIS OWN CLAN.
TOR WATCHES AS THE BOY IS PULLED AWAY... TEARFULLY PLEADING FOR HELP.
FILLED WITH MIXED EMOTIONS, TOR HESITATES. HELPFUL STRANGERS MAY SUFFER WORST IN SUCH DISPUTES. YET... THE BOY'S FATE WILL BE SEALED... UNLESS...
HE CANNOT STAND BY AND ALLOW THE BOY TO BE CONSIGNED TO SOME HORRIBLE FATE.
JUST THEN...
...EVERYTHING STOPS. TOR'S BODY TENSES AND HIS EYES NARROW. A TREMOR IS FELT UNDERFOOT. IT GROWS STRONGER...

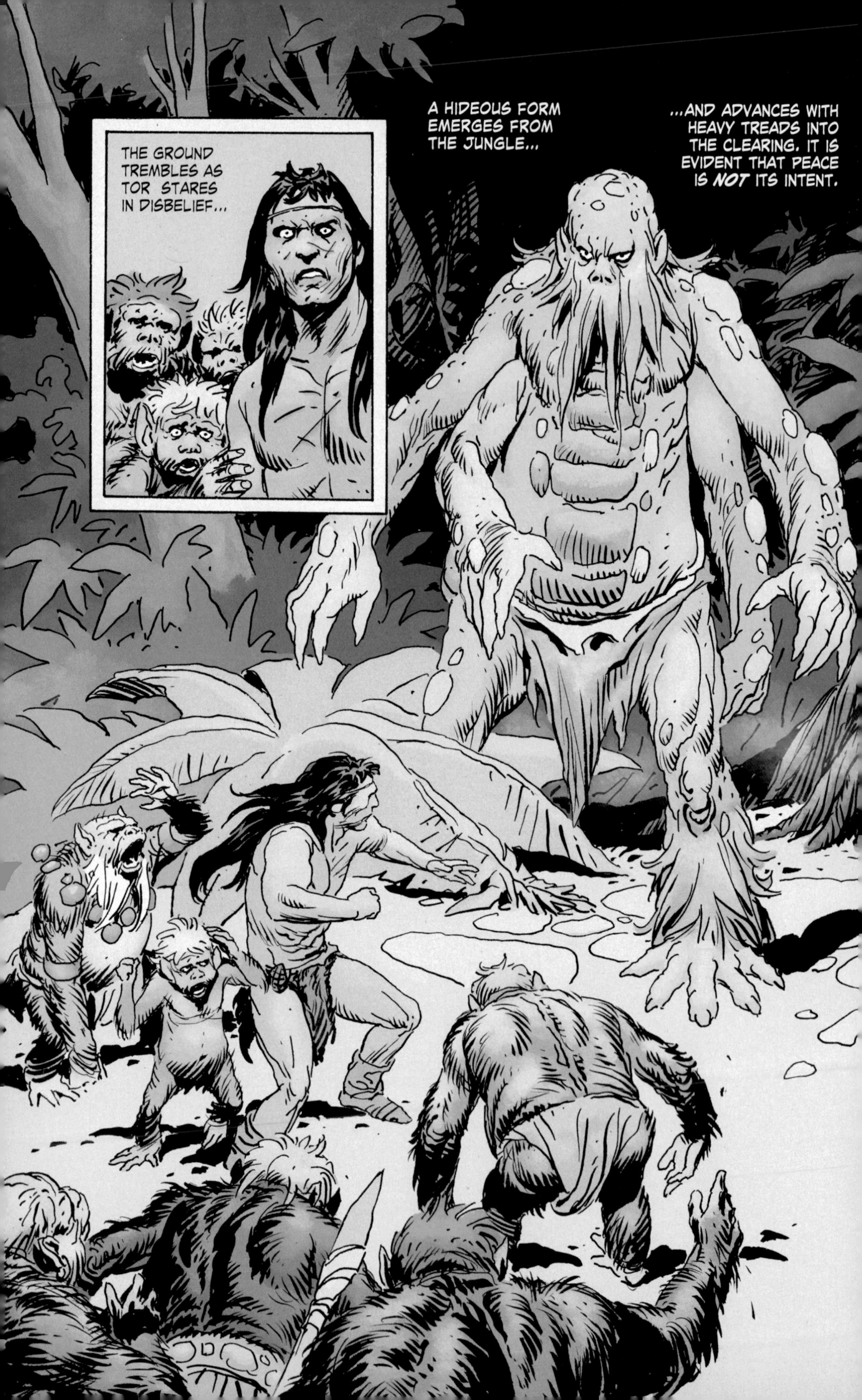
THE GROUND TREMBLES AS TOR STARES IN DISBELIEF...
A HIDEOUS FORM EMERGES FROM THE JUNGLE...
...AND ADVANCES WITH HEAVY TREADS INTO THE CLEARING. IT IS EVIDENT THAT PEACE IS NOT ITS INTENT.

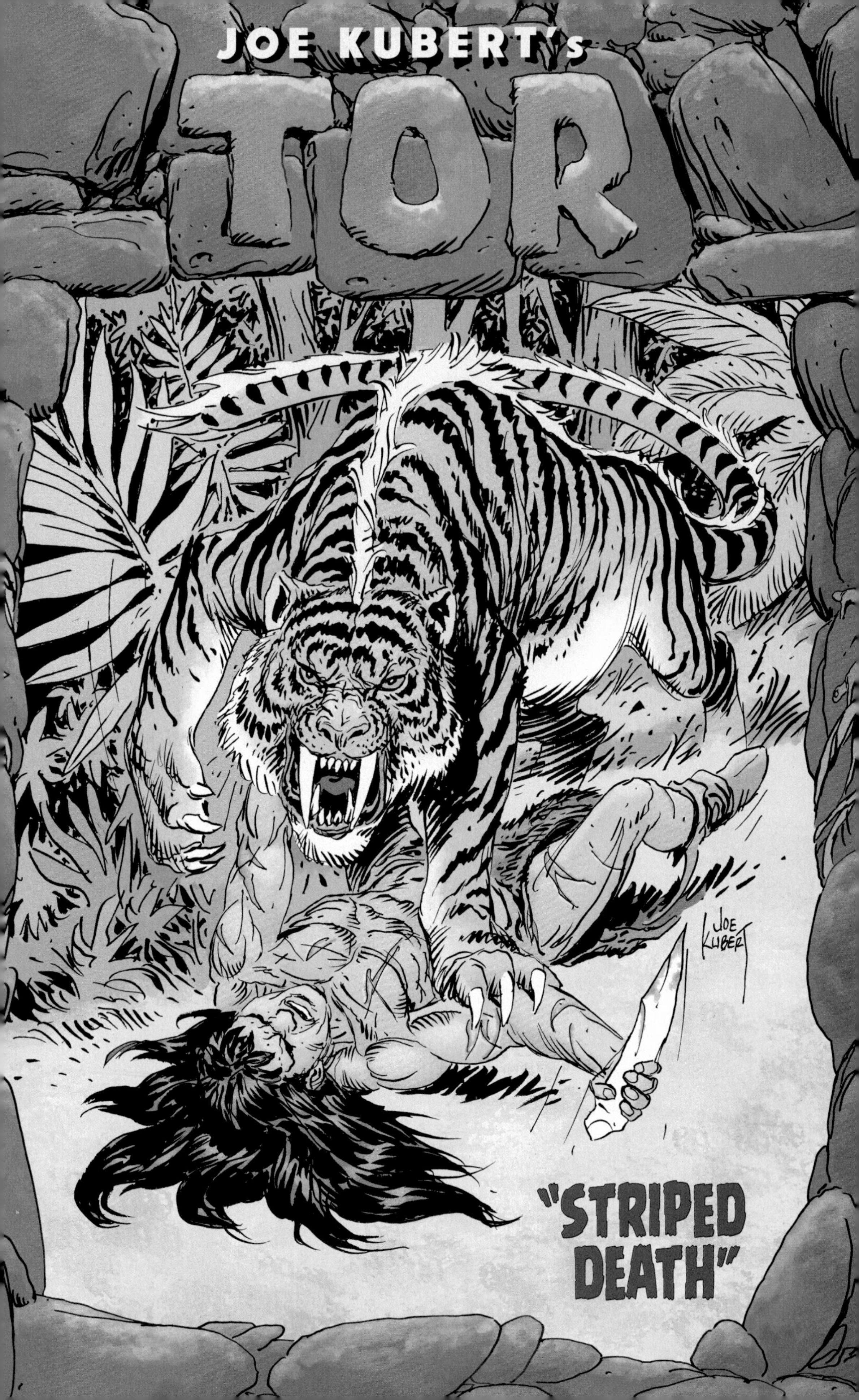
JOE KUBERT's
TOR
JOE KUBERT
"STRIPED DEATH"

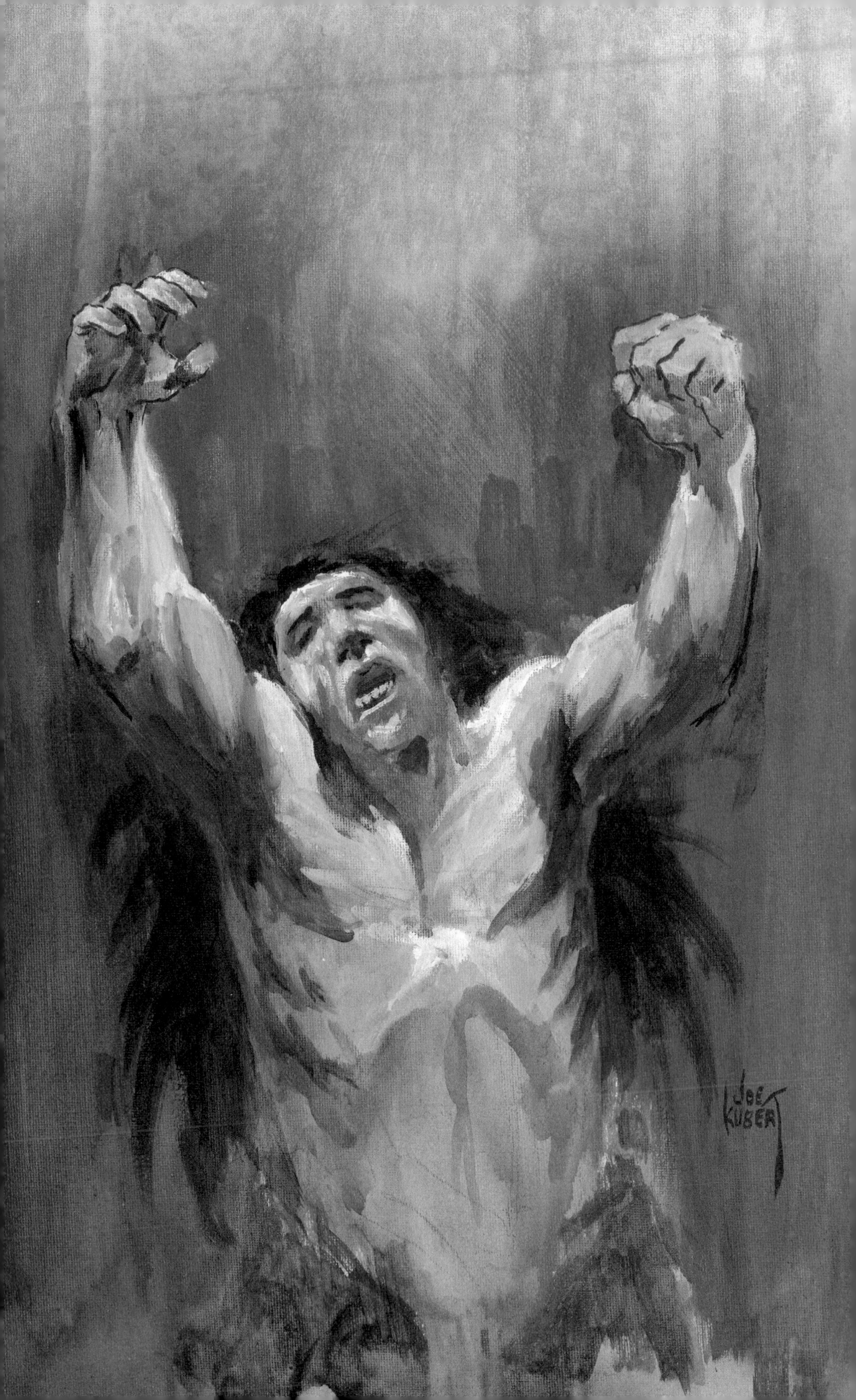
JOE KUBERT

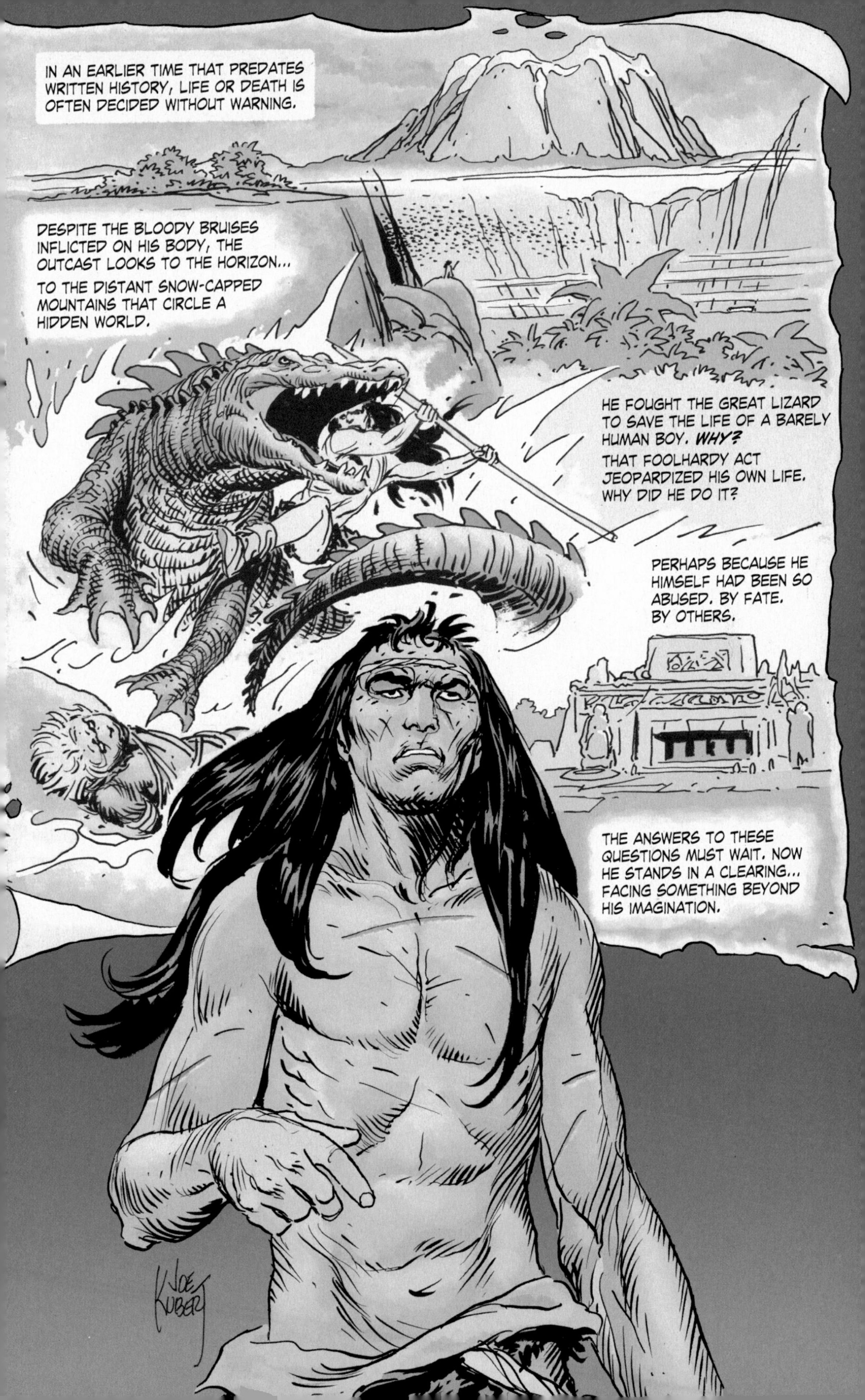
IN AN EARLIER TIME THAT PREDATES WRITTEN HISTORY, LIFE OR DEATH IS OFTEN DECIDED WITHOUT WARNING.
DESPITE THE BLOODY BRUISES INFLICTED ON HIS BODY, THE OUTCAST LOOKS TO THE HORIZON...
TO THE DISTANT SNOW-CAPPED MOUNTAINS THAT CIRCLE A HIDDEN WORLD.
HE FOUGHT THE GREAT LIZARD TO SAVE THE LIFE OF A BARELY HUMAN BOY. WHY?
THAT FOOLHARDY ACT JEOPARDIZED HIS OWN LIFE. WHY DID HE DO IT?
PERHAPS BECAUSE HE HIMSELF HAD BEEN SO ABUSED. BY FATE. BY OTHERS.
THE ANSWERS TO THESE QUESTIONS MUST WAIT. NOW HE STANDS IN A CLEARING... FACING SOMETHING BEYOND HIS IMAGINATION.
JOE KUBERT

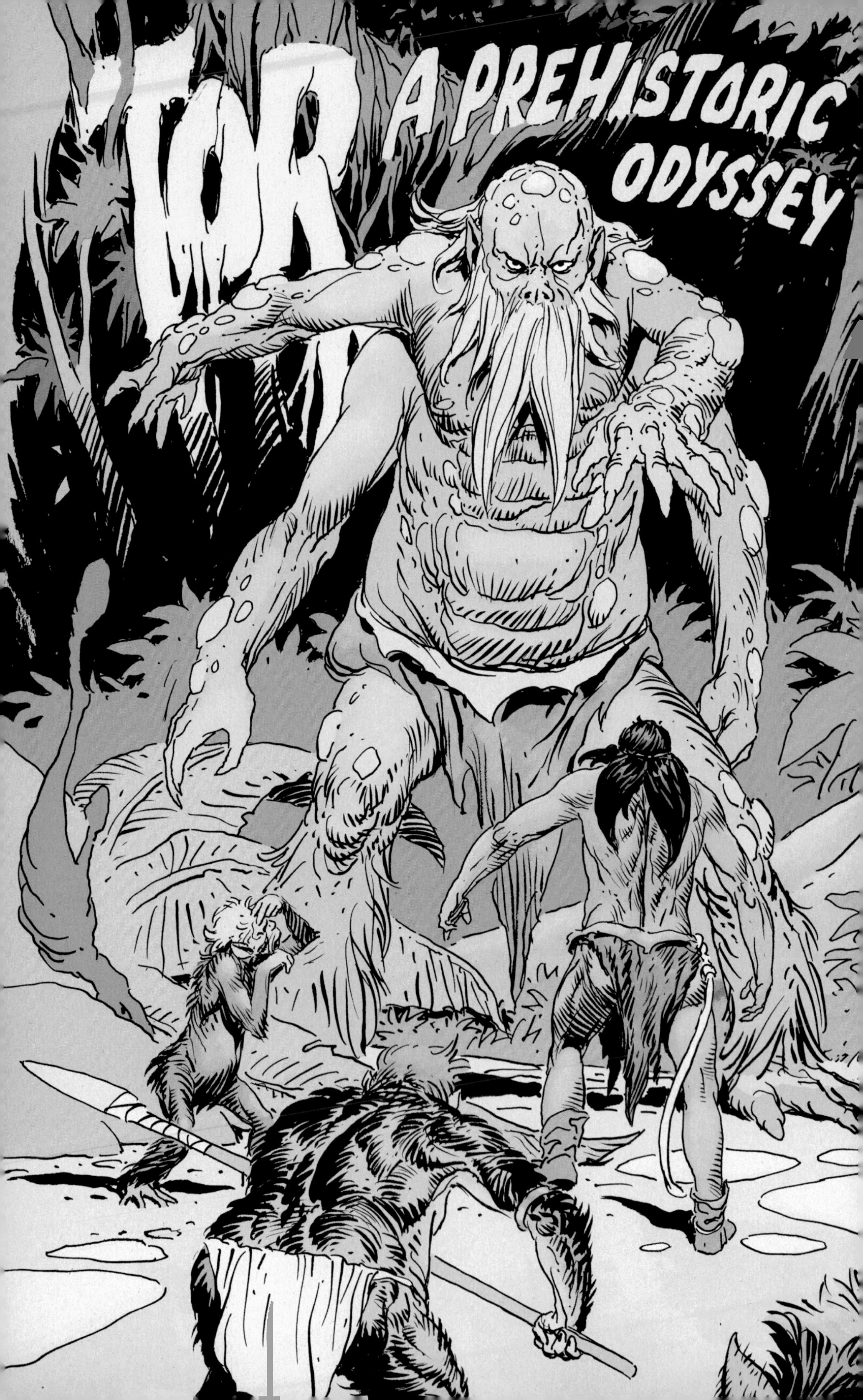
TOR
A PREHISTORIC ODYSSEY

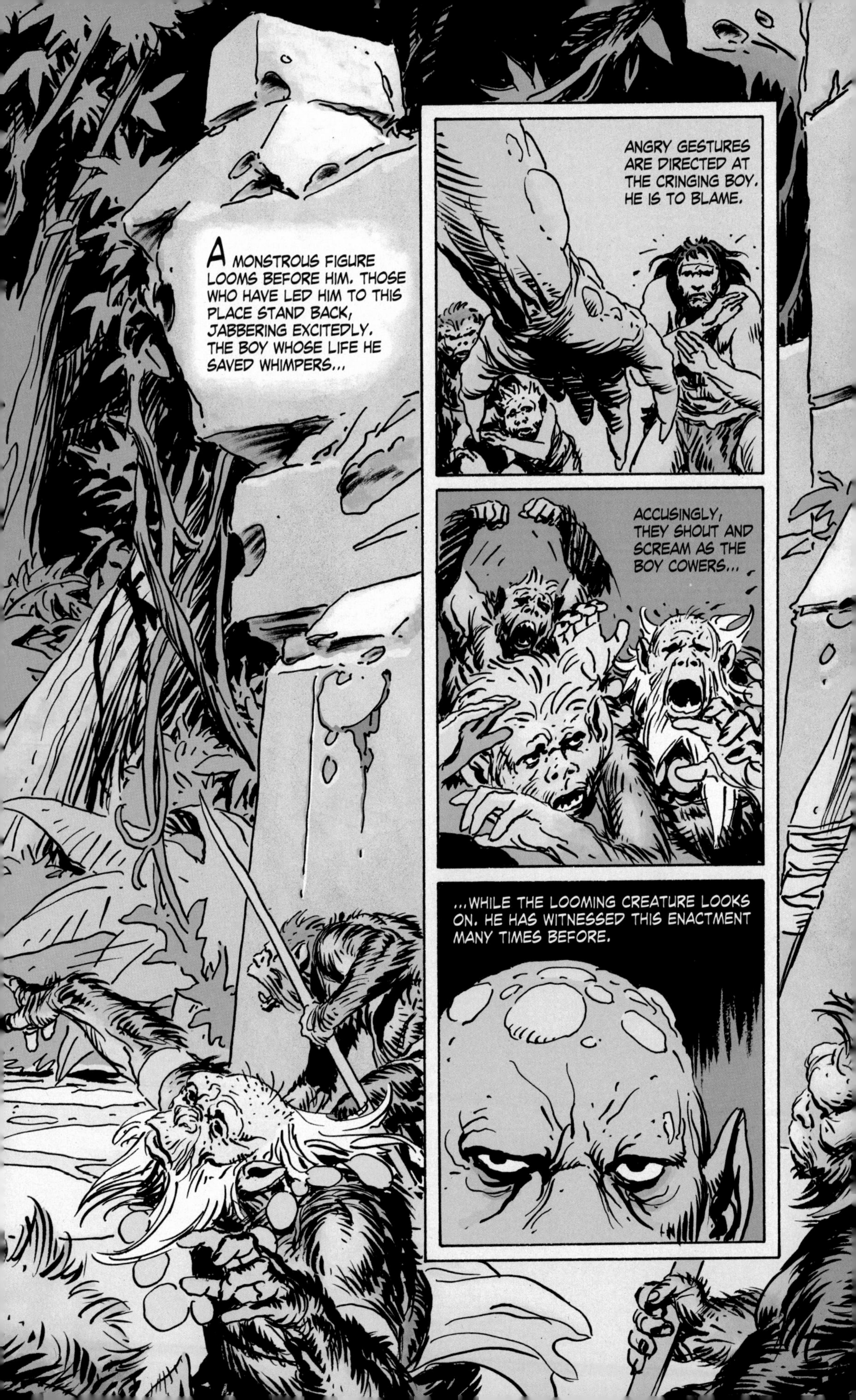
A MONSTROUS FIGURE LOOMS BEFORE HIM. THOSE WHO HAVE LED HIM TO THIS PLACE STAND BACK, JABBERING EXCITEDLY. THE BOY WHOSE LIFE HE SAVED WHIMPERS...
ANGRY GESTURES ARE DIRECTED AT THE CRINGING BOY. HE IS TO BLAME.
ACCUSINGLY, THEY SHOUT AND SCREAM AS THE BOY COWERS...
...WHILE THE LOOMING CREATURE LOOKS ON. HE HAS WITNESSED THIS ENACTMENT MANY TIMES BEFORE.

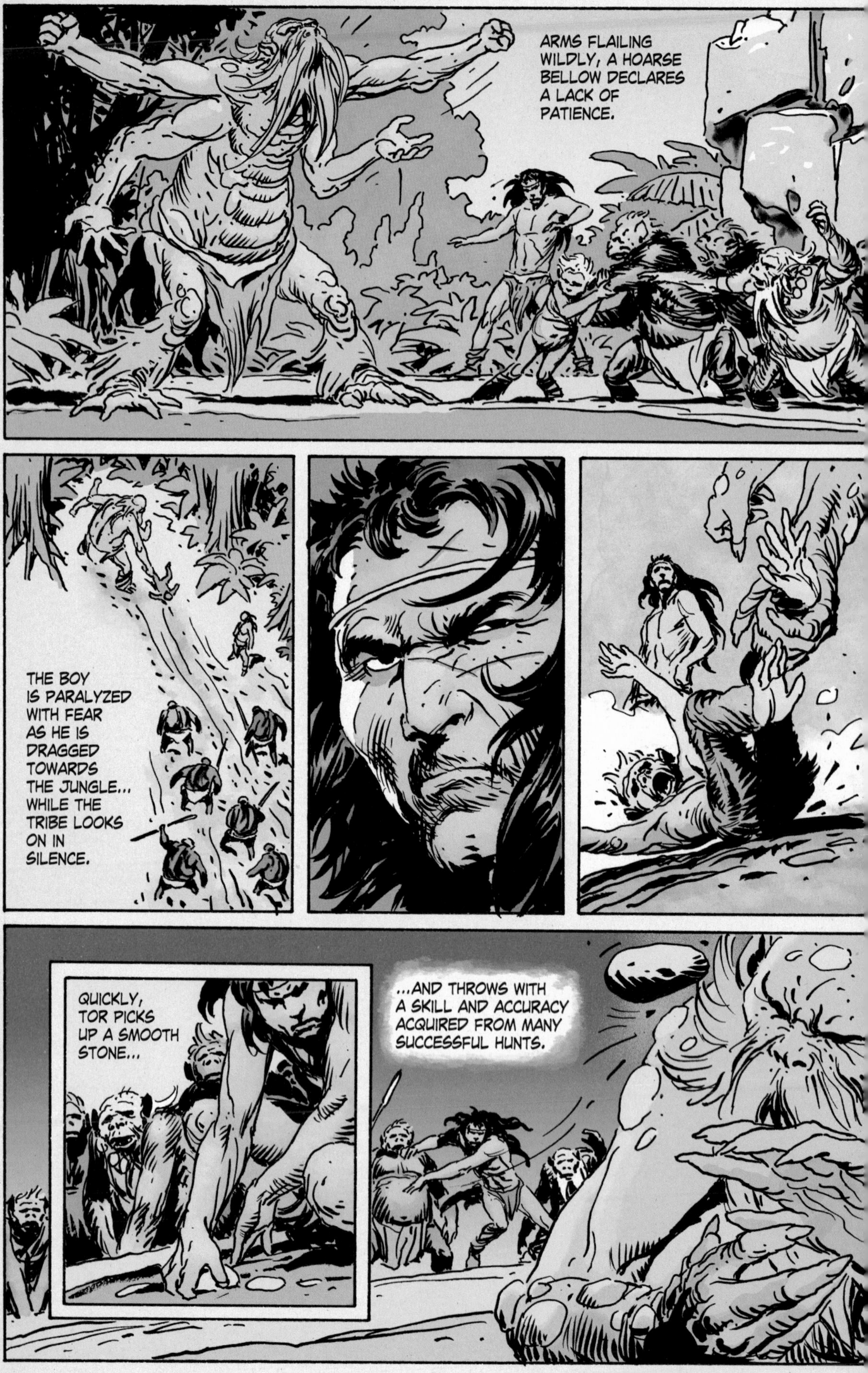
ARMS FLAILING WILDLY, A HOARSE BELLOW DECLARES A LACK OF PATIENCE.
THE BOY IS PARALYZED WITH FEAR AS HE IS DRAGGED TOWARDS THE JUNGLE... WHILE THE TRIBE LOOKS ON IN SILENCE.
QUICKLY, TOR PICKS UP A SMOOTH STONE...
...AND THROWS WITH A SKILL AND ACCURACY ACQUIRED FROM MANY SUCCESSFUL HUNTS.

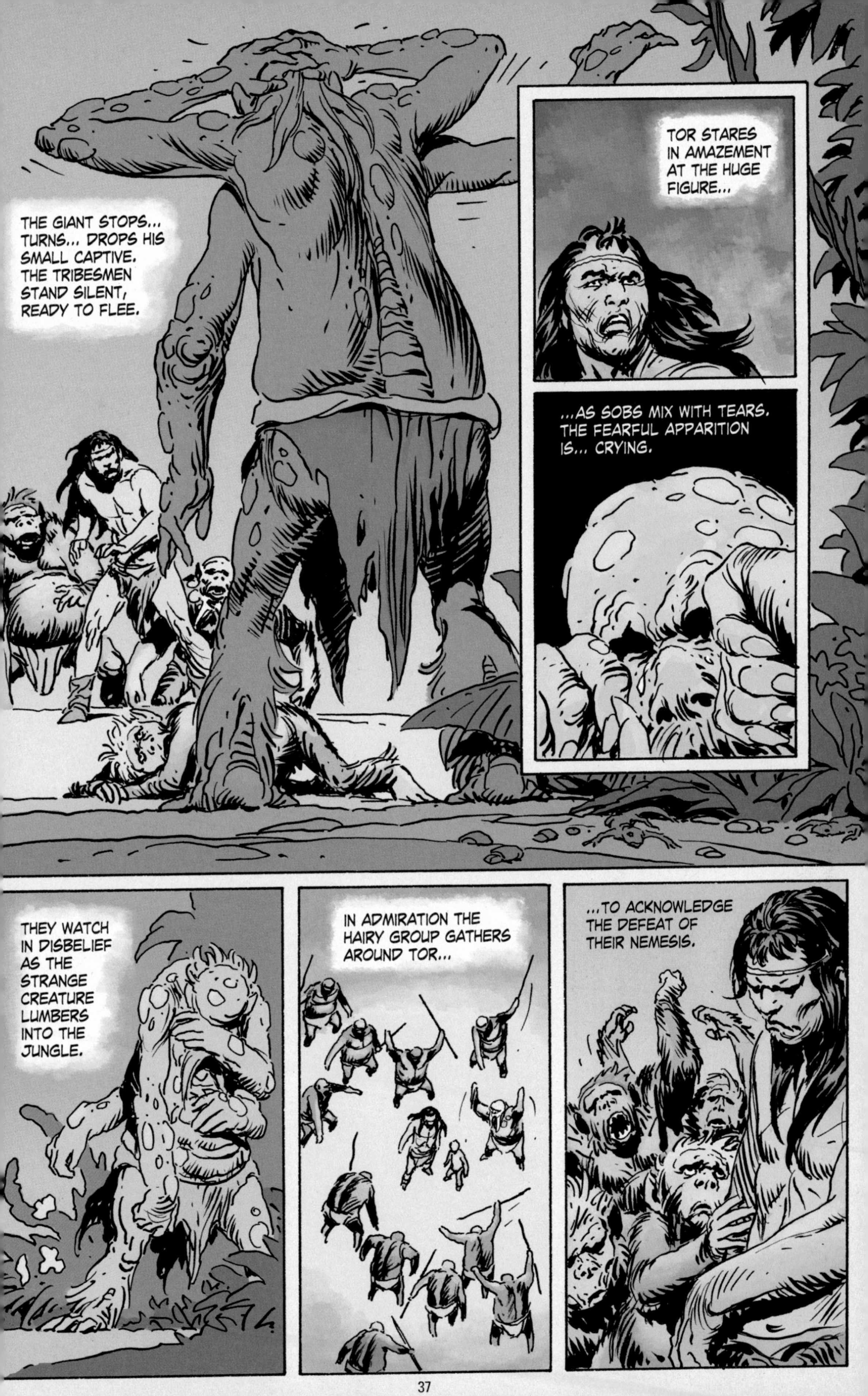
THE GIANT STOPS... TURNS... DROPS HIS SMALL CAPTIVE. THE TRIBESMEN STAND SILENT, READY TO FLEE.
TOR STARES IN AMAZEMENT AT THE HUGE FIGURE...
...AS SOBS MIX WITH TEARS. THE FEARFUL APPARITION IS... CRYING.
THEY WATCH IN DISBELIEF AS THE STRANGE CREATURE LUMBERS INTO THE JUNGLE.
IN ADMIRATION THE HAIRY GROUP GATHERS AROUND TOR...
...TO ACKNOWLEDGE THE DEFEAT OF THEIR NEMESIS.

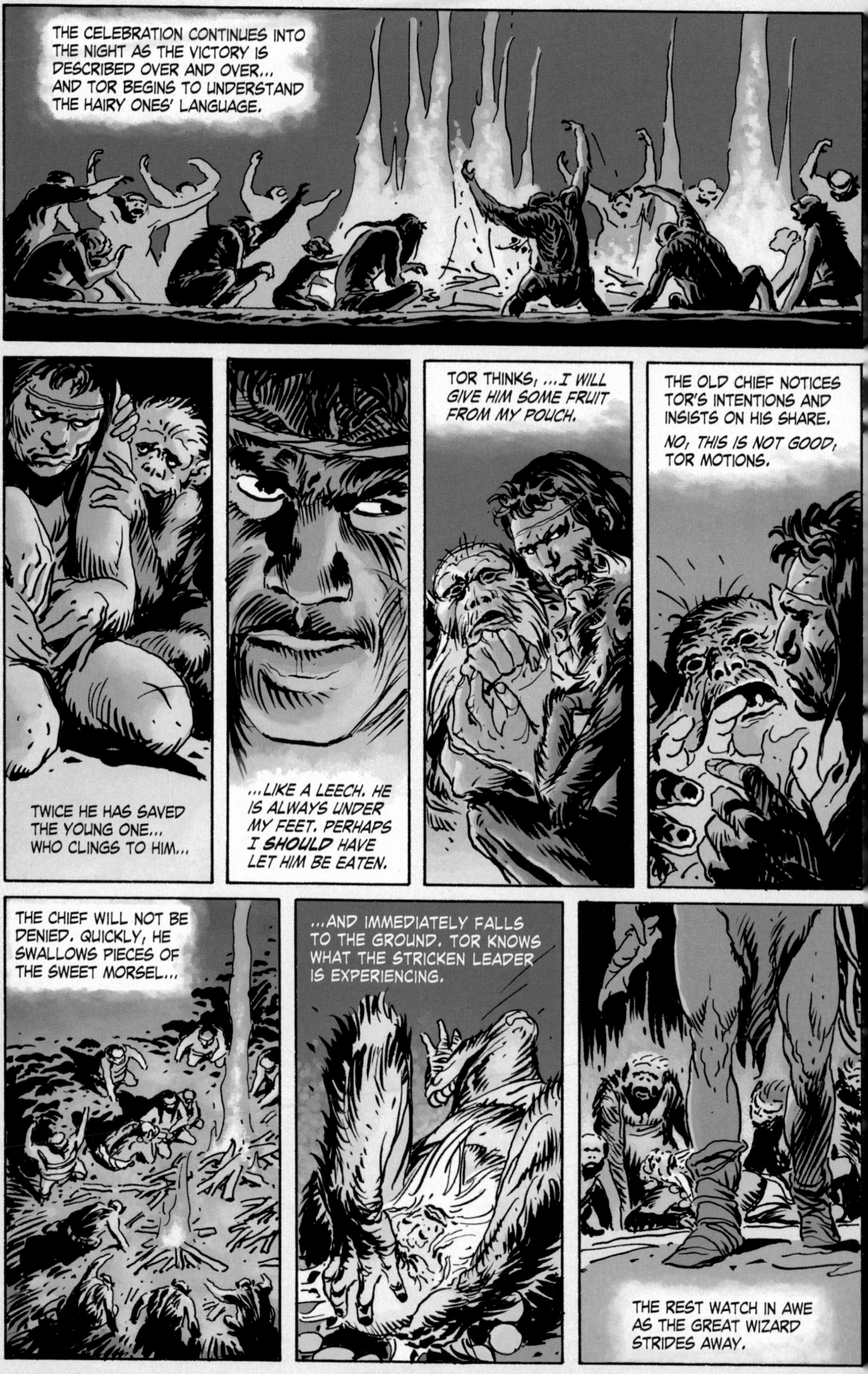
THE CELEBRATION CONTINUES INTO THE NIGHT AS THE VICTORY IS DESCRIBED OVER AND OVER... AND TOR BEGINS TO UNDERSTAND THE HAIRY ONES' LANGUAGE.
TWICE HE HAS SAVED THE YOUNG ONE... WHO CLINGS TO HIM...
...LIKE A LEECH. HE IS ALWAYS UNDER MY FEET. PERHAPS I SHOULD HAVE LET HIM BE EATEN.
TOR THINKS, ...I WILL GIVE HIM SOME FRUIT FROM MY POUCH.
THE OLD CHIEF NOTICES TOR'S INTENTIONS AND INSISTS ON HIS SHARE.
NO, THIS IS NOT GOOD, TOR MOTIONS.
THE CHIEF WILL NOT BE DENIED. QUICKLY, HE SWALLOWS PIECES OF THE SWEET MORSEL...
...AND IMMEDIATELY FALLS TO THE GROUND. TOR KNOWS WHAT THE STRICKEN LEADER IS EXPERIENCING.
THE REST WATCH IN AWE AS THE GREAT WIZARD STRIDES AWAY.

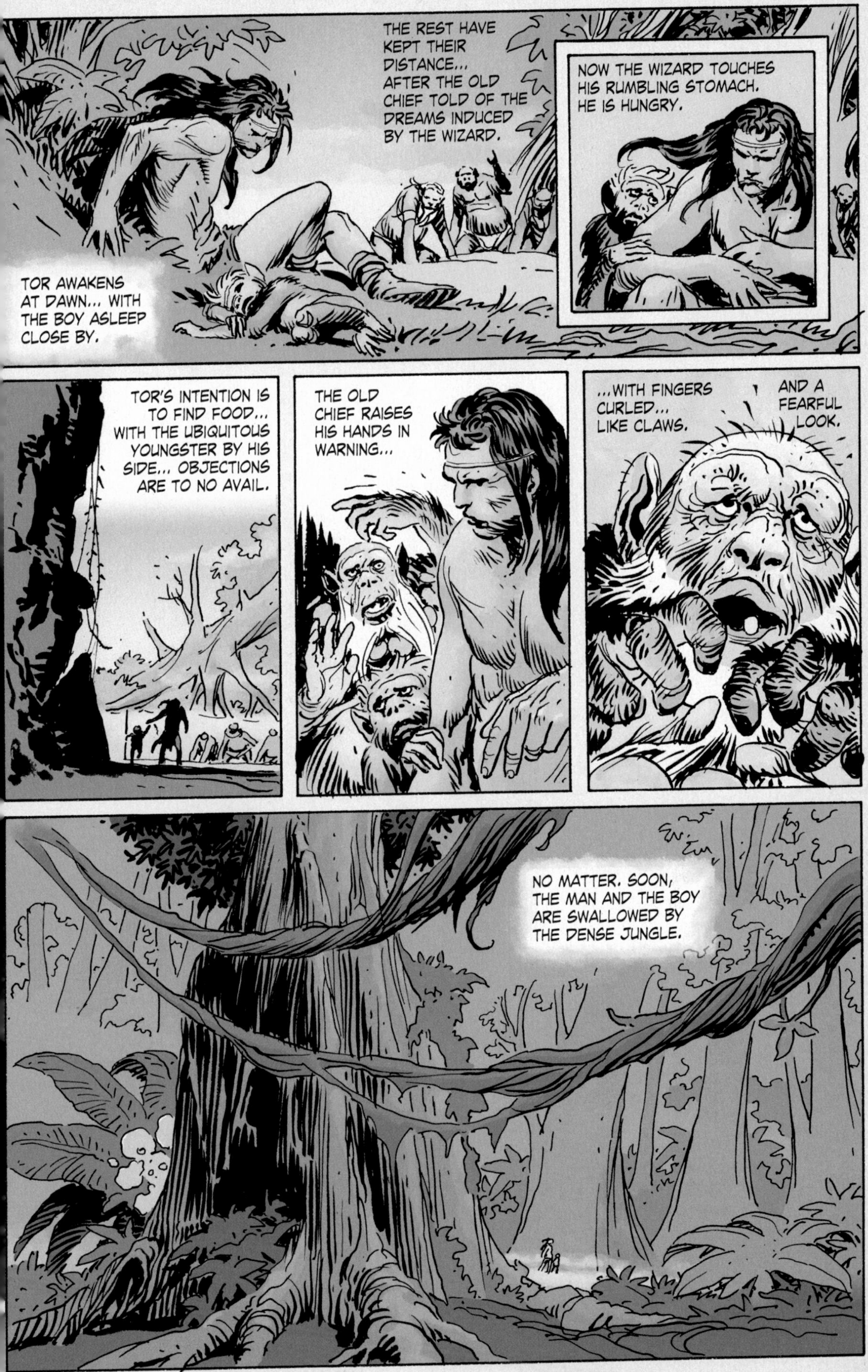
TOR AWAKENS AT DAWN... WITH THE BOY ASLEEP CLOSE BY.
THE REST HAVE KEPT THEIR DISTANCE... AFTER THE OLD CHIEF TOLD OF THE DREAMS INDUCED BY THE WIZARD.
NOW THE WIZARD TOUCHES HIS RUMBLING STOMACH. HE IS HUNGRY.
TOR'S INTENTION IS TO FIND FOOD... WITH THE UBIQUITOUS YOUNGSTER BY HIS SIDE... OBJECTIONS ARE TO NO AVAIL.
THE OLD CHIEF RAISES HIS HANDS IN WARNING...
...WITH FINGERS CURLED... LIKE CLAWS.
AND A FEARFUL LOOK.
NO MATTER. SOON, THE MAN AND THE BOY ARE SWALLOWED BY THE DENSE JUNGLE.

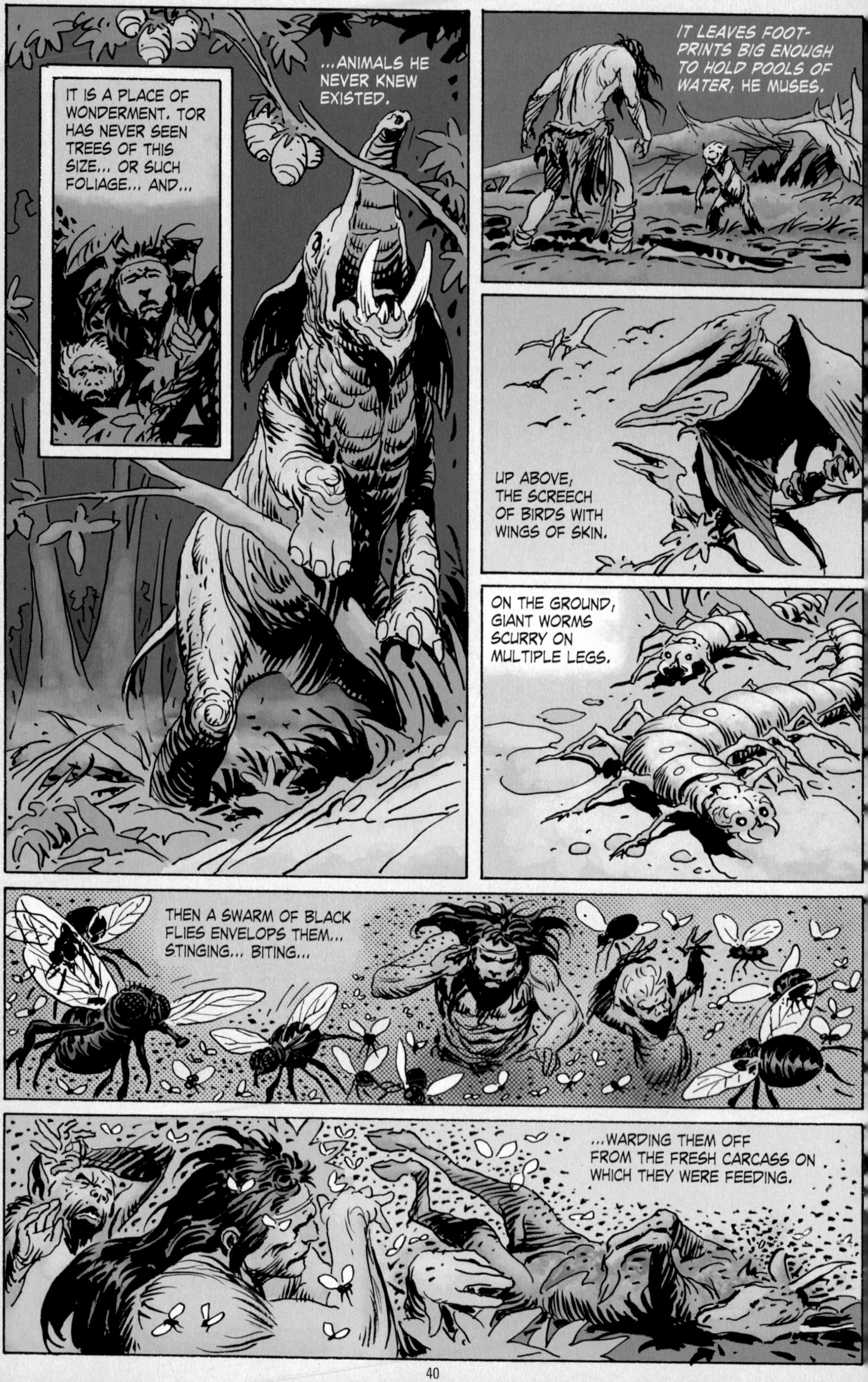
IT IS A PLACE OF WONDERMENT. TOR HAS NEVER SEEN TREES OF THIS SIZE... OR SUCH FOLIAGE... AND...
...ANIMALS HE NEVER KNEW EXISTED.
IT LEAVES FOOT-PRINTS BIG ENOUGH TO HOLD POOLS OF WATER, HE MUSES.
UP ABOVE, THE SCREECH OF BIRDS WITH WINGS OF SKIN.
ON THE GROUND, GIANT WORMS SCURRY ON MULTIPLE LEGS.
THEN A SWARM OF BLACK FLIES ENVELOPS THEM... STINGING... BITING...
...WARDING THEM OFF FROM THE FRESH CARCASS ON WHICH THEY WERE FEEDING.

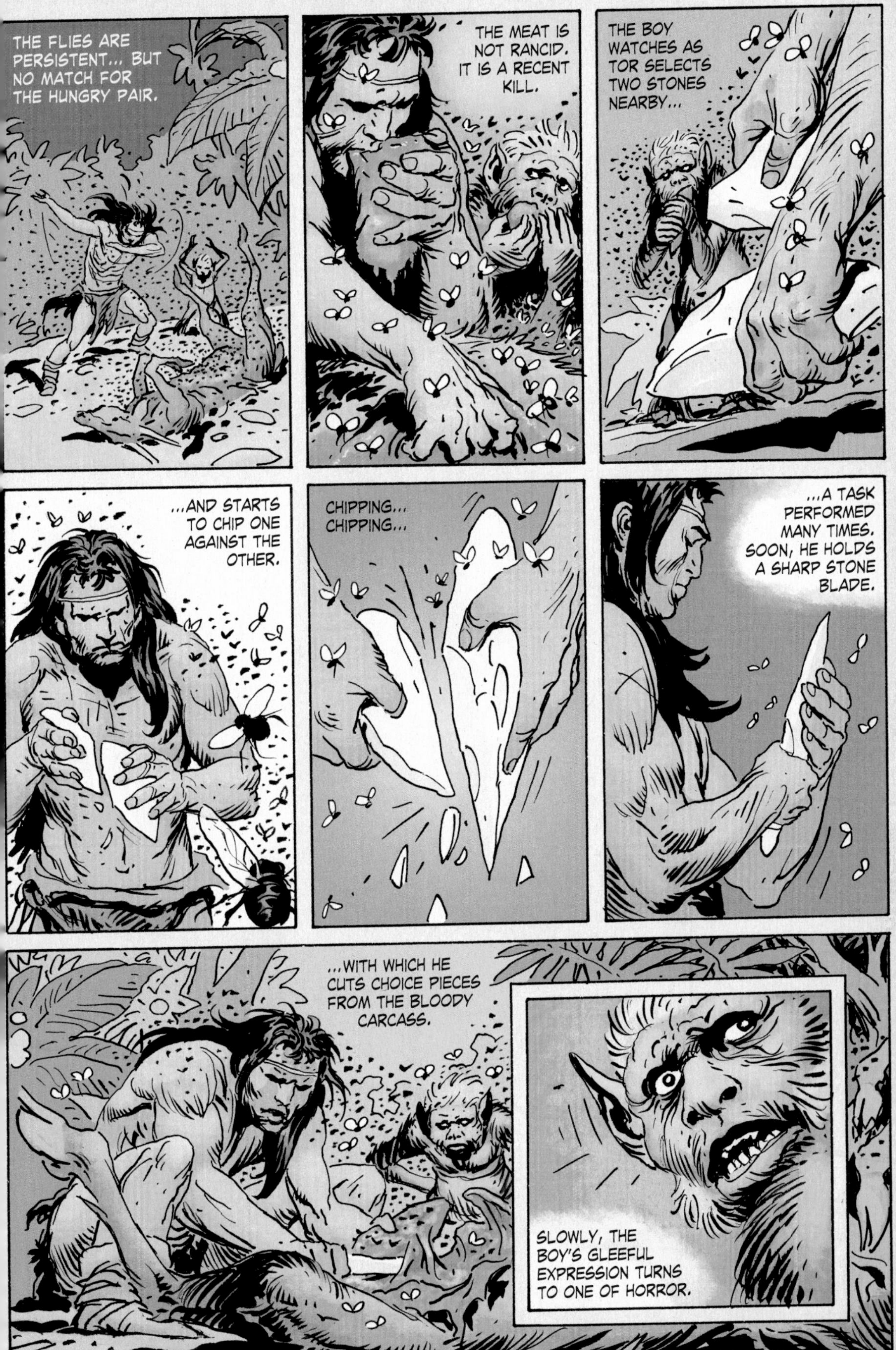
THE FLIES ARE PERSISTENT... BUT NO MATCH FOR THE HUNGRY PAIR.
THE MEAT IS NOT RANCID. IT IS A RECENT KILL.
THE BOY WATCHES AS TOR SELECTS TWO STONES NEARBY...
...AND STARTS TO CHIP ONE AGAINST THE OTHER.
CHIPPING... CHIPPING...
...A TASK PERFORMED MANY TIMES. SOON, HE HOLDS A SHARP STONE BLADE.
...WITH WHICH HE CUTS CHOICE PIECES FROM THE BLOODY CARCASS.
SLOWLY, THE BOY'S GLEEFUL EXPRESSION TURNS TO ONE OF HORROR.

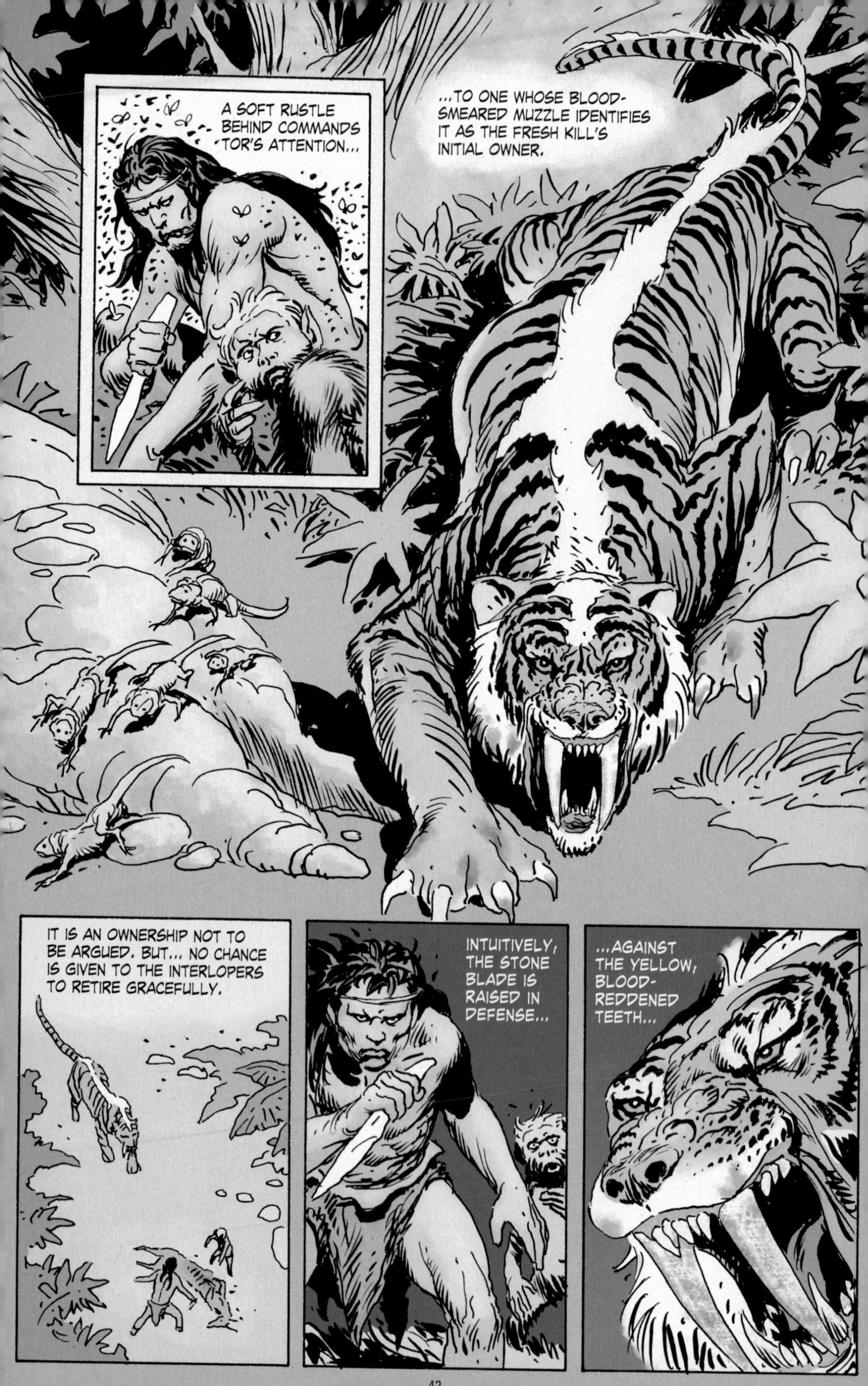

A SOFT RUSTLE BEHIND COMMANDS TOR'S ATTENTION...
...TO ONE WHOSE BLOOD-SMEARED MUZZLE IDENTIFIES IT AS THE FRESH KILL'S INITIAL OWNER.
IT IS AN OWNERSHIP NOT TO BE ARGUED. BUT... NO CHANCE IS GIVEN TO THE INTERLOPERS TO RETIRE GRACEFULLY.
INTUITIVELY, THE STONE BLADE IS RAISED IN DEFENSE...
...AGAINST THE YELLOW, BLOOD-REDDENED TEETH...

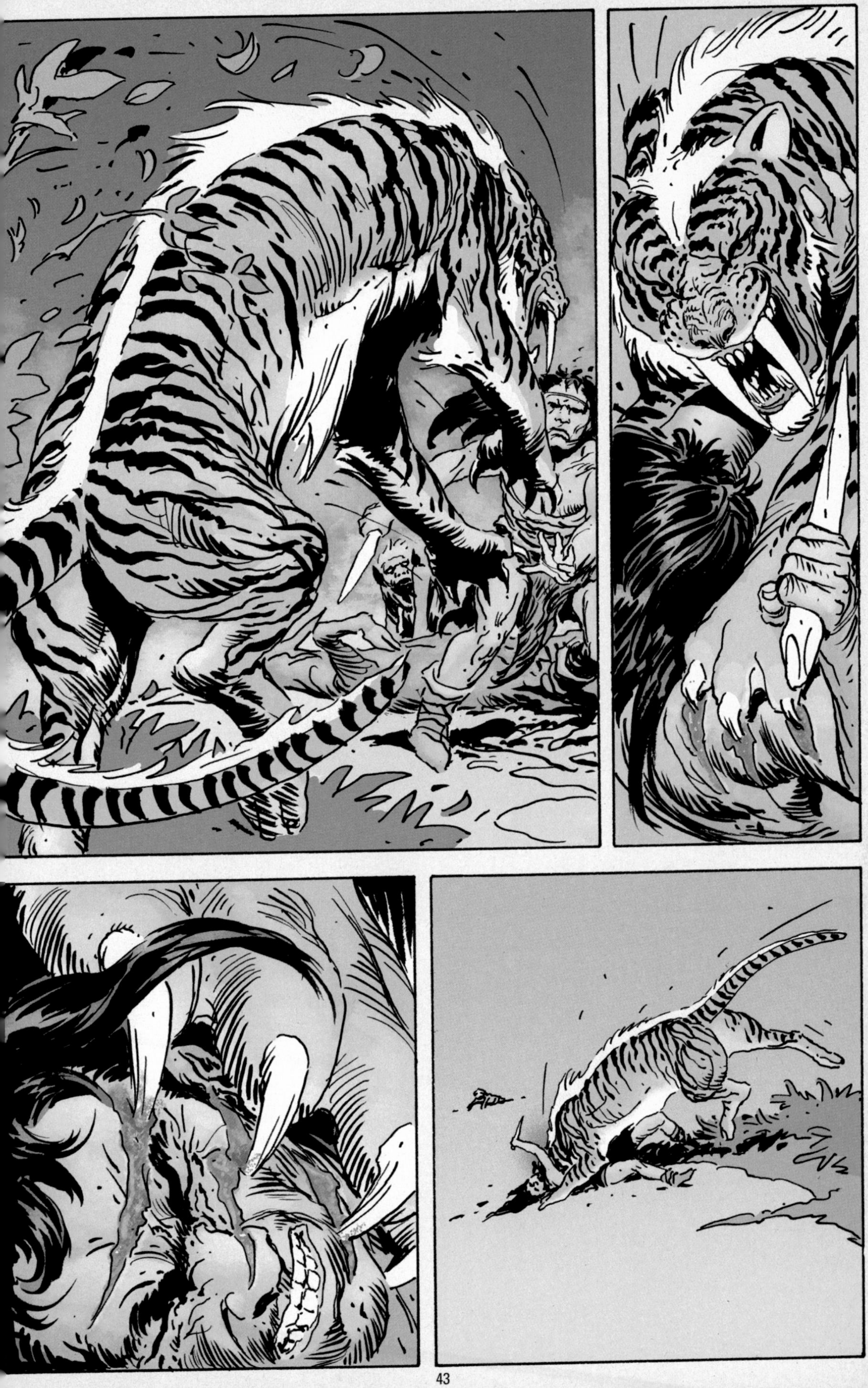

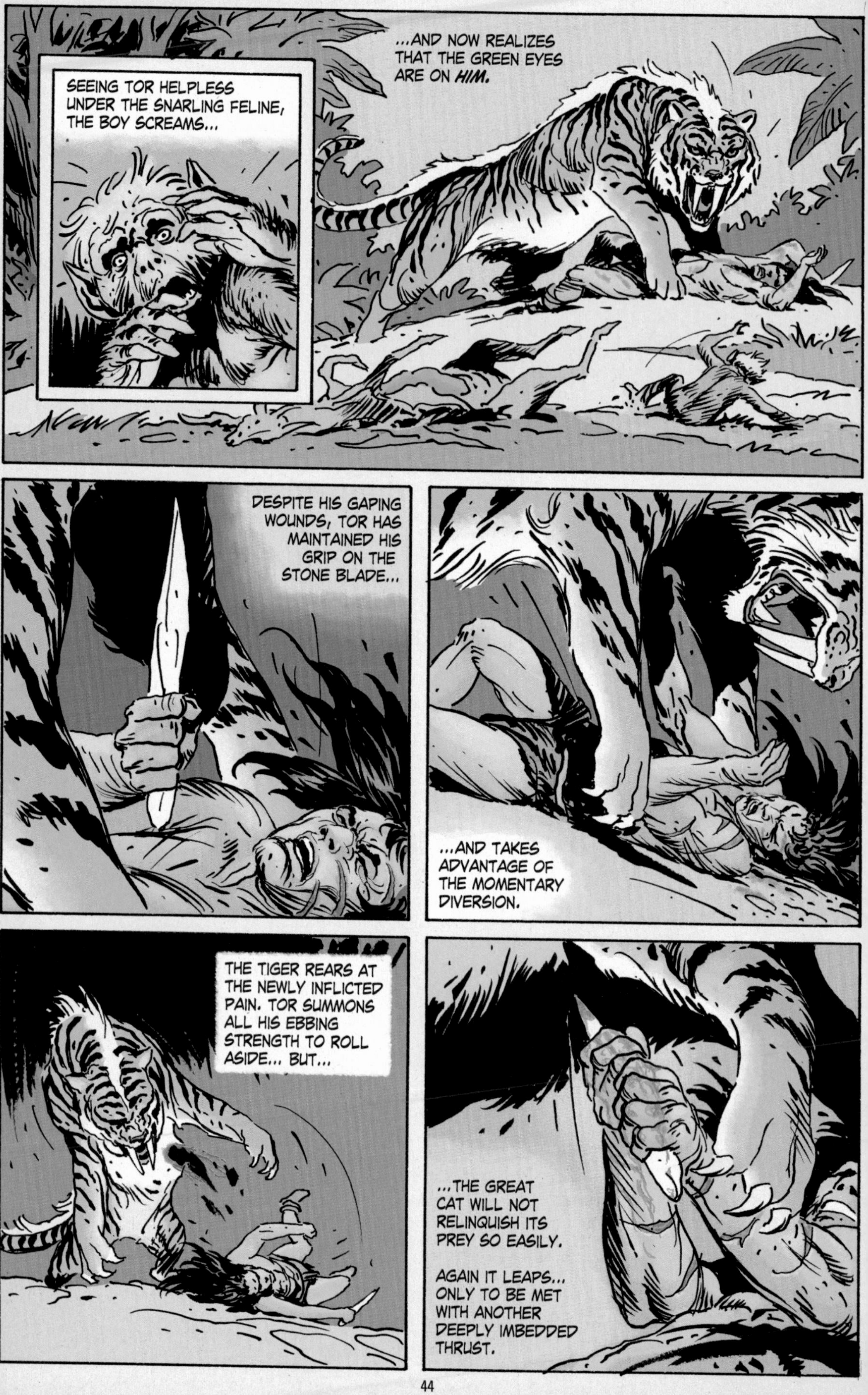
SEEING TOR HELPLESS UNDER THE SNARLING FELINE, THE BOY SCREAMS...
...AND NOW REALIZES THAT THE GREEN EYES ARE ON *HIM.*
DESPITE HIS GAPING WOUNDS, TOR HAS MAINTAINED HIS GRIP ON THE STONE BLADE...
...AND TAKES ADVANTAGE OF THE MOMENTARY DIVERSION.
THE TIGER REARS AT THE NEWLY INFLICTED PAIN. TOR SUMMONS ALL HIS EBBING STRENGTH TO ROLL ASIDE... BUT...
...THE GREAT CAT WILL NOT RELINQUISH ITS PREY SO EASILY.
AGAIN IT LEAPS... ONLY TO BE MET WITH ANOTHER DEEPLY IMBEDDED THRUST.

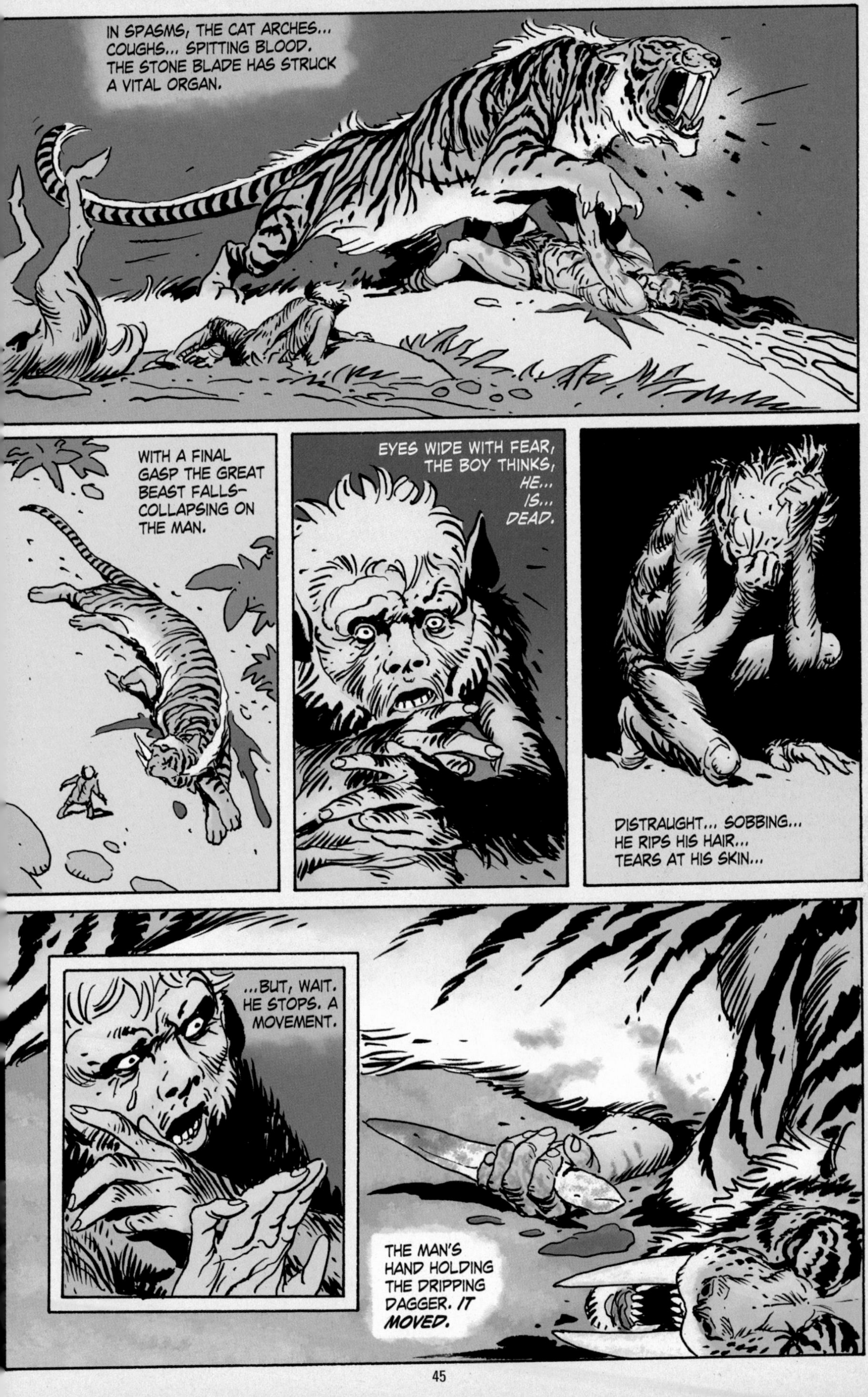
IN SPASMS, THE CAT ARCHES... COUGHS... SPITTING BLOOD. THE STONE BLADE HAS STRUCK A VITAL ORGAN.
WITH A FINAL GASP THE GREAT BEAST FALLS—COLLAPSING ON THE MAN.
EYES WIDE WITH FEAR, THE BOY THINKS, *HE... IS... DEAD.*
DISTRAUGHT... SOBBING... HE RIPS HIS HAIR... TEARS AT HIS SKIN...
...BUT, WAIT. HE STOPS. A MOVEMENT.
THE MAN'S HAND HOLDING THE DRIPPING DAGGER. *IT MOVED.*

HE RUNS TO THE INERT ANIMAL... PRESSING... PUSHING WITH ALL HIS MIGHT. AGAIN, THE MAN'S HAND AND LEG MOVE.

DESPERATELY, HE PULLS ON THE LOOSE, THICK SKIN... UNTIL....

...WITH SOME HELP FROM THE MAN UNDERNEATH, THE HEAVY BODY ROLLS...

...TO REVEAL THE BLOOD-SOAKED FIGURE. IS HE ALIVE? *YES.* HE BREATHES... MOANS...

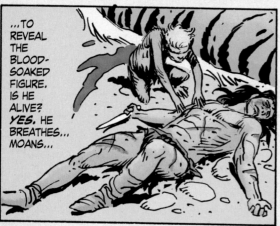

WITH ONLY A QUICK GLANCE, THE BOY SCAMPERS INTO THE JUNGLE. *THE HEALING LEAVES. WITHOUT THEM, HE WILL SURELY DIE.*

TOR FEELS THE THROBBING PAIN... SMELLS THE SICKENING SWEET ODOR OF BLOOD.

HE FORCES HIS THOUGHTS BACK TO THE LOW HILLS CLOSE TO THE CLEAR WATER... WHERE HIS JOURNEY BEGAN...

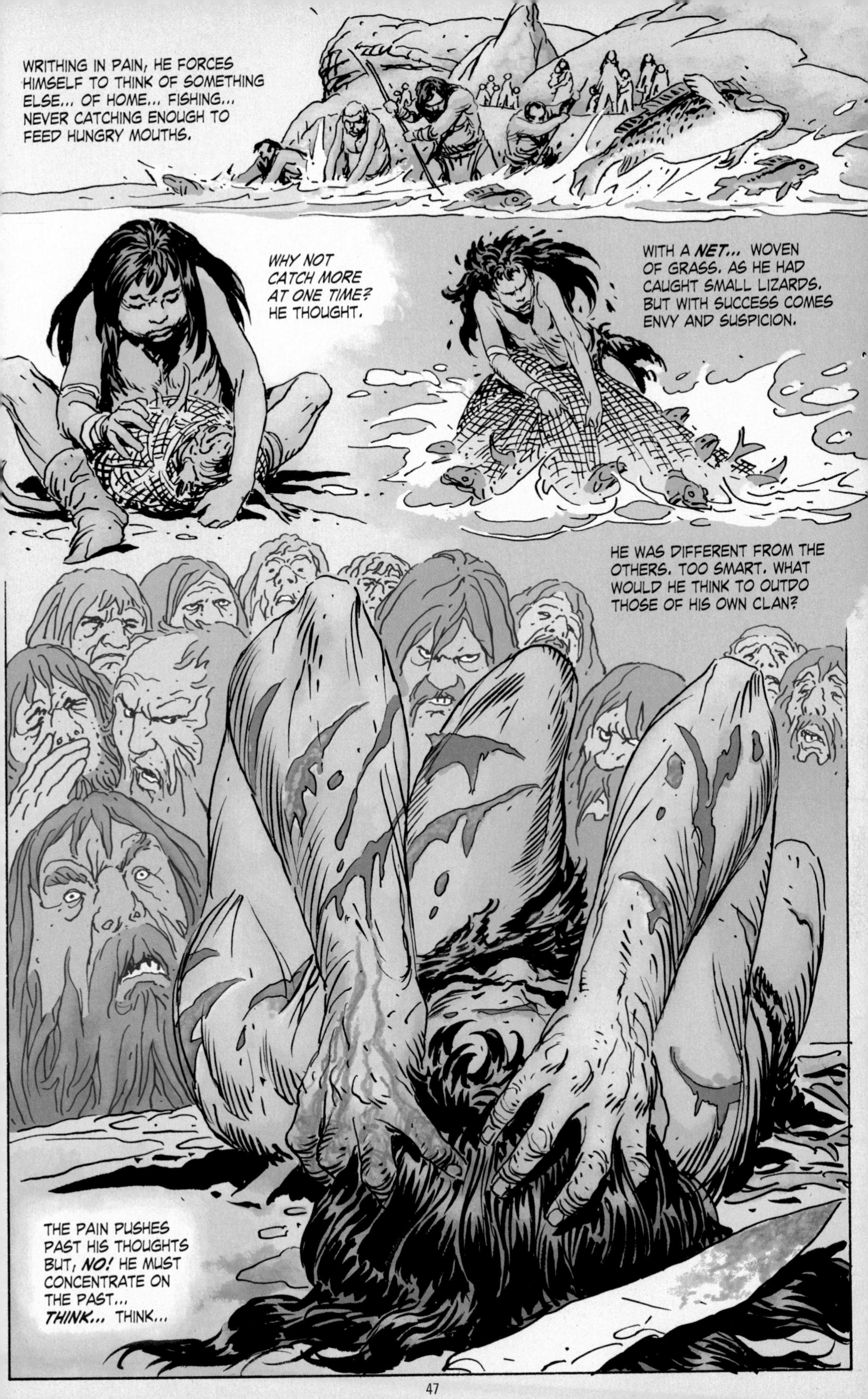
WRITHING IN PAIN, HE FORCES HIMSELF TO THINK OF SOMETHING ELSE... OF HOME... FISHING... NEVER CATCHING ENOUGH TO FEED HUNGRY MOUTHS.
WHY NOT CATCH MORE AT ONE TIME? HE THOUGHT.
WITH A NET... WOVEN OF GRASS. AS HE HAD CAUGHT SMALL LIZARDS. BUT WITH SUCCESS COMES ENVY AND SUSPICION.
HE WAS DIFFERENT FROM THE OTHERS. TOO SMART. WHAT WOULD HE THINK TO OUTDO THOSE OF HIS OWN CLAN?
THE PAIN PUSHES PAST HIS THOUGHTS BUT, NO! HE MUST CONCENTRATE ON THE PAST... THINK... THINK...

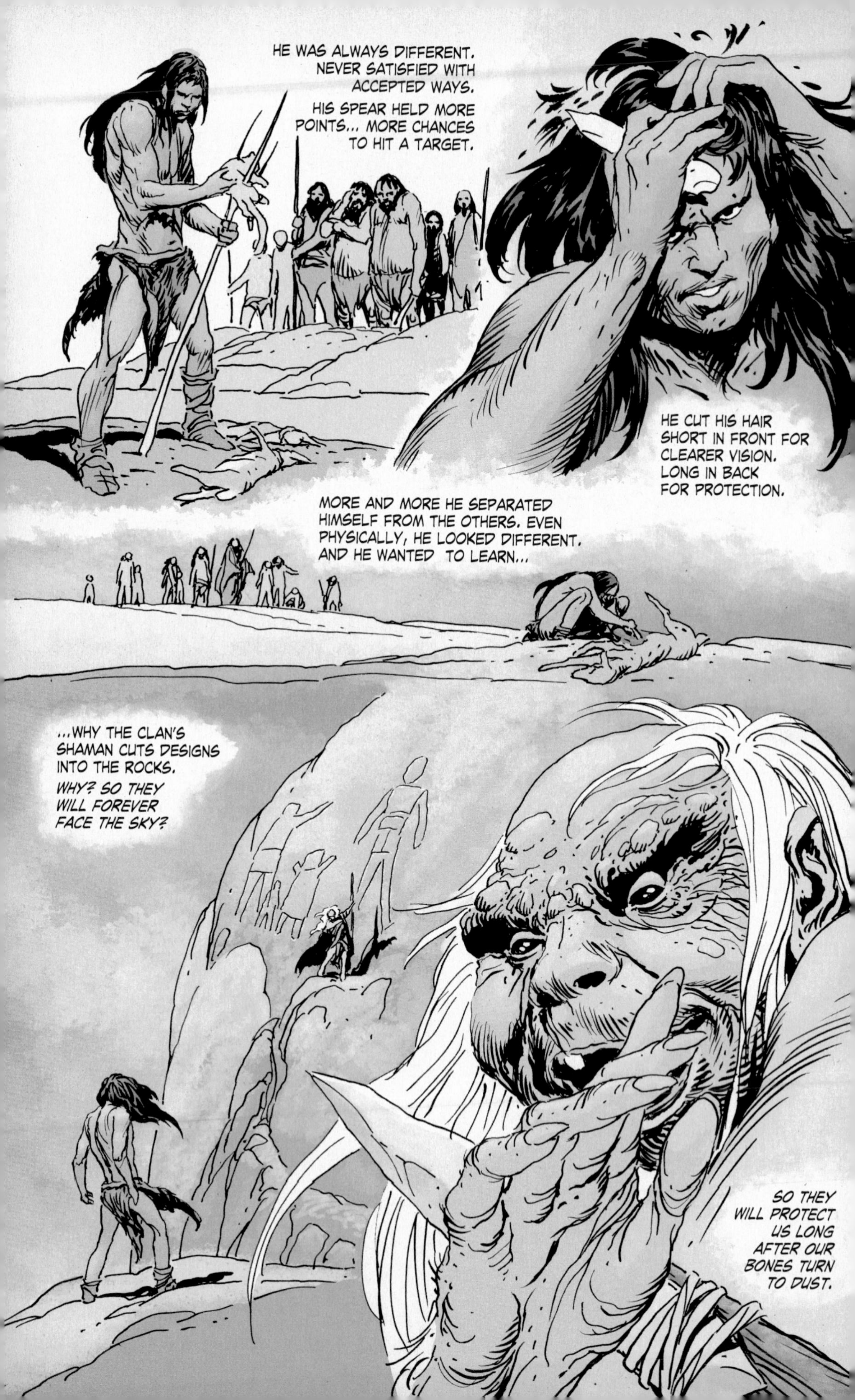
HE WAS ALWAYS DIFFERENT. NEVER SATISFIED WITH ACCEPTED WAYS.
HIS SPEAR HELD MORE POINTS... MORE CHANCES TO HIT A TARGET.
HE CUT HIS HAIR SHORT IN FRONT FOR CLEARER VISION. LONG IN BACK FOR PROTECTION.
MORE AND MORE HE SEPARATED HIMSELF FROM THE OTHERS. EVEN PHYSICALLY, HE LOOKED DIFFERENT. AND HE WANTED TO LEARN...
...WHY THE CLAN'S SHAMAN CUTS DESIGNS INTO THE ROCKS.
WHY? SO THEY WILL FOREVER FACE THE SKY?
SO THEY WILL PROTECT US LONG AFTER OUR BONES TURN TO DUST.

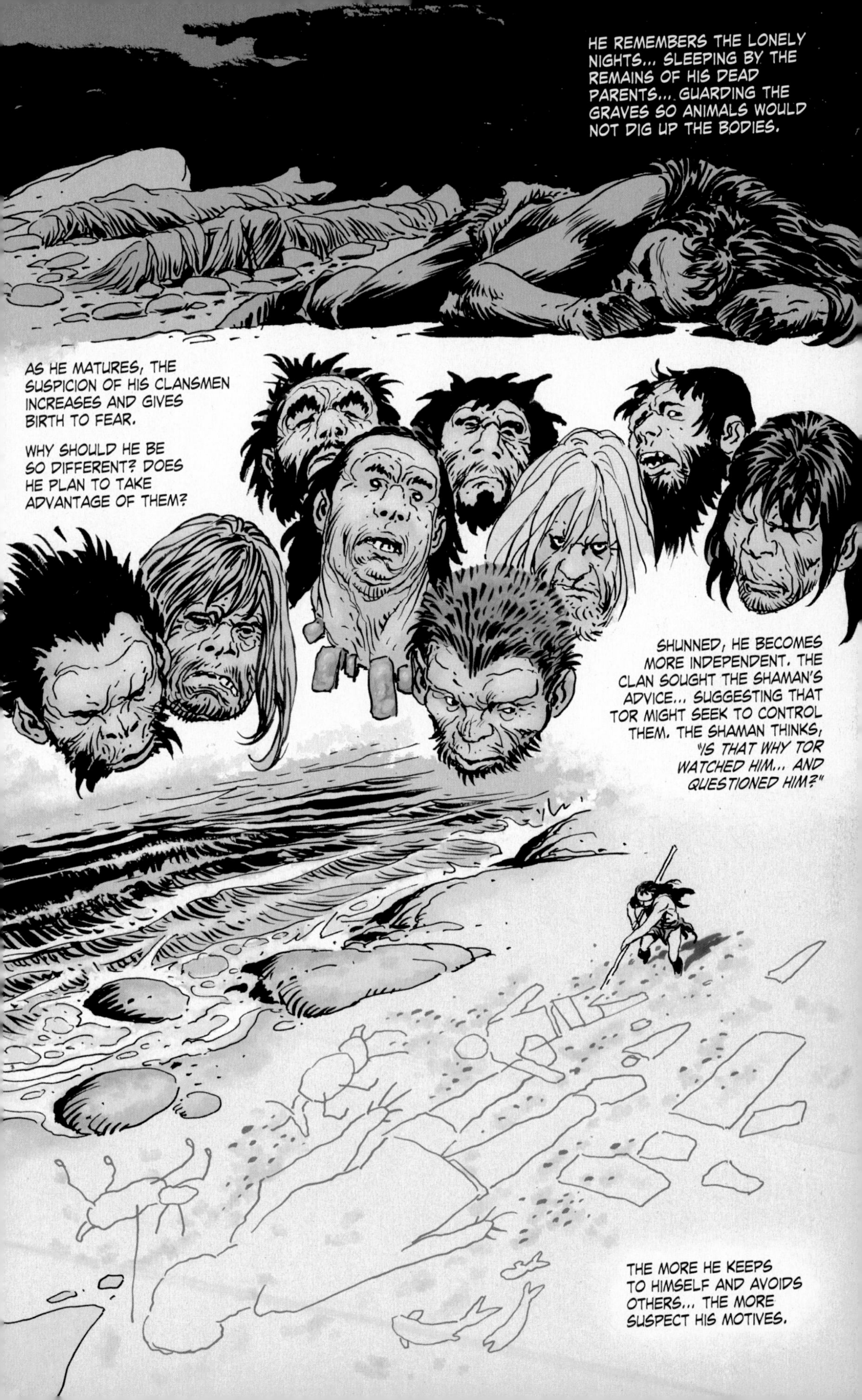
HE REMEMBERS THE LONELY NIGHTS... SLEEPING BY THE REMAINS OF HIS DEAD PARENTS... GUARDING THE GRAVES SO ANIMALS WOULD NOT DIG UP THE BODIES.
AS HE MATURES, THE SUSPICION OF HIS CLANSMEN INCREASES AND GIVES BIRTH TO FEAR.
WHY SHOULD HE BE SO DIFFERENT? DOES HE PLAN TO TAKE ADVANTAGE OF THEM?
SHUNNED, HE BECOMES MORE INDEPENDENT. THE CLAN SOUGHT THE SHAMAN'S ADVICE... SUGGESTING THAT TOR MIGHT SEEK TO CONTROL THEM. THE SHAMAN THINKS, "IS THAT WHY TOR WATCHED HIM... AND QUESTIONED HIM?"
THE MORE HE KEEPS TO HIMSELF AND AVOIDS OTHERS... THE MORE SUSPECT HIS MOTIVES.

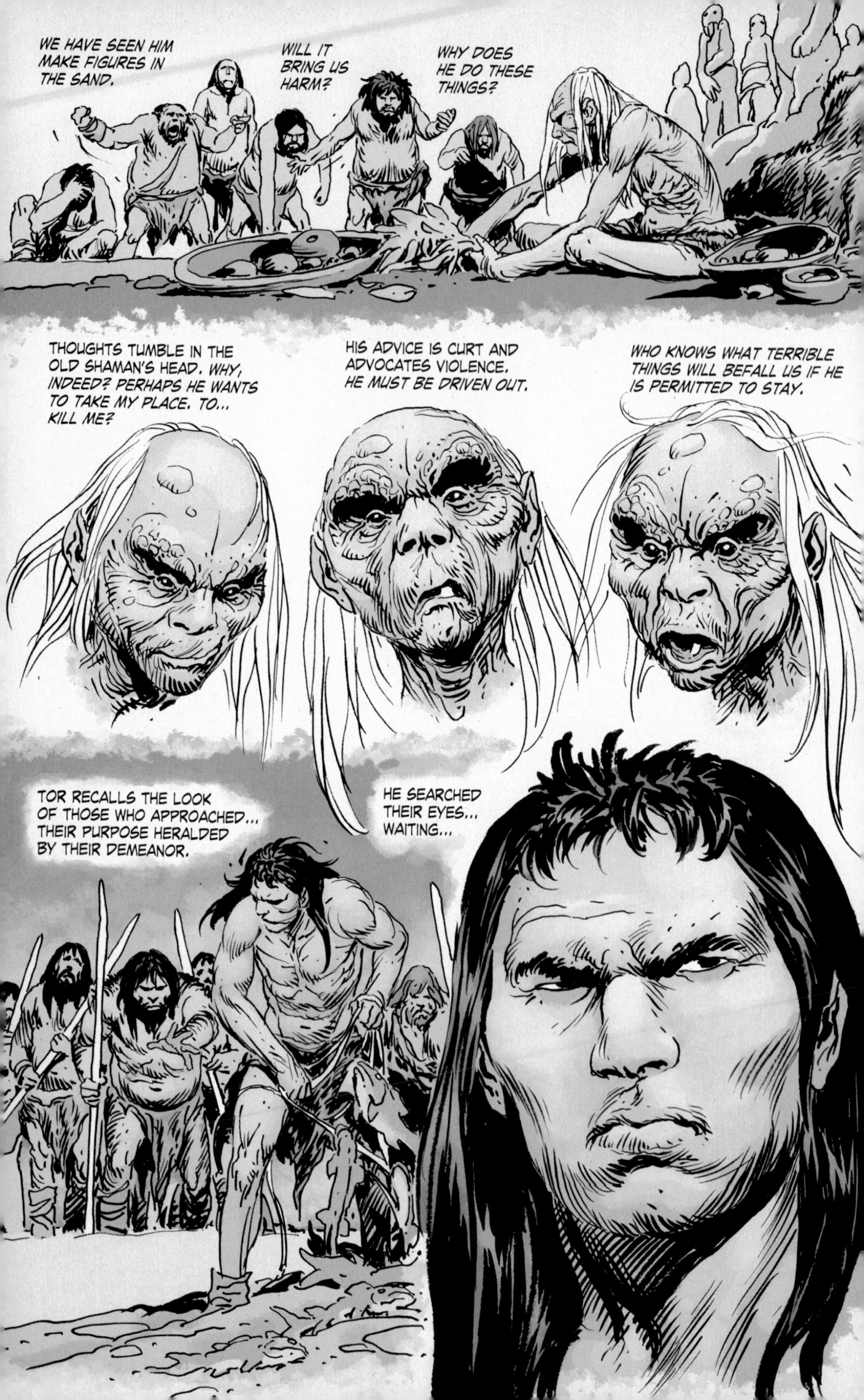
WE HAVE SEEN HIM MAKE FIGURES IN THE SAND.
WILL IT BRING US HARM?
WHY DOES HE DO THESE THINGS?
THOUGHTS TUMBLE IN THE OLD SHAMAN'S HEAD. WHY, INDEED? PERHAPS HE WANTS TO TAKE MY PLACE. TO... KILL ME?
HIS ADVICE IS CURT AND ADVOCATES VIOLENCE. HE MUST BE DRIVEN OUT.
WHO KNOWS WHAT TERRIBLE THINGS WILL BEFALL US IF HE IS PERMITTED TO STAY.
TOR RECALLS THE LOOK OF THOSE WHO APPROACHED... THEIR PURPOSE HERALDED BY THEIR DEMEANOR.
HE SEARCHED THEIR EYES... WAITING...

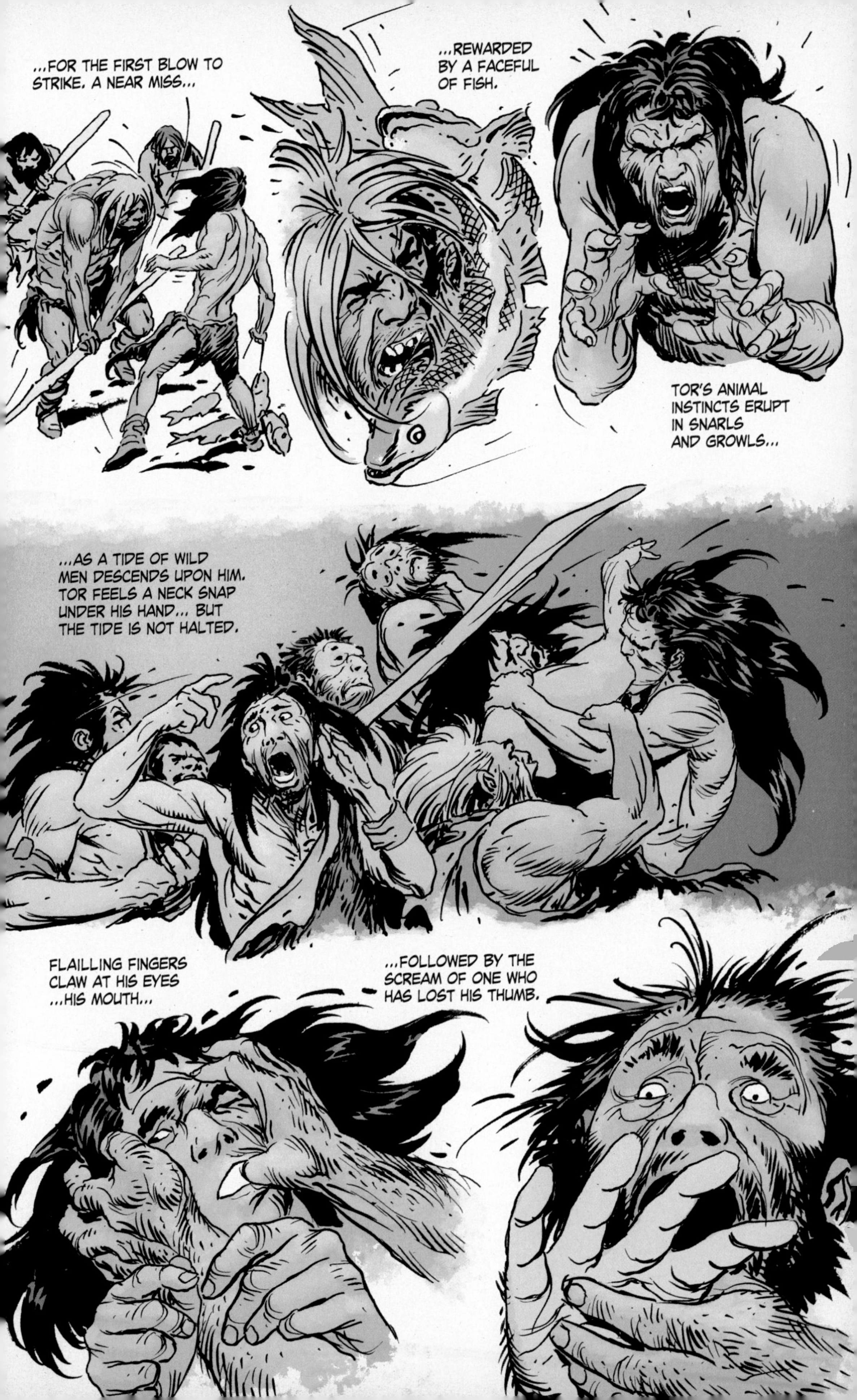
...FOR THE FIRST BLOW TO STRIKE. A NEAR MISS...
...REWARDED BY A FACEFUL OF FISH.
TOR'S ANIMAL INSTINCTS ERUPT IN SNARLS AND GROWLS...
...AS A TIDE OF WILD MEN DESCENDS UPON HIM. TOR FEELS A NECK SNAP UNDER HIS HAND... BUT THE TIDE IS NOT HALTED.
FLAILLING FINGERS CLAW AT HIS EYES ...HIS MOUTH...
...FOLLOWED BY THE SCREAM OF ONE WHO HAS LOST HIS THUMB.

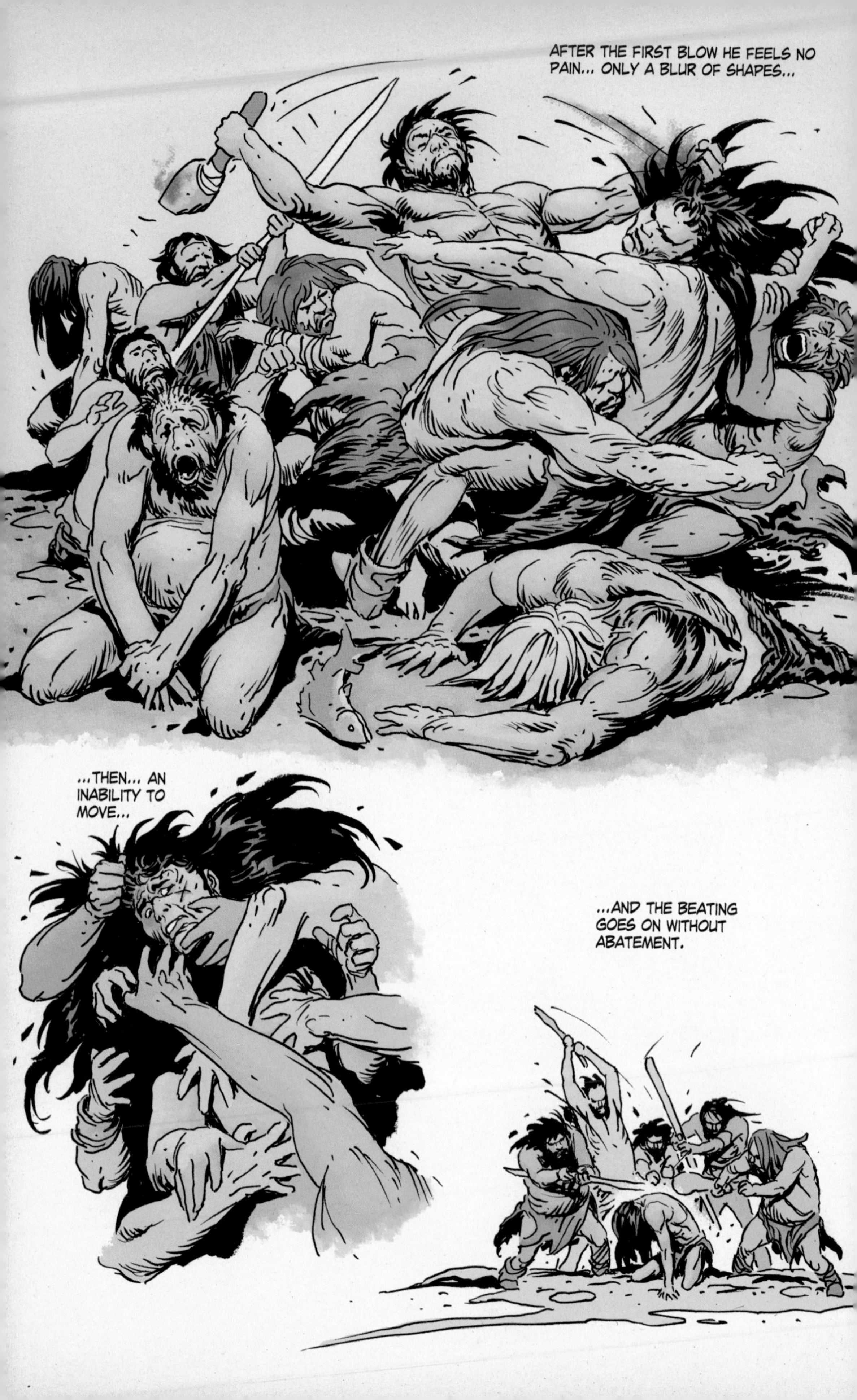
AFTER THE FIRST BLOW HE FEELS NO PAIN... ONLY A BLUR OF SHAPES...
...THEN... AN INABILITY TO MOVE...
...AND THE BEATING GOES ON WITHOUT ABATEMENT.

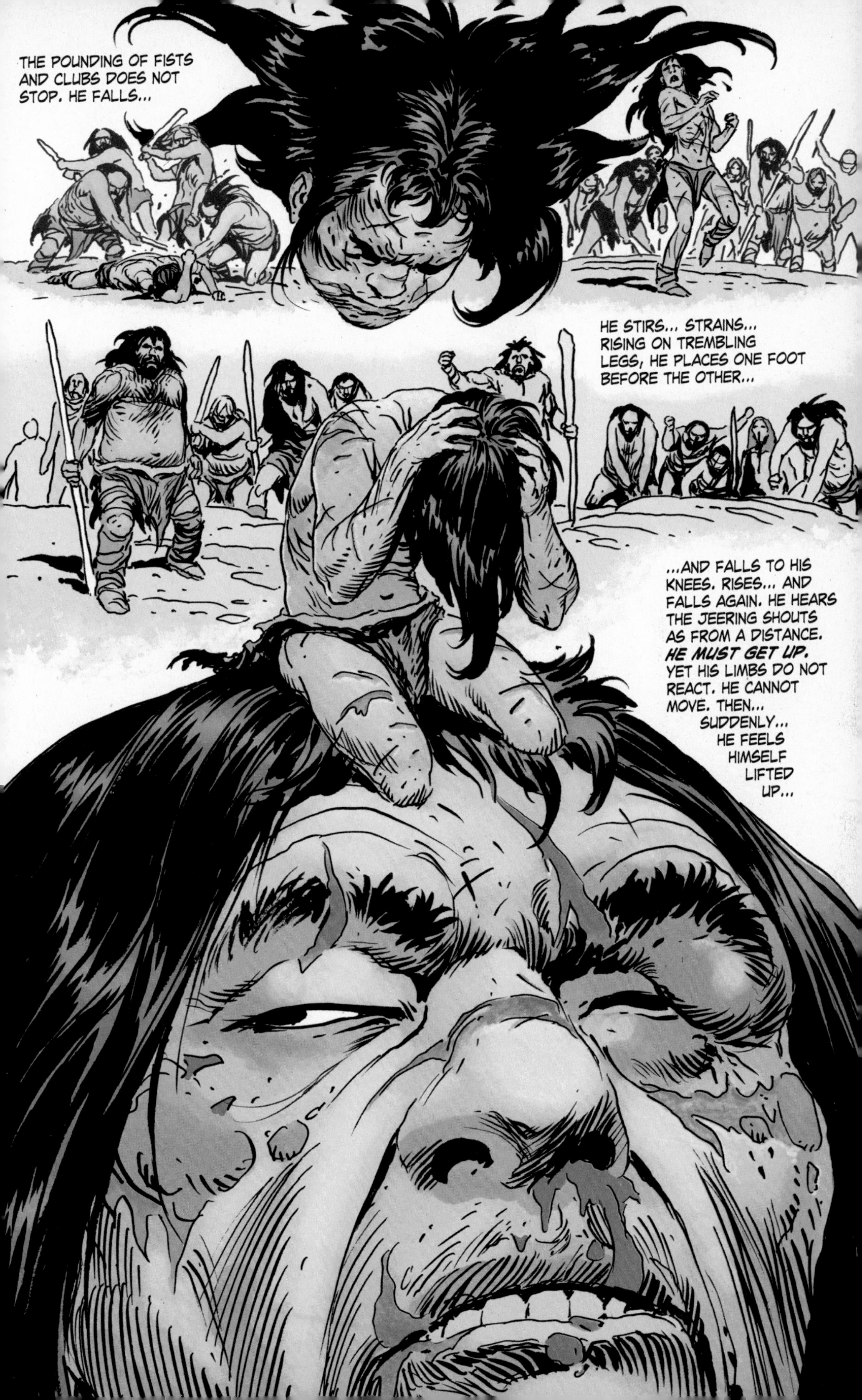
THE POUNDING OF FISTS AND CLUBS DOES NOT STOP. HE FALLS...
HE STIRS... STRAINS... RISING ON TREMBLING LEGS, HE PLACES ONE FOOT BEFORE THE OTHER...
...AND FALLS TO HIS KNEES. RISES... AND FALLS AGAIN. HE HEARS THE JEERING SHOUTS AS FROM A DISTANCE. *HE MUST GET UP.* YET HIS LIMBS DO NOT REACT. HE CANNOT MOVE. THEN... SUDDENLY... HE FEELS HIMSELF LIFTED UP...

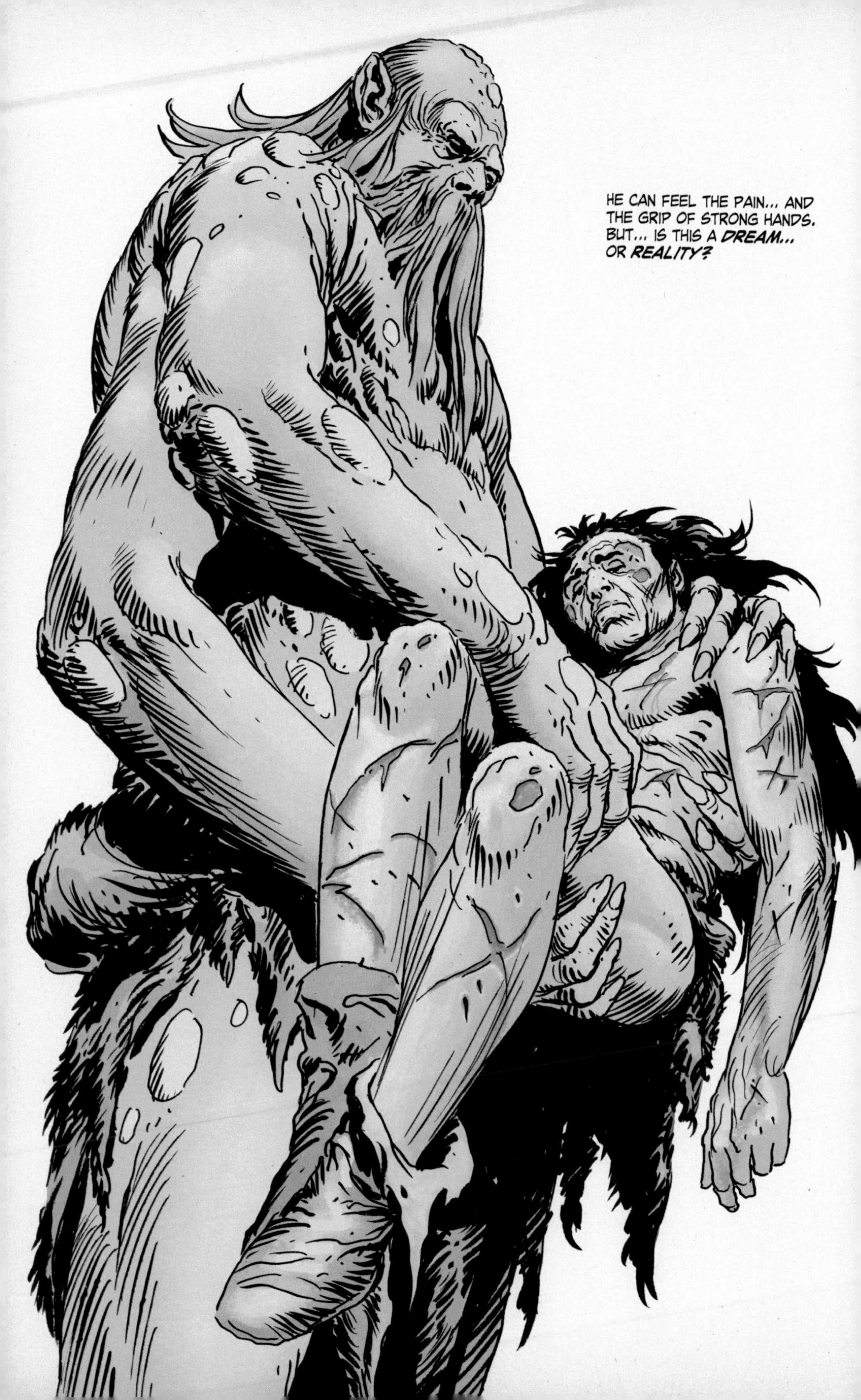
HE CAN FEEL THE PAIN... AND THE GRIP OF STRONG HANDS. BUT... IS THIS A *DREAM...* OR *REALITY?*

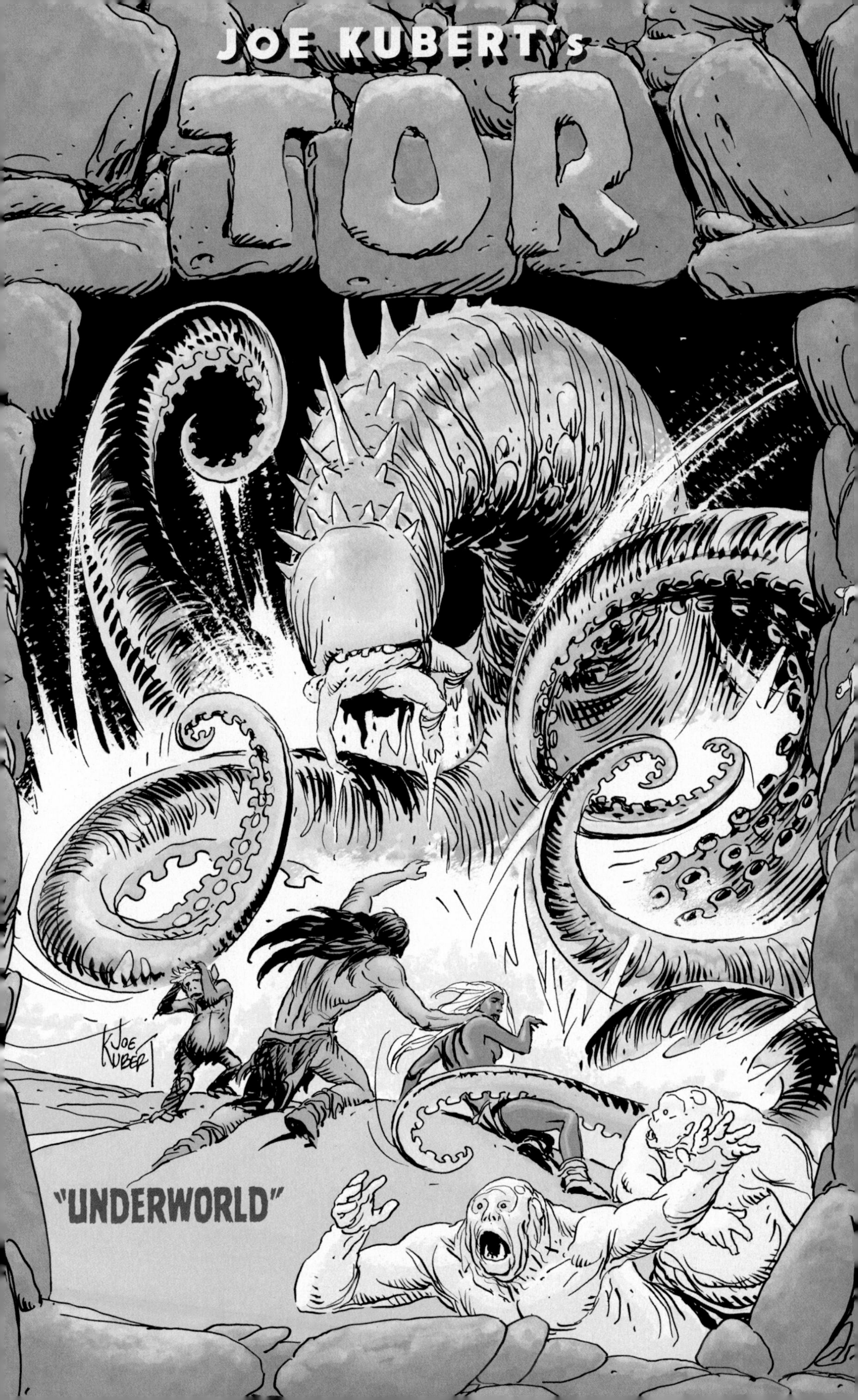
JOE KUBERT's
TOR
JOE KUBERT
"UNDERWORLD"

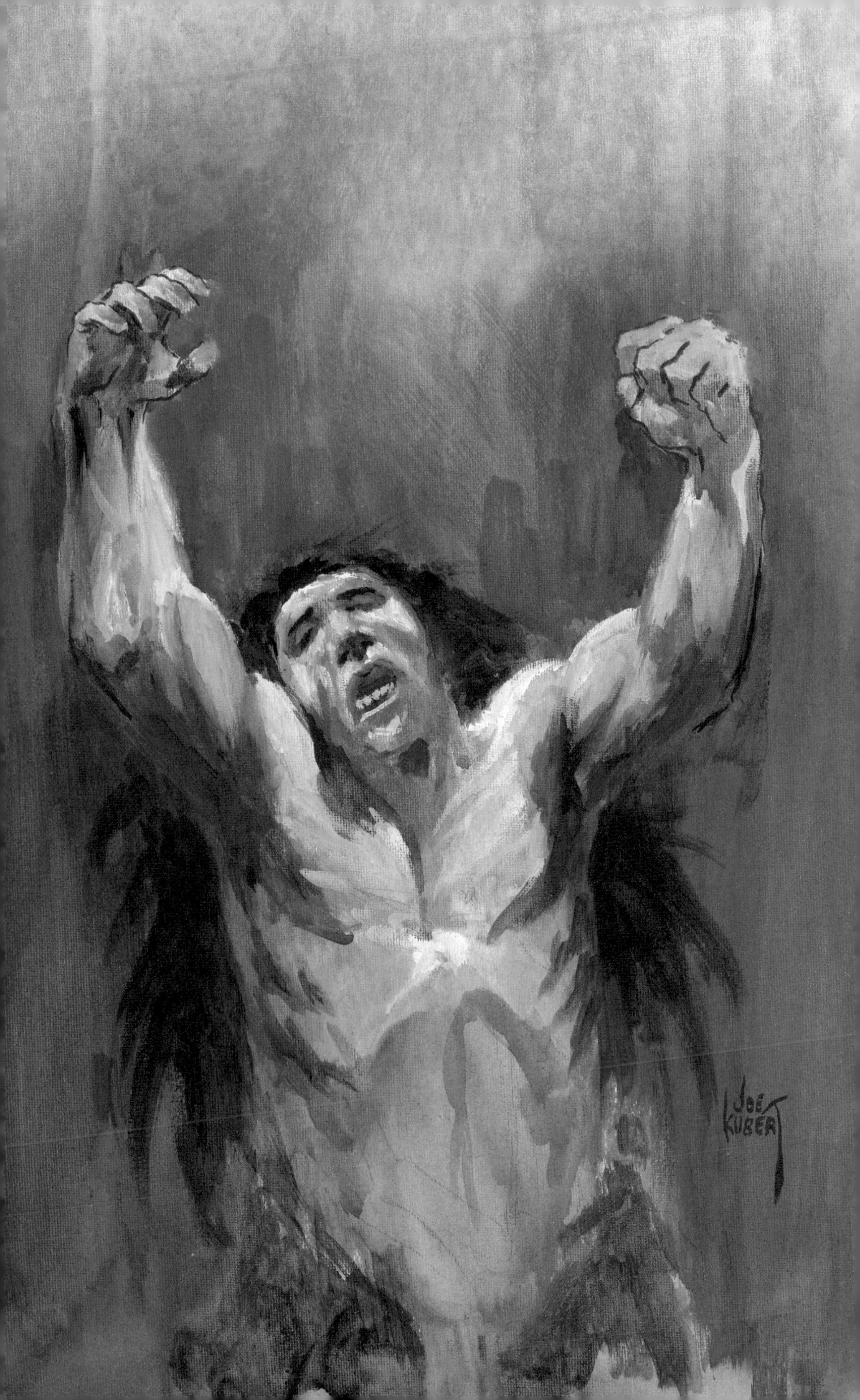
JOE
KUBERT

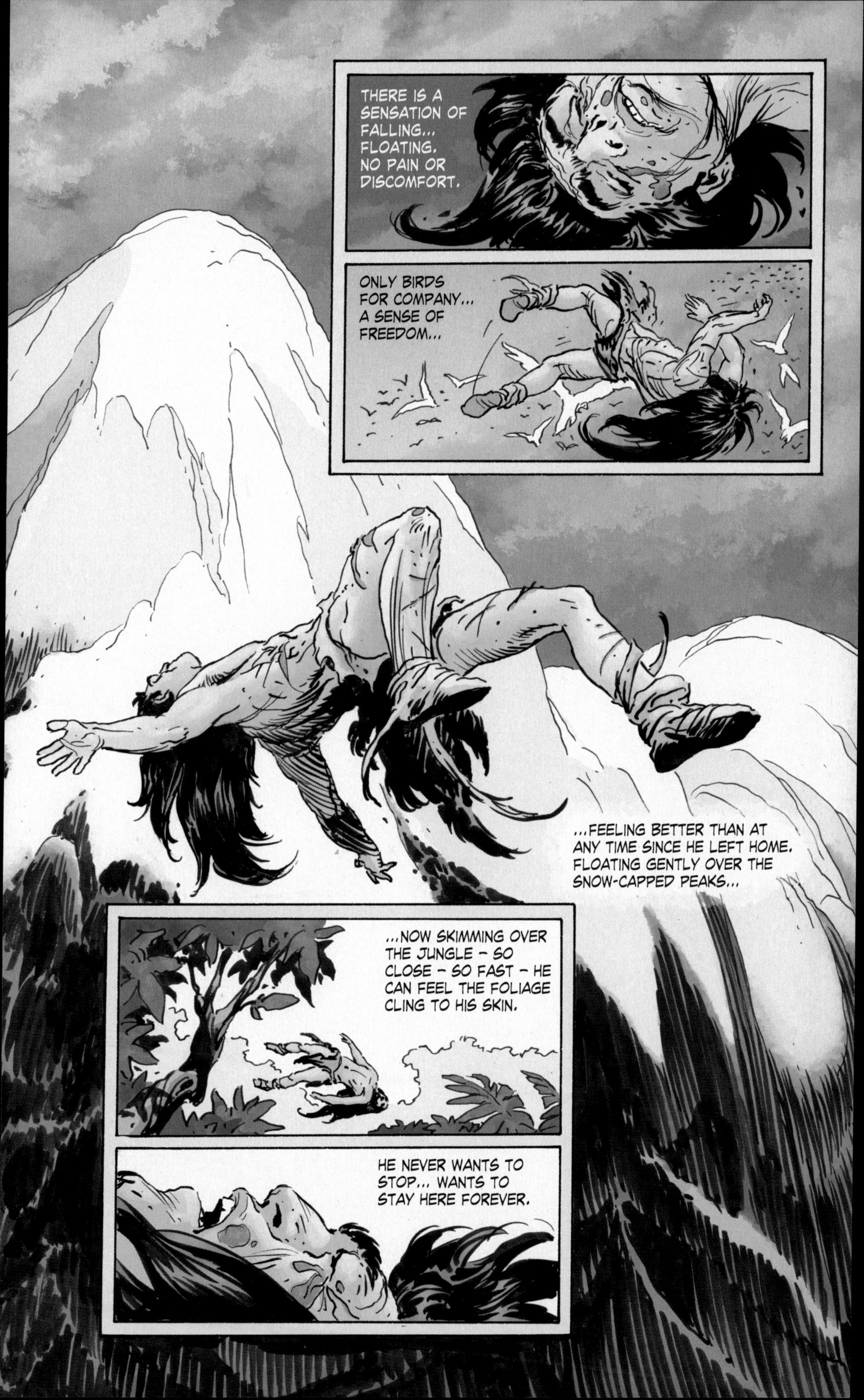

THERE IS A SENSATION OF FALLING... FLOATING. NO PAIN OR DISCOMFORT.
ONLY BIRDS FOR COMPANY... A SENSE OF FREEDOM...
...FEELING BETTER THAN AT ANY TIME SINCE HE LEFT HOME. FLOATING GENTLY OVER THE SNOW-CAPPED PEAKS...
...NOW SKIMMING OVER THE JUNGLE - SO CLOSE - SO FAST - HE CAN FEEL THE FOLIAGE CLING TO HIS SKIN.
HE NEVER WANTS TO STOP... WANTS TO STAY HERE FOREVER.

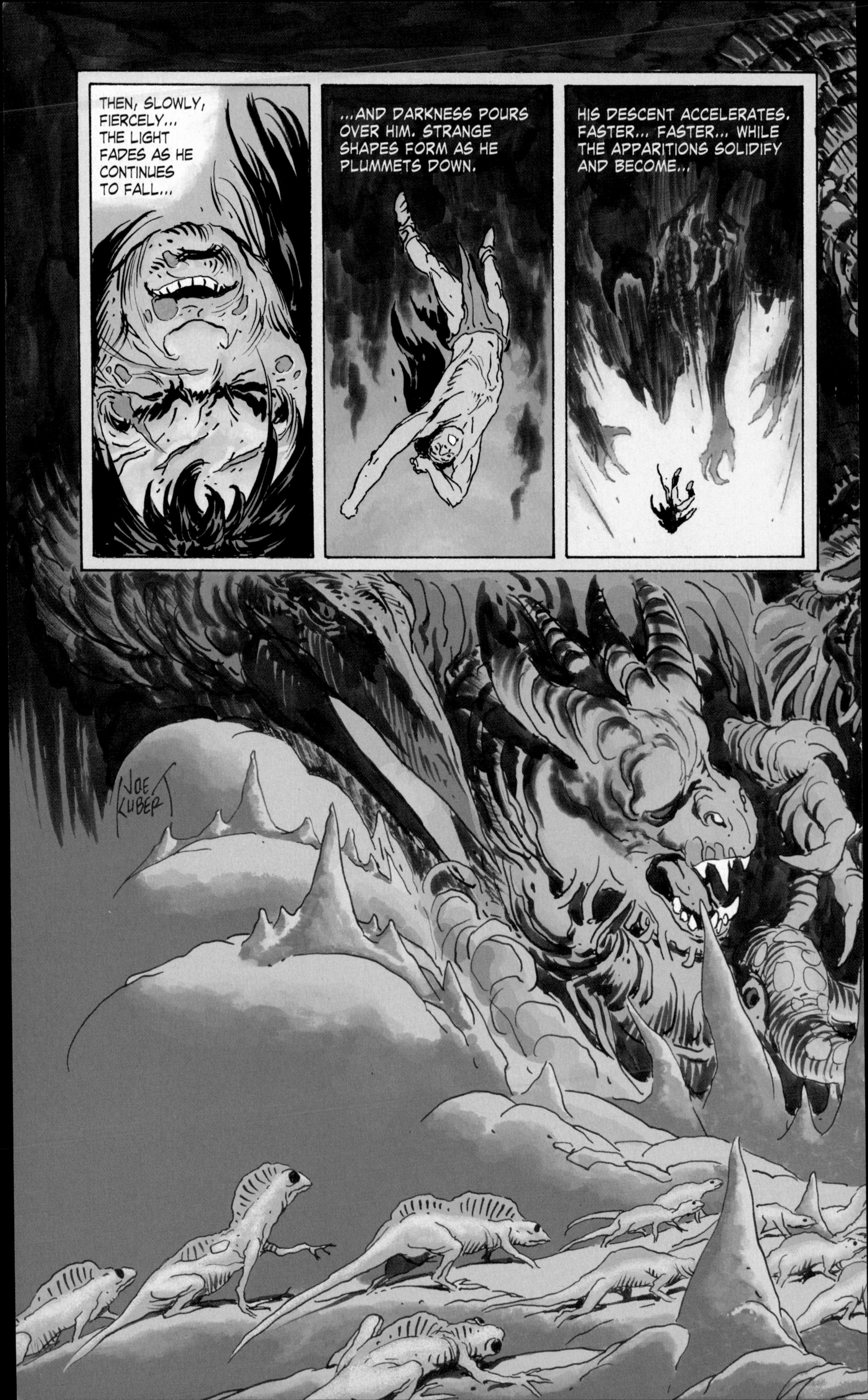
THEN, SLOWLY, FIERCELY... THE LIGHT FADES AS HE CONTINUES TO FALL...
...AND DARKNESS POURS OVER HIM. STRANGE SHAPES FORM AS HE PLUMMETS DOWN.
HIS DESCENT ACCELERATES. FASTER... FASTER... WHILE THE APPARITIONS SOLIDIFY AND BECOME...
JOE KUBERT

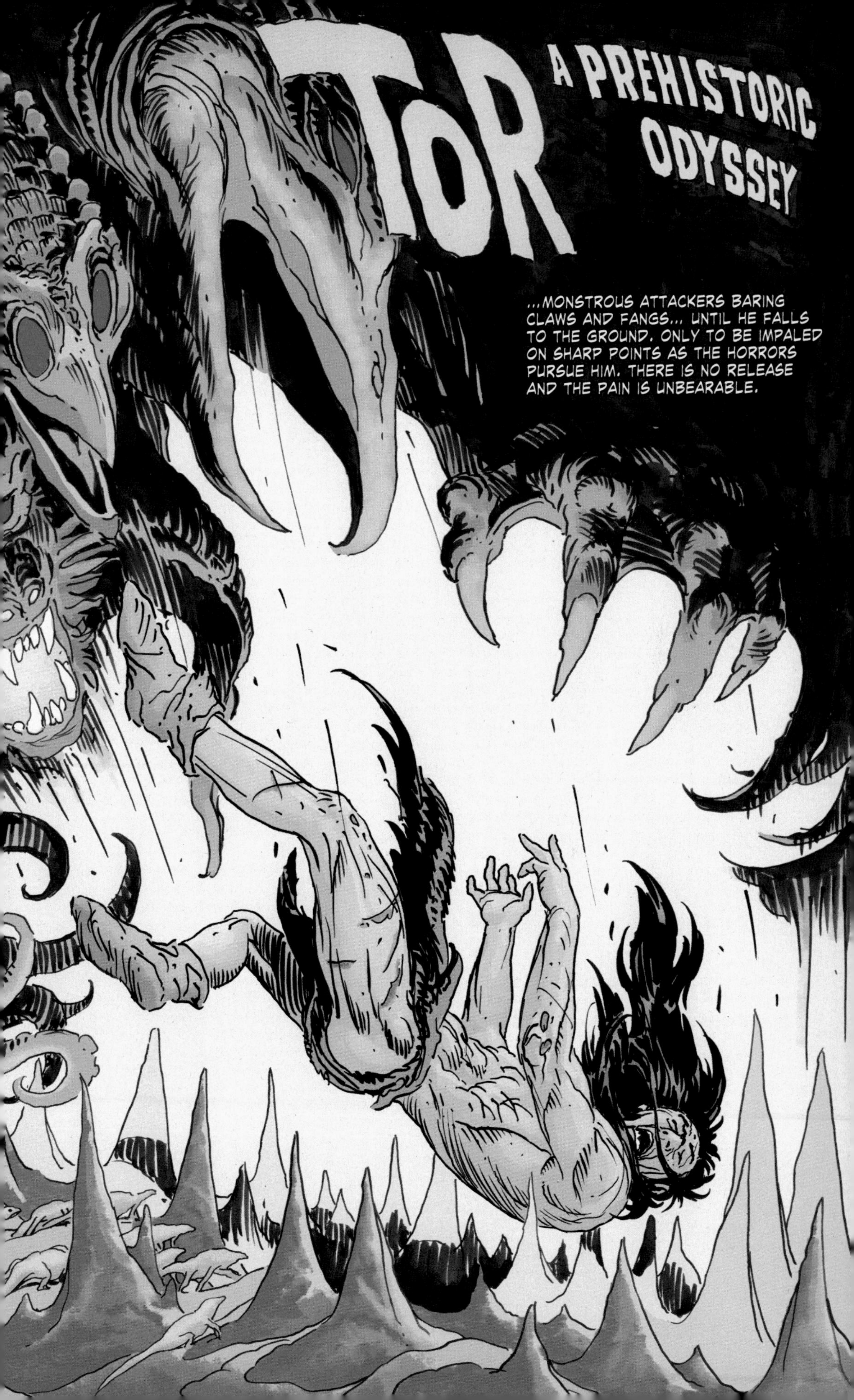
TOR
A PREHISTORIC ODYSSEY
...MONSTROUS ATTACKERS BARING CLAWS AND FANGS... UNTIL HE FALLS TO THE GROUND. ONLY TO BE IMPALED ON SHARP POINTS AS THE HORRORS PURSUE HIM. THERE IS NO RELEASE AND THE PAIN IS UNBEARABLE.

HE TRIES TO OPEN HIS EYES. ONLY ONE WILL OPEN...

HE TRIES TO SIT UP. HE CANNOT MOVE HIS ARM OR HIS LEG.

ANY ATTEMPT TO MOVE RESULTS IN EXCRUCIATING PAIN. NOW HE REALIZES SOMEONE IS NEAR.

HE TURNS HIS HEAD, AND PAIN ERUPTS THROUGH HIS BODY. A GIANT FIGURE LOOMS... BUT HE IS UNABLE TO MOVE OR PROTECT HIMSELF.

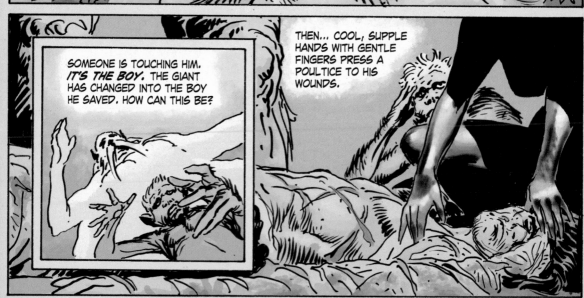

SOMEONE IS TOUCHING HIM. *IT'S THE BOY.* THE GIANT HAS CHANGED INTO THE BOY HE SAVED. HOW CAN THIS BE?

THEN... COOL, SUPPLE HANDS WITH GENTLE FINGERS PRESS A POULTICE TO HIS WOUNDS.

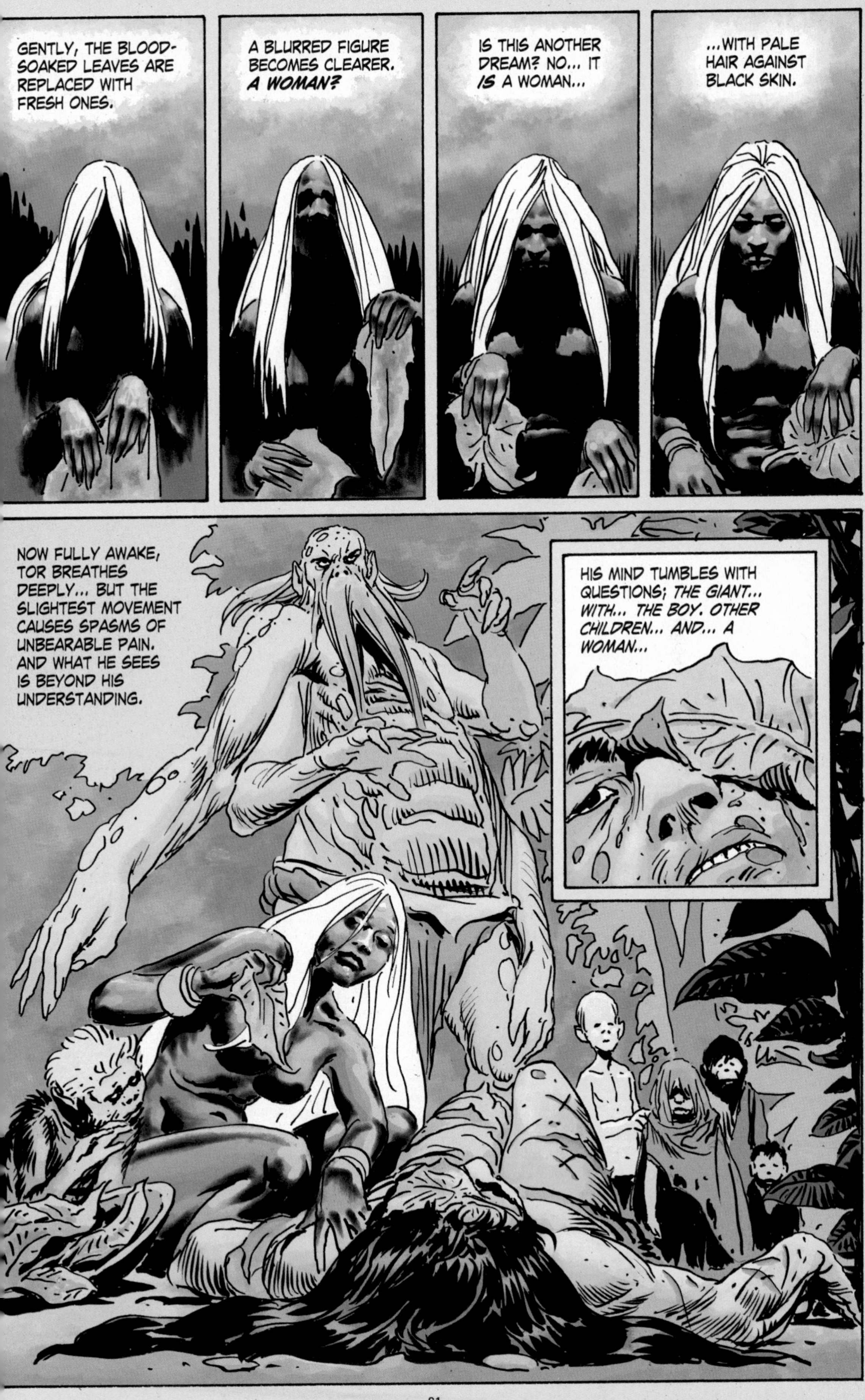
GENTLY, THE BLOOD-SOAKED LEAVES ARE REPLACED WITH FRESH ONES.
A BLURRED FIGURE BECOMES CLEARER. *A WOMAN?*
IS THIS ANOTHER DREAM? NO... IT *IS* A WOMAN...
...WITH PALE HAIR AGAINST BLACK SKIN.
NOW FULLY AWAKE, TOR BREATHES DEEPLY... BUT THE SLIGHTEST MOVEMENT CAUSES SPASMS OF UNBEARABLE PAIN. AND WHAT HE SEES IS BEYOND HIS UNDERSTANDING.
HIS MIND TUMBLES WITH QUESTIONS; *THE GIANT... WITH... THE BOY. OTHER CHILDREN... AND... A WOMAN...*

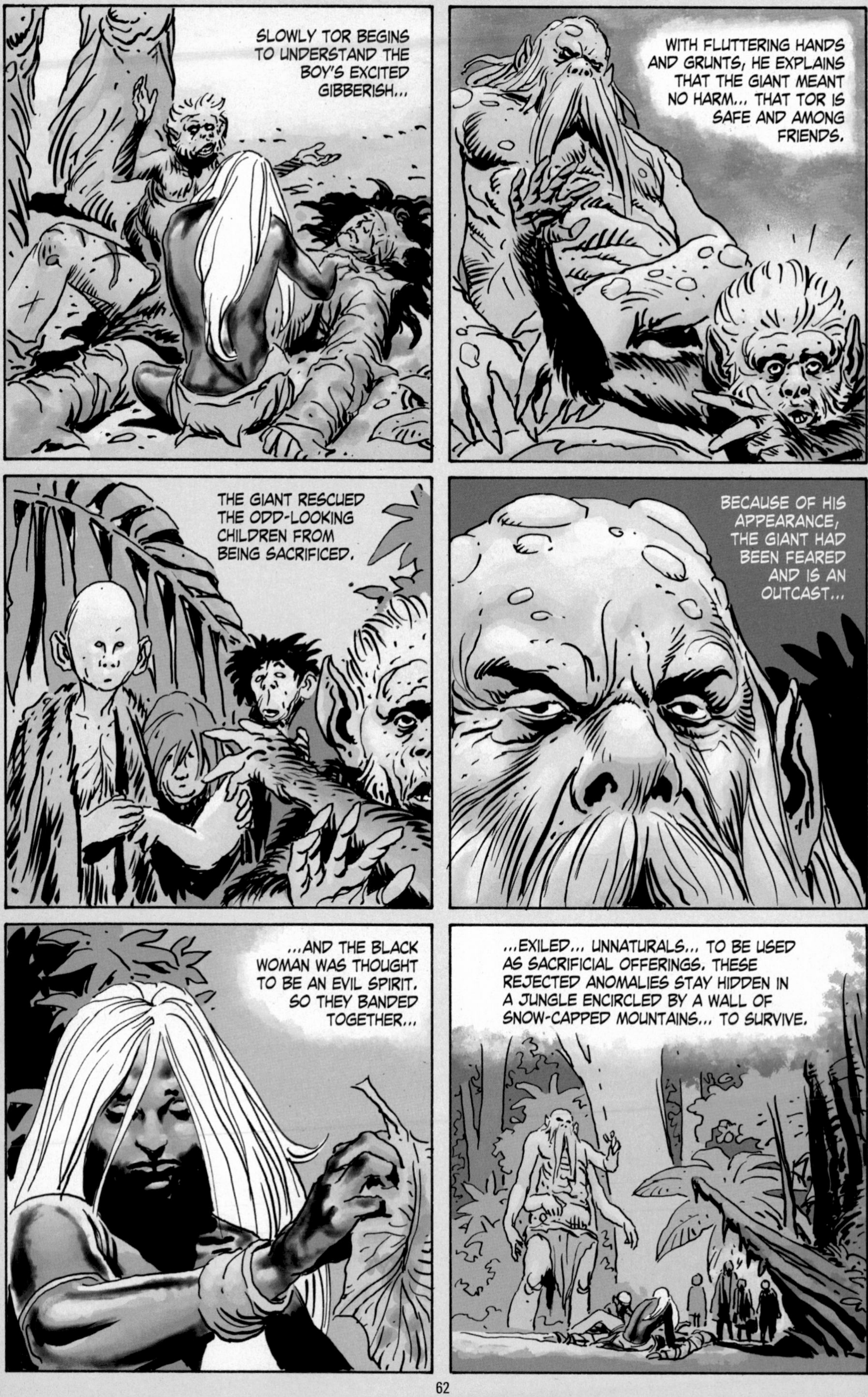
SLOWLY TOR BEGINS TO UNDERSTAND THE BOY'S EXCITED GIBBERISH...
WITH FLUTTERING HANDS AND GRUNTS, HE EXPLAINS THAT THE GIANT MEANT NO HARM... THAT TOR IS SAFE AND AMONG FRIENDS.
THE GIANT RESCUED THE ODD-LOOKING CHILDREN FROM BEING SACRIFICED.
BECAUSE OF HIS APPEARANCE, THE GIANT HAD BEEN FEARED AND IS AN OUTCAST...
...AND THE BLACK WOMAN WAS THOUGHT TO BE AN EVIL SPIRIT. SO THEY BANDED TOGETHER...
...EXILED... UNNATURALS... TO BE USED AS SACRIFICIAL OFFERINGS. THESE REJECTED ANOMALIES STAY HIDDEN IN A JUNGLE ENCIRCLED BY A WALL OF SNOW-CAPPED MOUNTAINS... TO SURVIVE.

TOR IS CARRIED INTO THE SUNLIGHT BY THOSE WHO HAVE THE TASK OF CARING FOR HIM.

ALTHOUGH ACHING FROM HIS LACERATIONS, TOR IS GRATEFUL... YET... IT IS DIFFICULT TO UNDERSTAND SUCH KINDNESS AND CARE.

EVERY DAY THE CHILDREN BRING HIM THE SWEETEST FRUIT... WATER... AND TEND HIS WOUNDS.

SOMETIMES, THEY BRING FOOD HE HAS NEVER SEEN BEFORE.

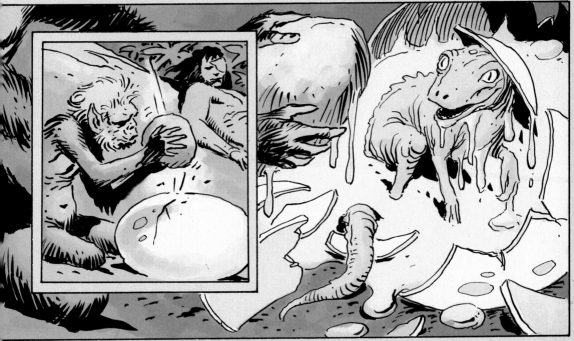

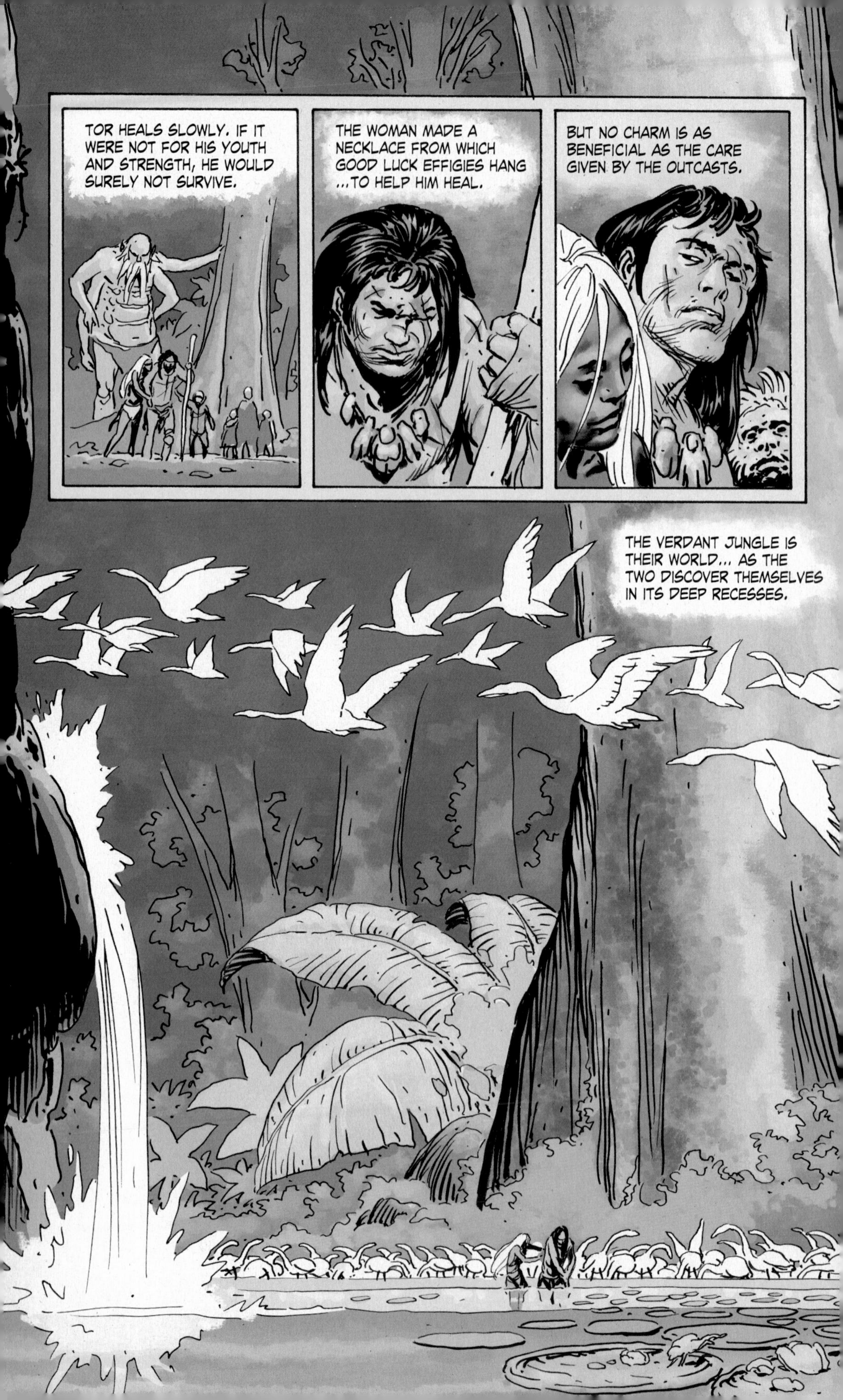
TOR HEALS SLOWLY. IF IT WERE NOT FOR HIS YOUTH AND STRENGTH, HE WOULD SURELY NOT SURVIVE.
THE WOMAN MADE A NECKLACE FROM WHICH GOOD LUCK EFFIGIES HANG ...TO HELP HIM HEAL.
BUT NO CHARM IS AS BENEFICIAL AS THE CARE GIVEN BY THE OUTCASTS.
THE VERDANT JUNGLE IS THEIR WORLD... AS THE TWO DISCOVER THEMSELVES IN ITS DEEP RECESSES.

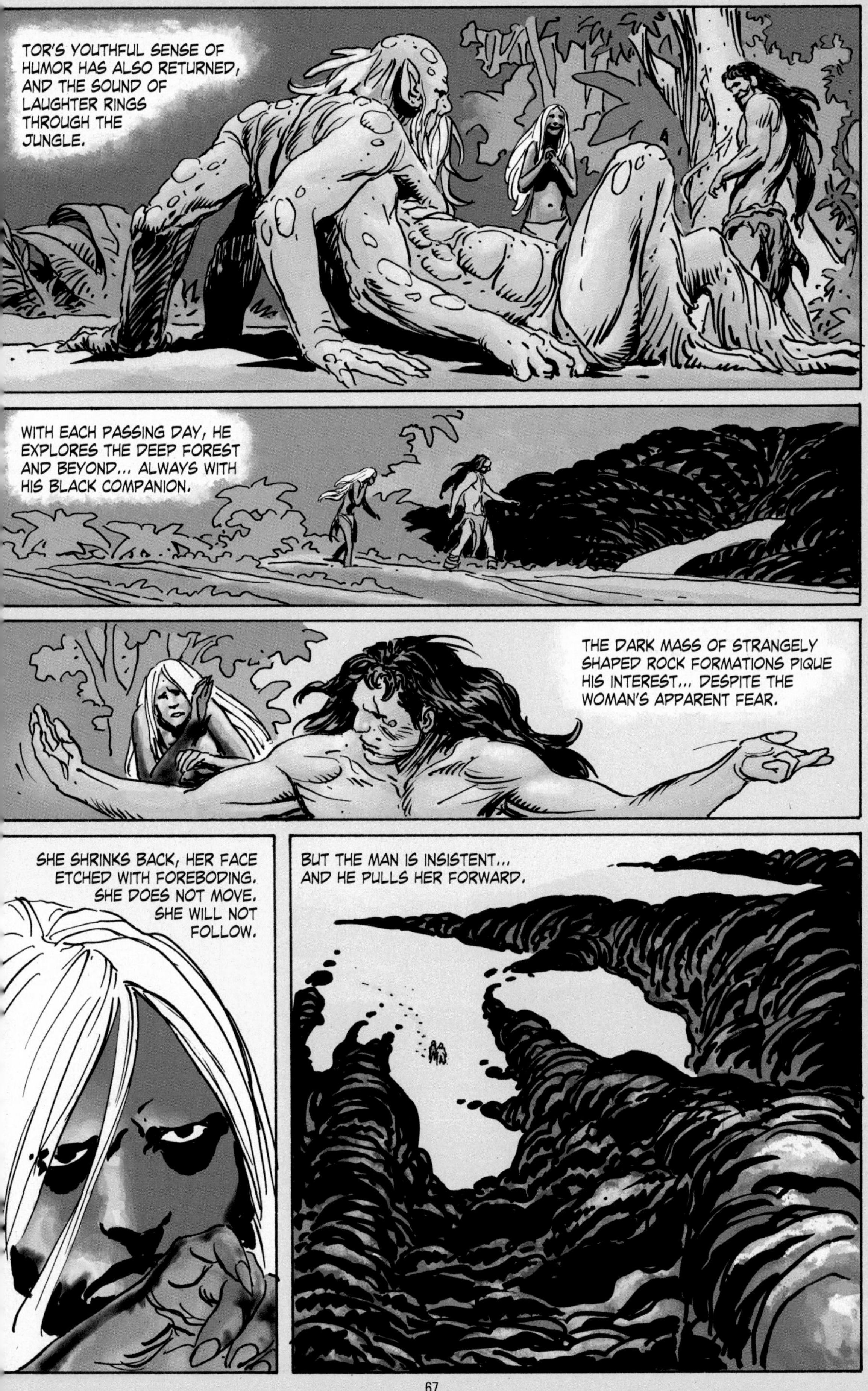
TOR'S YOUTHFUL SENSE OF HUMOR HAS ALSO RETURNED, AND THE SOUND OF LAUGHTER RINGS THROUGH THE JUNGLE.
WITH EACH PASSING DAY, HE EXPLORES THE DEEP FOREST AND BEYOND... ALWAYS WITH HIS BLACK COMPANION.
THE DARK MASS OF STRANGELY SHAPED ROCK FORMATIONS PIQUE HIS INTEREST... DESPITE THE WOMAN'S APPARENT FEAR.
SHE SHRINKS BACK, HER FACE ETCHED WITH FOREBODING. SHE DOES NOT MOVE. SHE WILL NOT FOLLOW.
BUT THE MAN IS INSISTENT... AND HE PULLS HER FORWARD.

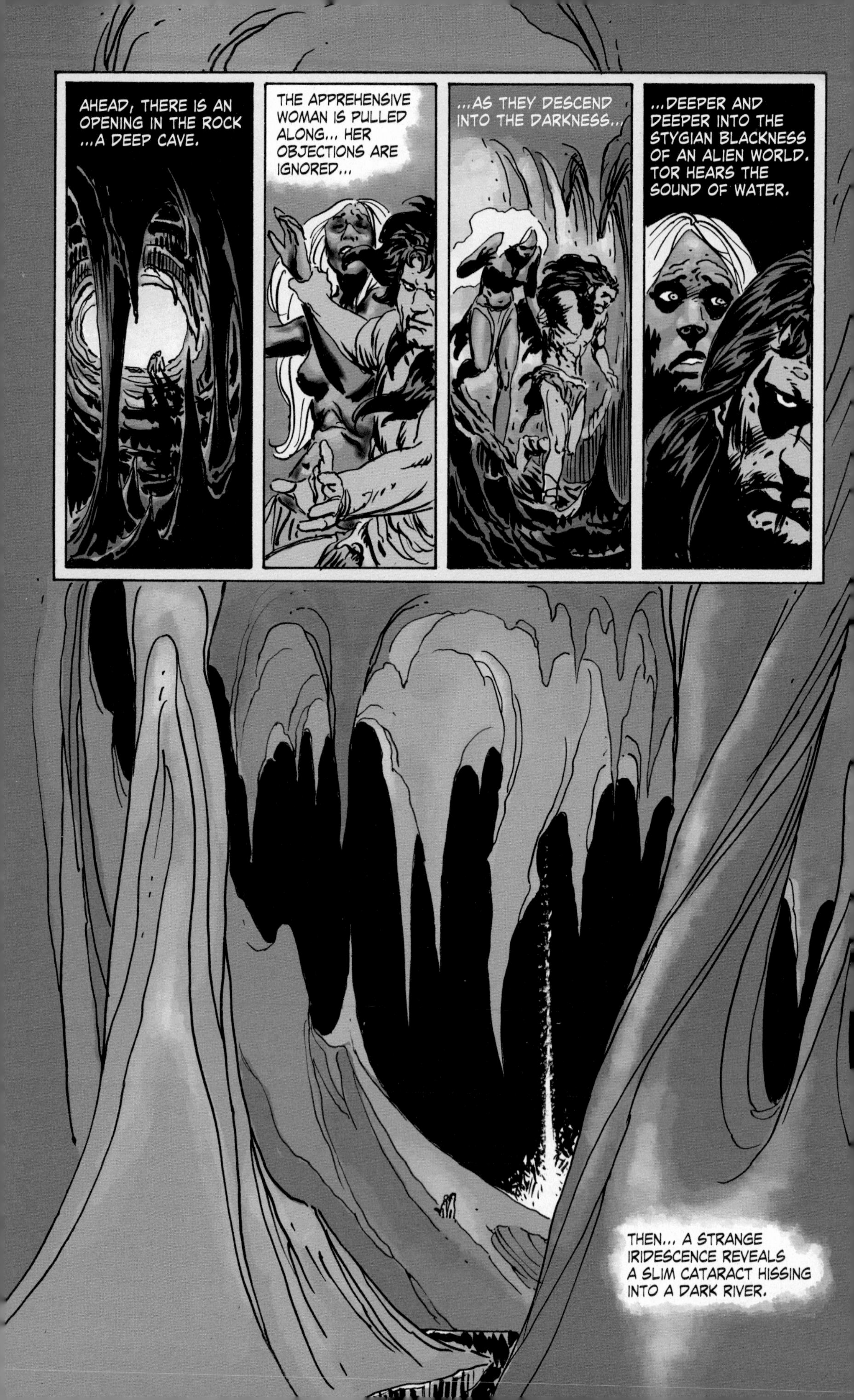
AHEAD, THERE IS AN OPENING IN THE ROCK ...A DEEP CAVE.
THE APPREHENSIVE WOMAN IS PULLED ALONG... HER OBJECTIONS ARE IGNORED...
...AS THEY DESCEND INTO THE DARKNESS...
...DEEPER AND DEEPER INTO THE STYGIAN BLACKNESS OF AN ALIEN WORLD. TOR HEARS THE SOUND OF WATER.
THEN... A STRANGE IRIDESCENCE REVEALS A SLIM CATARACT HISSING INTO A DARK RIVER.

THERE... IN THE SOFT LUMINESCENCE... *WATER.* UNDER THE GROUND. HOW COULD THIS BE?

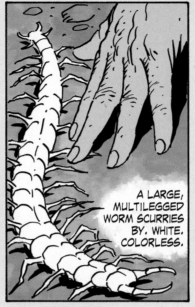

A LARGE, MULTILEGGED WORM SCURRIES BY. WHITE. COLORLESS.

A FLUTTER OF INSECT WINGS. PALE... ALMOST INVISIBLE AGAINST THE STONE PILLARS.

HE REACTS INTUITIVELY AT A MOVEMENT THAT CATCHES HIS EYE...

...AND SNATCHES A SMALL WHITE LIZARD ...THAT HAS NO EYES.

SUCH A STRANGE PLACE. TOR KNEELS TO QUENCH HIS THIRST...

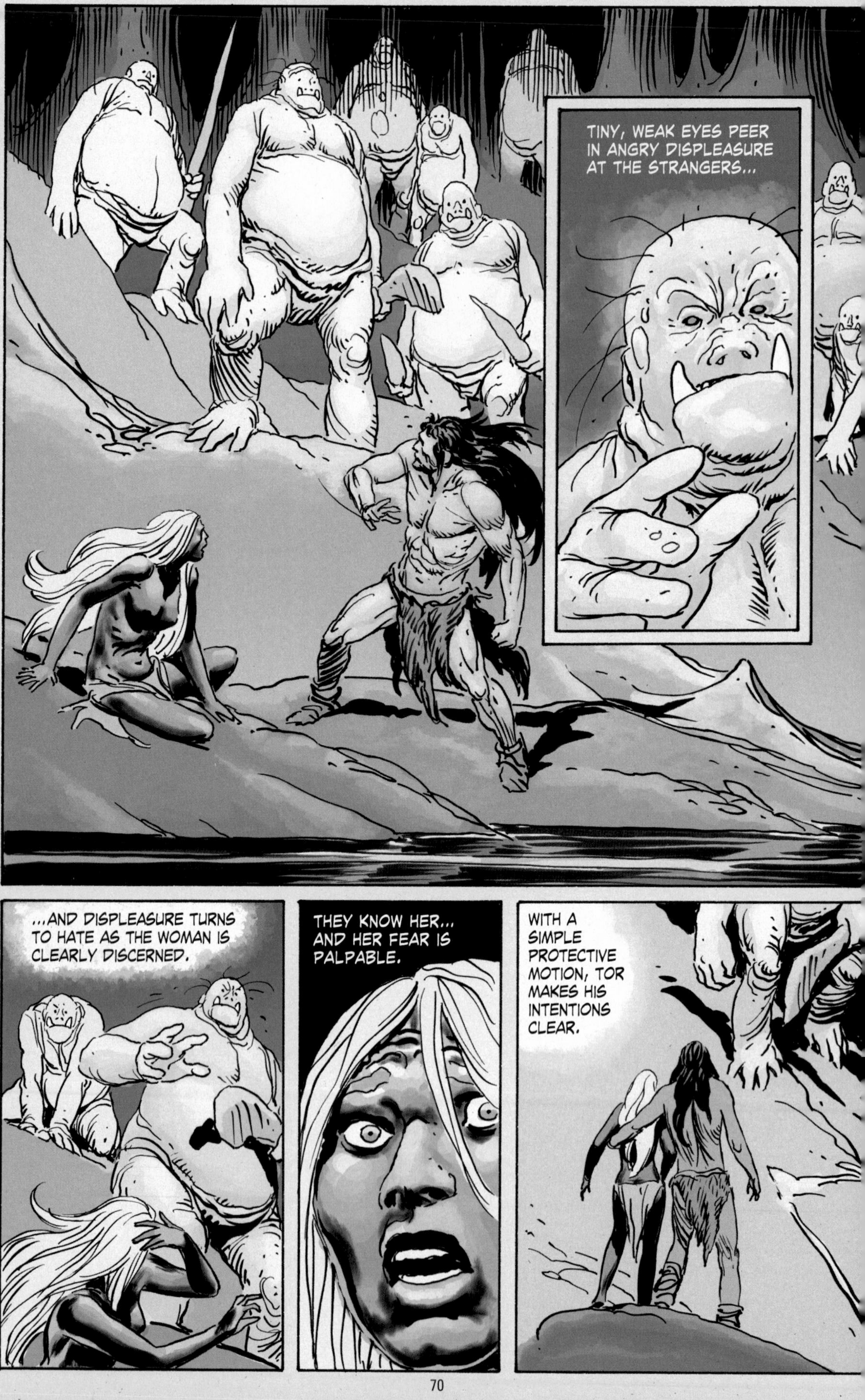
TINY, WEAK EYES PEER IN ANGRY DISPLEASURE AT THE STRANGERS...
...AND DISPLEASURE TURNS TO HATE AS THE WOMAN IS CLEARLY DISCERNED.
THEY KNOW HER... AND HER FEAR IS PALPABLE.
WITH A SIMPLE PROTECTIVE MOTION, TOR MAKES HIS INTENTIONS CLEAR.

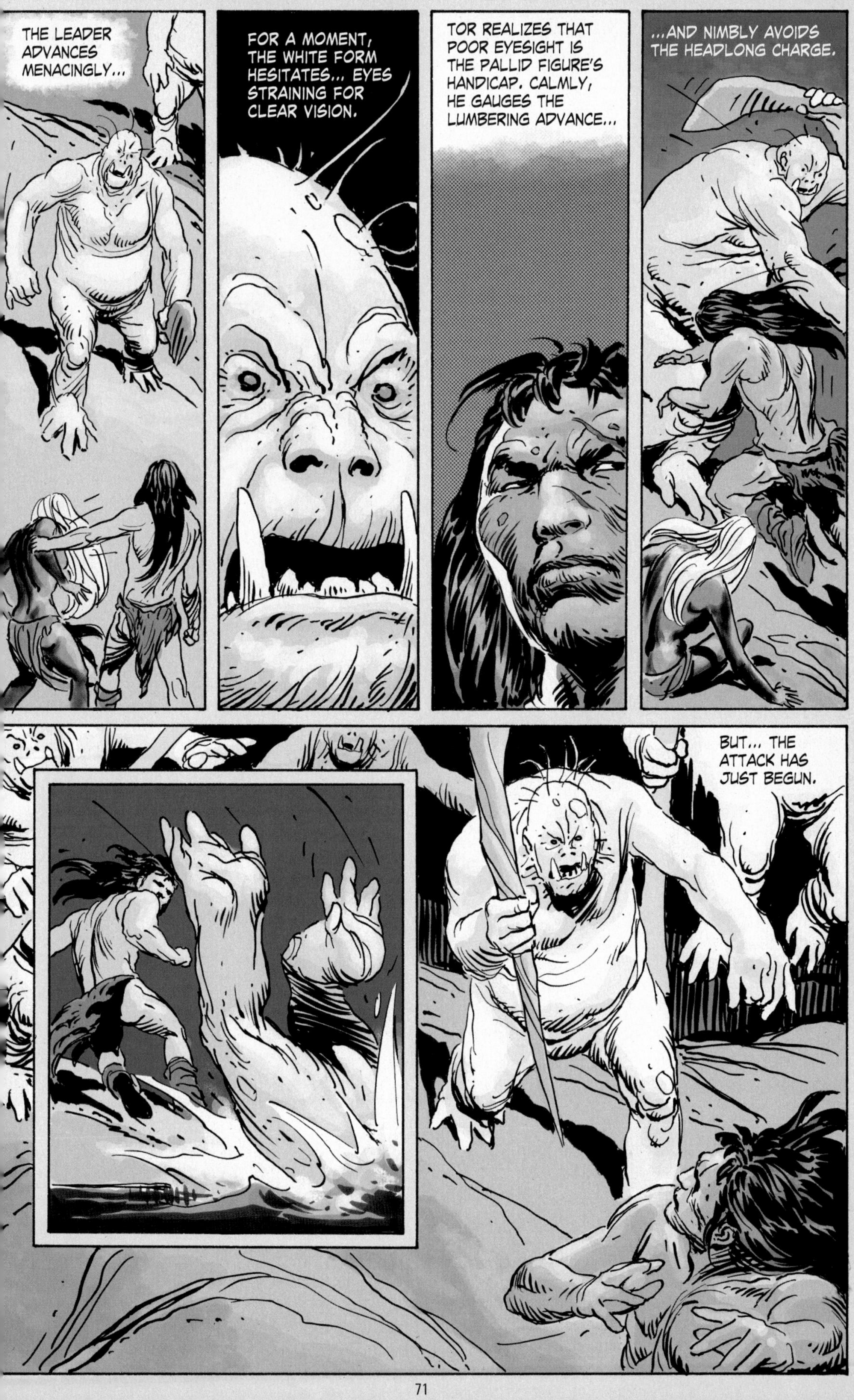
THE LEADER ADVANCES MENACINGLY...
FOR A MOMENT, THE WHITE FORM HESITATES... EYES STRAINING FOR CLEAR VISION.
TOR REALIZES THAT POOR EYESIGHT IS THE PALLID FIGURE'S HANDICAP. CALMLY, HE GAUGES THE LUMBERING ADVANCE...
...AND NIMBLY AVOIDS THE HEADLONG CHARGE.
BUT... THE ATTACK HAS JUST BEGUN.

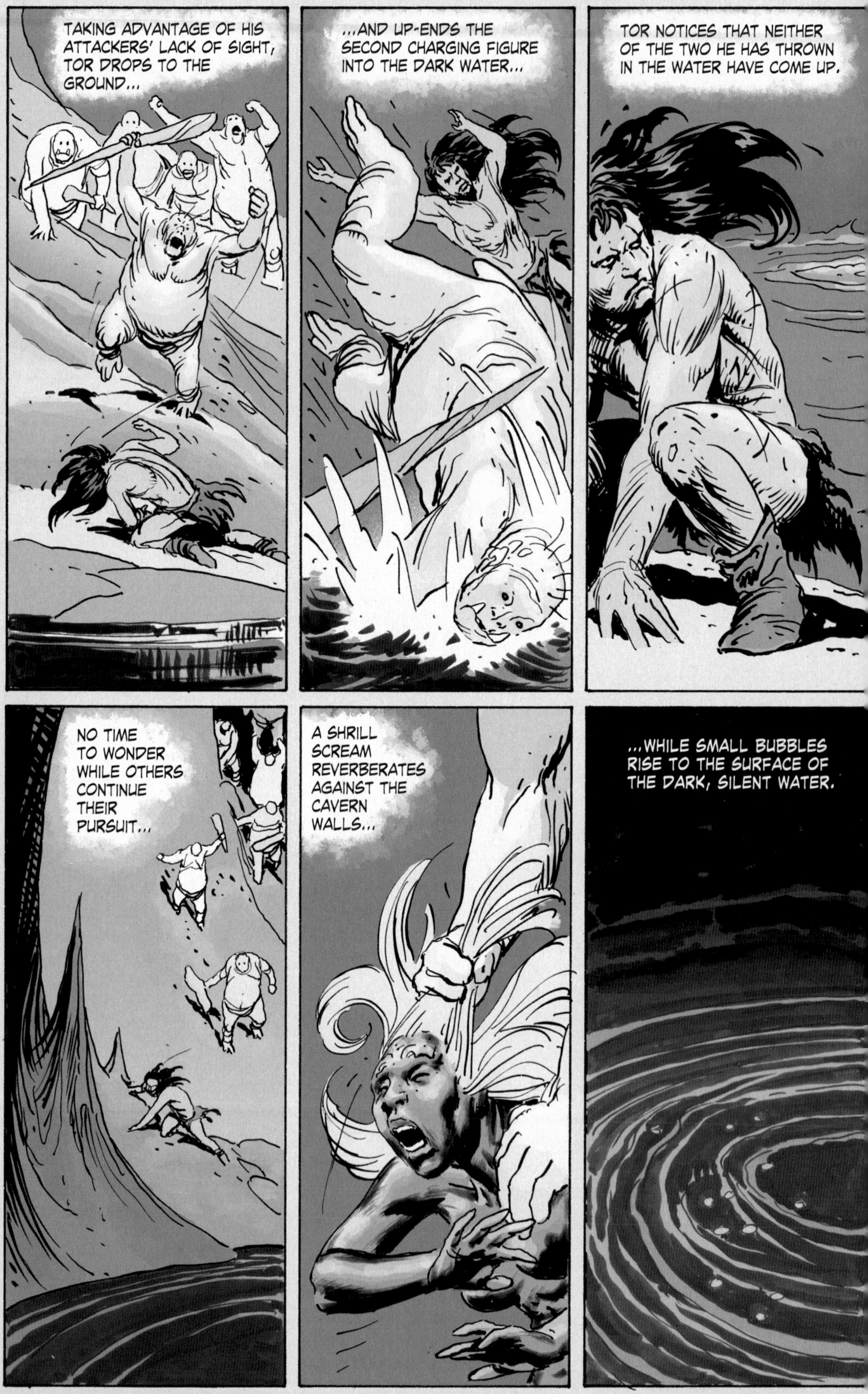
TAKING ADVANTAGE OF HIS ATTACKERS' LACK OF SIGHT, TOR DROPS TO THE GROUND...
...AND UP-ENDS THE SECOND CHARGING FIGURE INTO THE DARK WATER...
TOR NOTICES THAT NEITHER OF THE TWO HE HAS THROWN IN THE WATER HAVE COME UP.
NO TIME TO WONDER WHILE OTHERS CONTINUE THEIR PURSUIT...
A SHRILL SCREAM REVERBERATES AGAINST THE CAVERN WALLS...
...WHILE SMALL BUBBLES RISE TO THE SURFACE OF THE DARK, SILENT WATER.

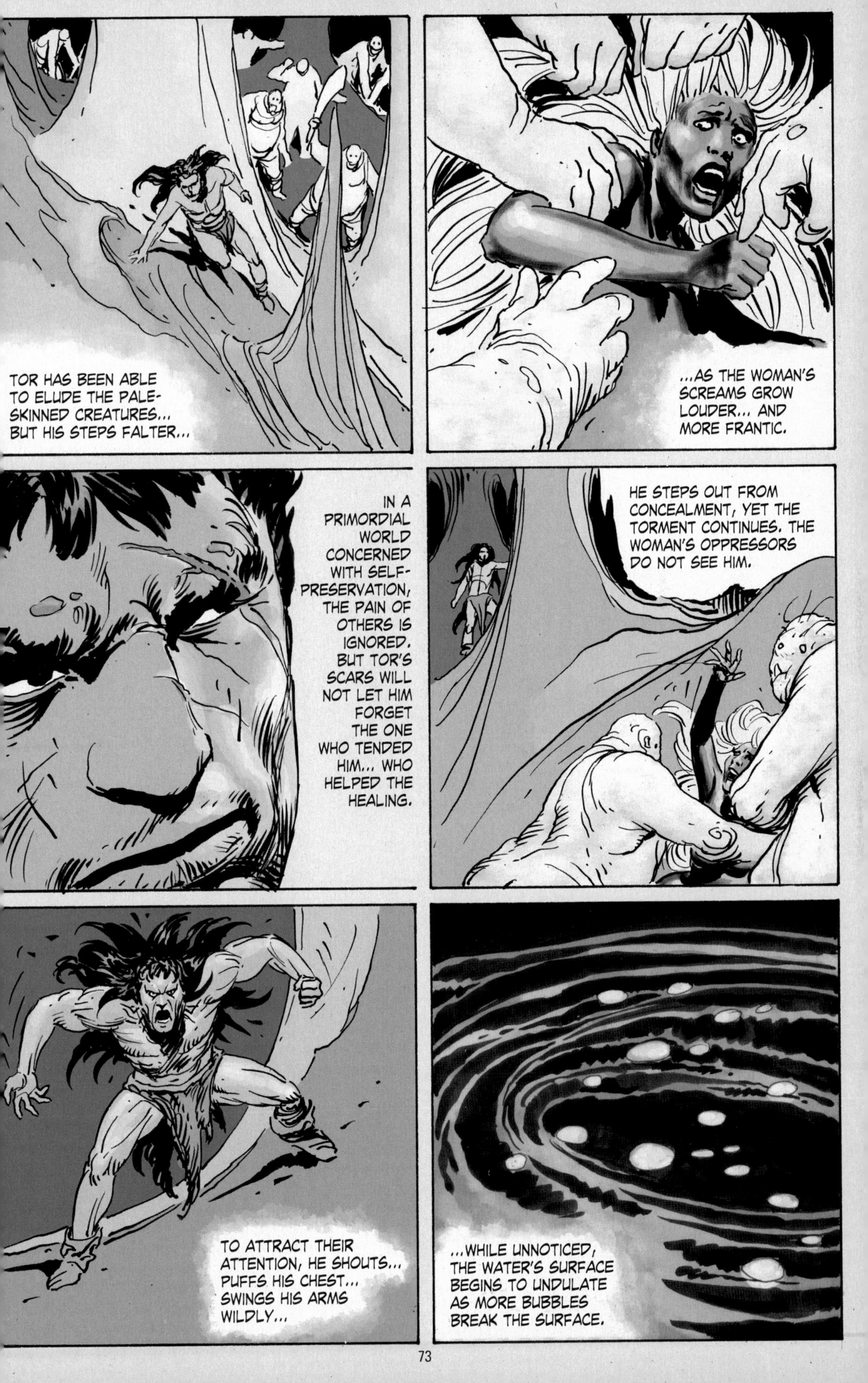
TOR HAS BEEN ABLE TO ELUDE THE PALE-SKINNED CREATURES... BUT HIS STEPS FALTER...
...AS THE WOMAN'S SCREAMS GROW LOUDER... AND MORE FRANTIC.
IN A PRIMORDIAL WORLD CONCERNED WITH SELF-PRESERVATION, THE PAIN OF OTHERS IS IGNORED. BUT TOR'S SCARS WILL NOT LET HIM FORGET THE ONE WHO TENDED HIM... WHO HELPED THE HEALING.
HE STEPS OUT FROM CONCEALMENT, YET THE TORMENT CONTINUES. THE WOMAN'S OPPRESSORS DO NOT SEE HIM.
TO ATTRACT THEIR ATTENTION, HE SHOUTS... PUFFS HIS CHEST... SWINGS HIS ARMS WILDLY...
...WHILE UNNOTICED, THE WATER'S SURFACE BEGINS TO UNDULATE AS MORE BUBBLES BREAK THE SURFACE.

WITH AN EAR-PIERCING CRY...

...TOR HURTLES ACROSS THE DIM CAVERN...

...ONLY TO BE MET BY A WALL OF SLIPPERY WHITE FLESH.

FINGERS DEVOID OF NAILS PULL AND MAUL AS MULTIPLE BODIES PRESS TOR TO THE GROUND.

HE SHOUTS TO THE WOMAN TO RUN... ESCAPE...

BUT, INSTEAD, SHE TEARS AT THE WHITE MOUNDS THAT ENGULF TOR.

AND THE BUBBLES CONTINUE TO RISE... LARGER... MORE FREQUENT...

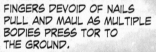

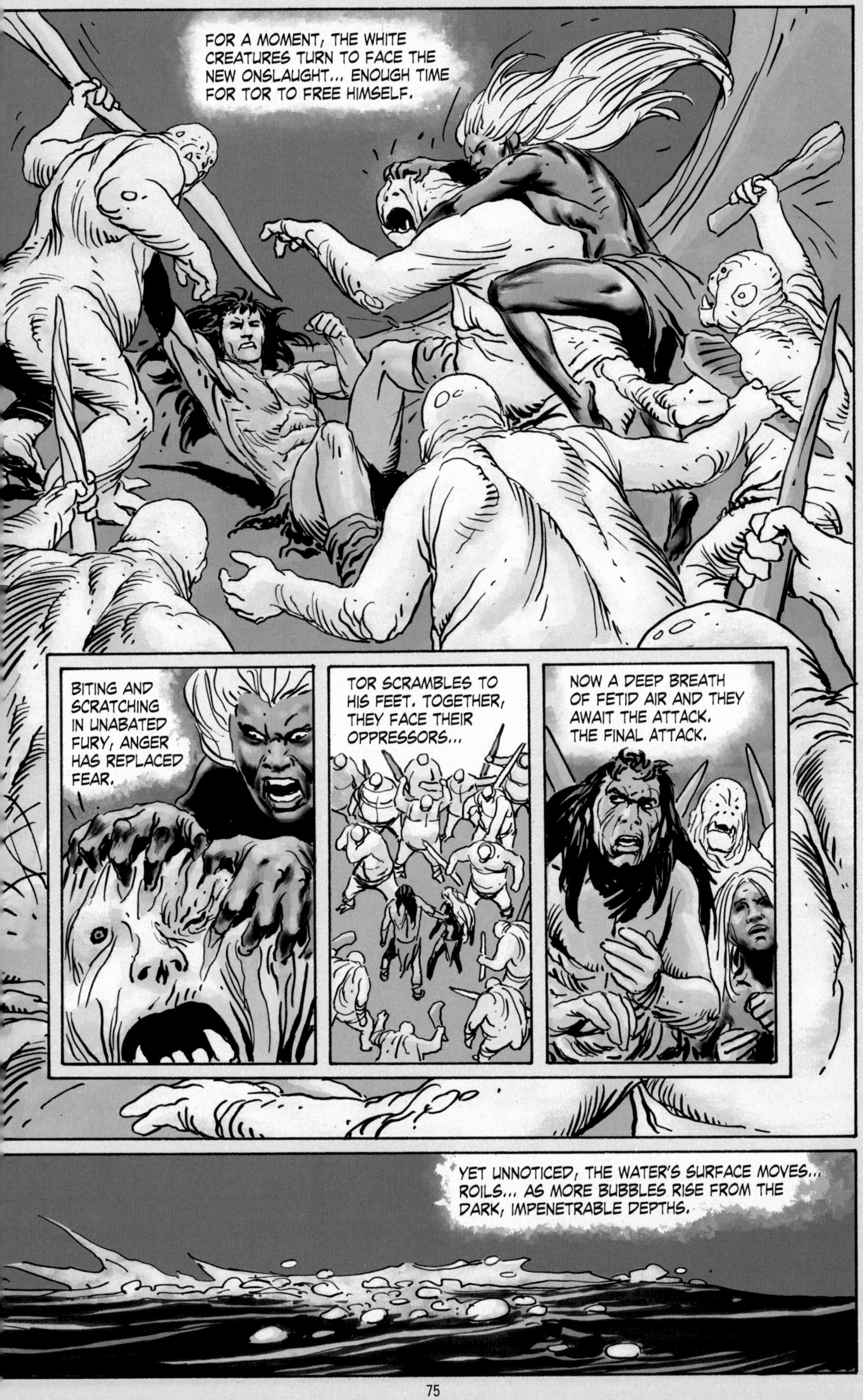
FOR A MOMENT, THE WHITE CREATURES TURN TO FACE THE NEW ONSLAUGHT... ENOUGH TIME FOR TOR TO FREE HIMSELF.
BITING AND SCRATCHING IN UNABATED FURY, ANGER HAS REPLACED FEAR.
TOR SCRAMBLES TO HIS FEET. TOGETHER, THEY FACE THEIR OPPRESSORS...
NOW A DEEP BREATH OF FETID AIR AND THEY AWAIT THE ATTACK. THE FINAL ATTACK.
YET UNNOTICED, THE WATER'S SURFACE MOVES... ROILS... AS MORE BUBBLES RISE FROM THE DARK, IMPENETRABLE DEPTHS.

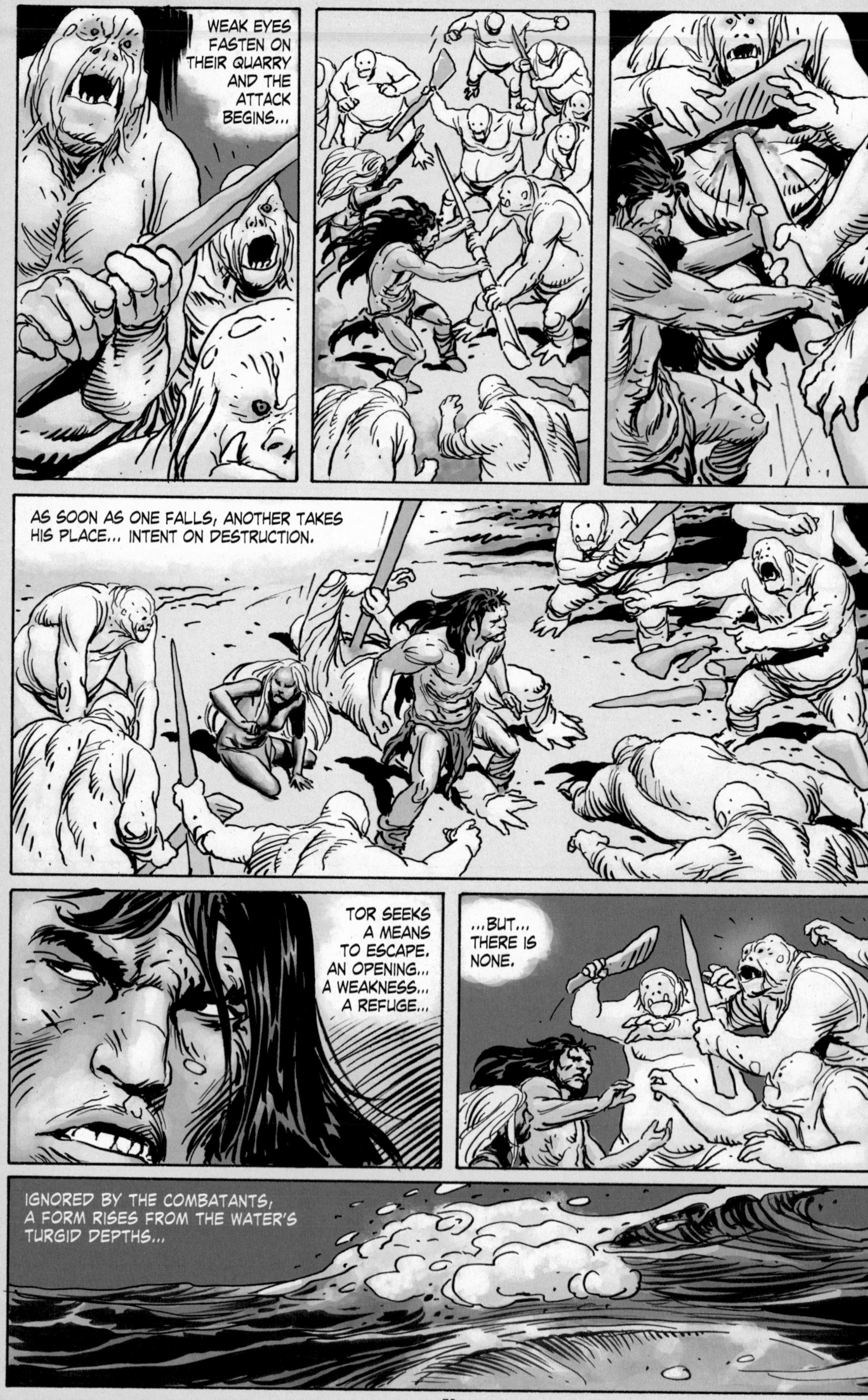
WEAK EYES FASTEN ON THEIR QUARRY AND THE ATTACK BEGINS...
AS SOON AS ONE FALLS, ANOTHER TAKES HIS PLACE... INTENT ON DESTRUCTION.
TOR SEEKS A MEANS TO ESCAPE. AN OPENING... A WEAKNESS... A REFUGE...
...BUT... THERE IS NONE.
IGNORED BY THE COMBATANTS, A FORM RISES FROM THE WATER'S TURGID DEPTHS...

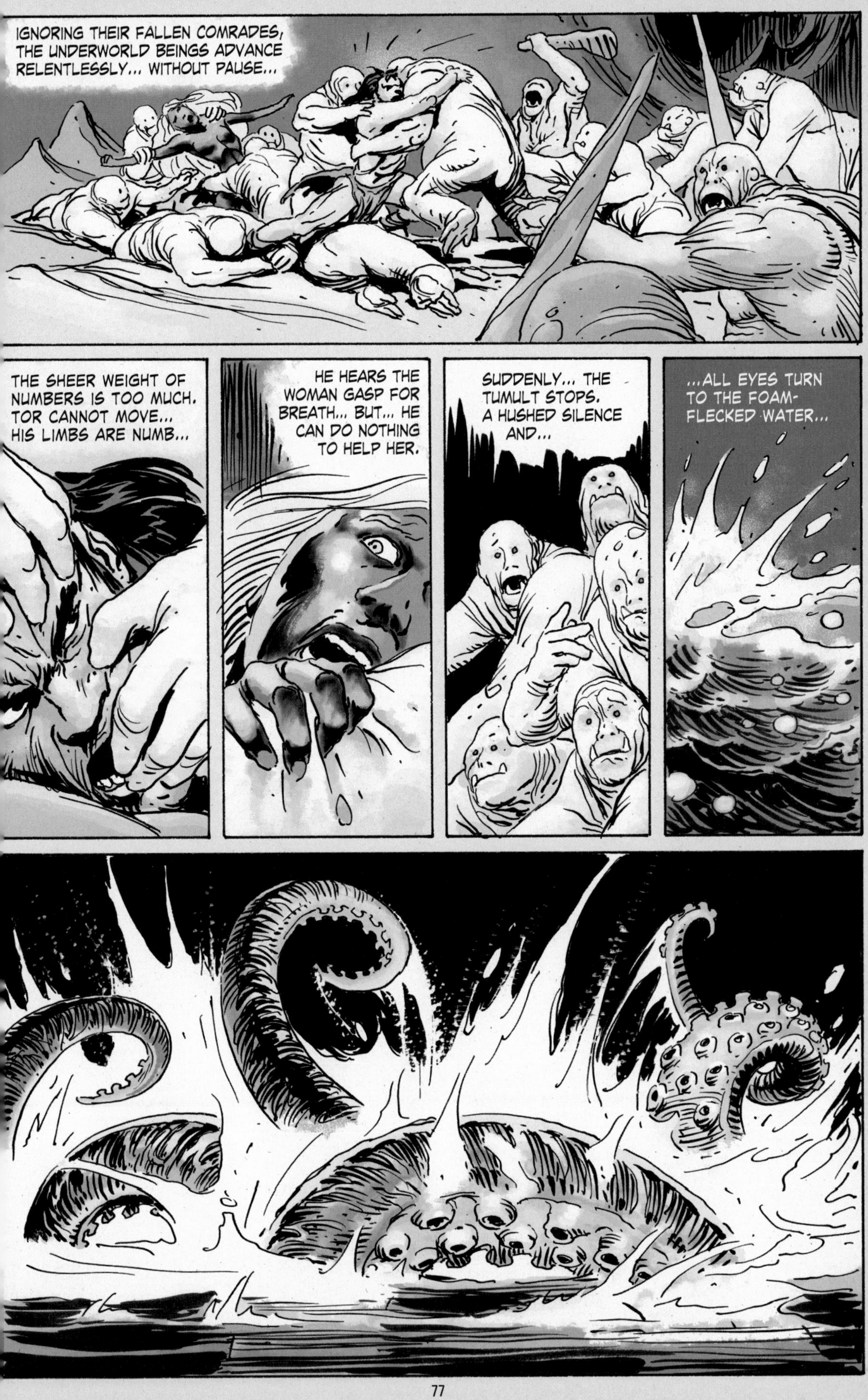
IGNORING THEIR FALLEN COMRADES, THE UNDERWORLD BEINGS ADVANCE RELENTLESSLY... WITHOUT PAUSE...
THE SHEER WEIGHT OF NUMBERS IS TOO MUCH. TOR CANNOT MOVE... HIS LIMBS ARE NUMB...
HE HEARS THE WOMAN GASP FOR BREATH... BUT... HE CAN DO NOTHING TO HELP HER.
SUDDENLY... THE TUMULT STOPS. A HUSHED SILENCE AND...
...ALL EYES TURN TO THE FOAM-FLECKED WATER...

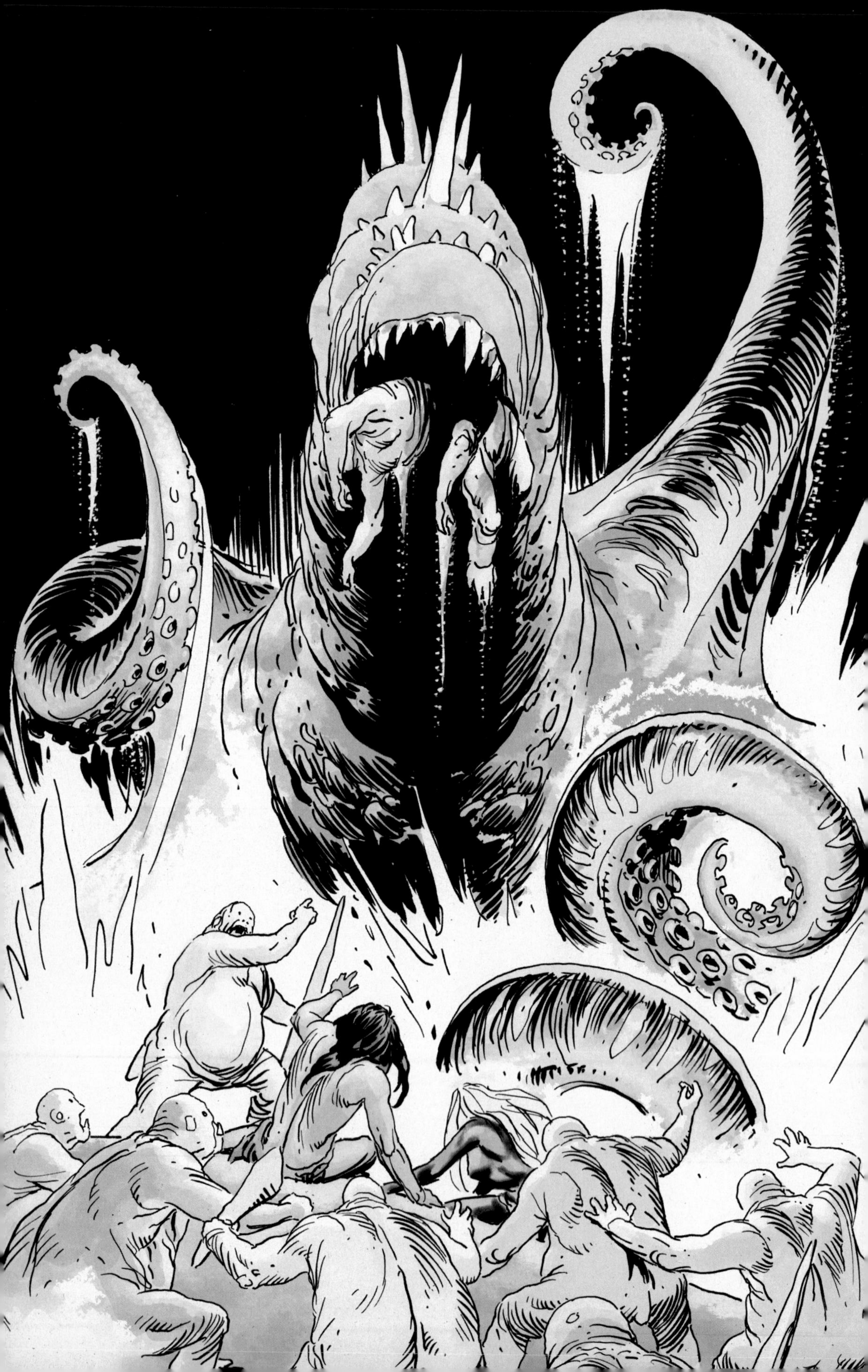

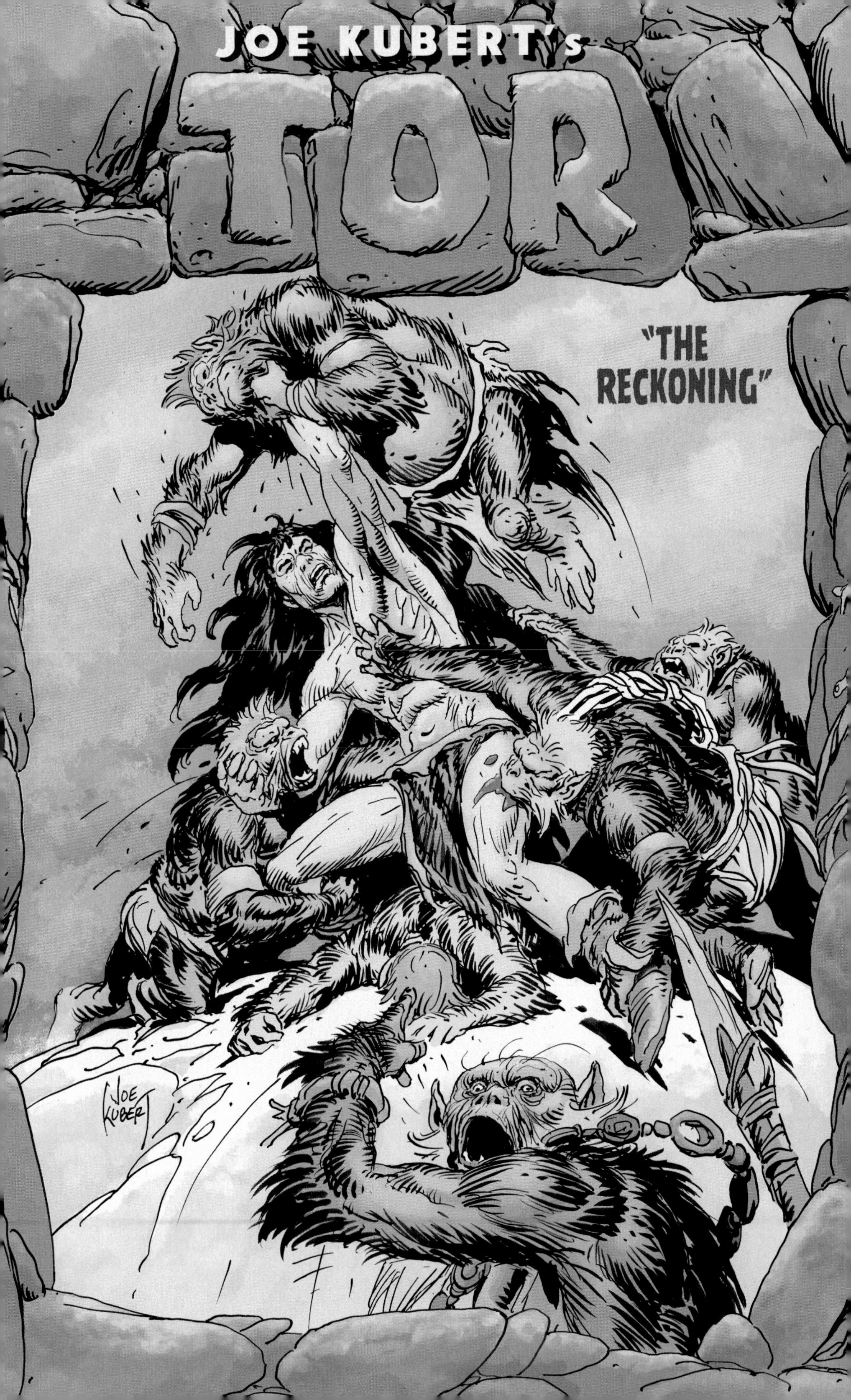
JOE KUBERT's
TOR
"THE RECKONING"
JOE KUBERT

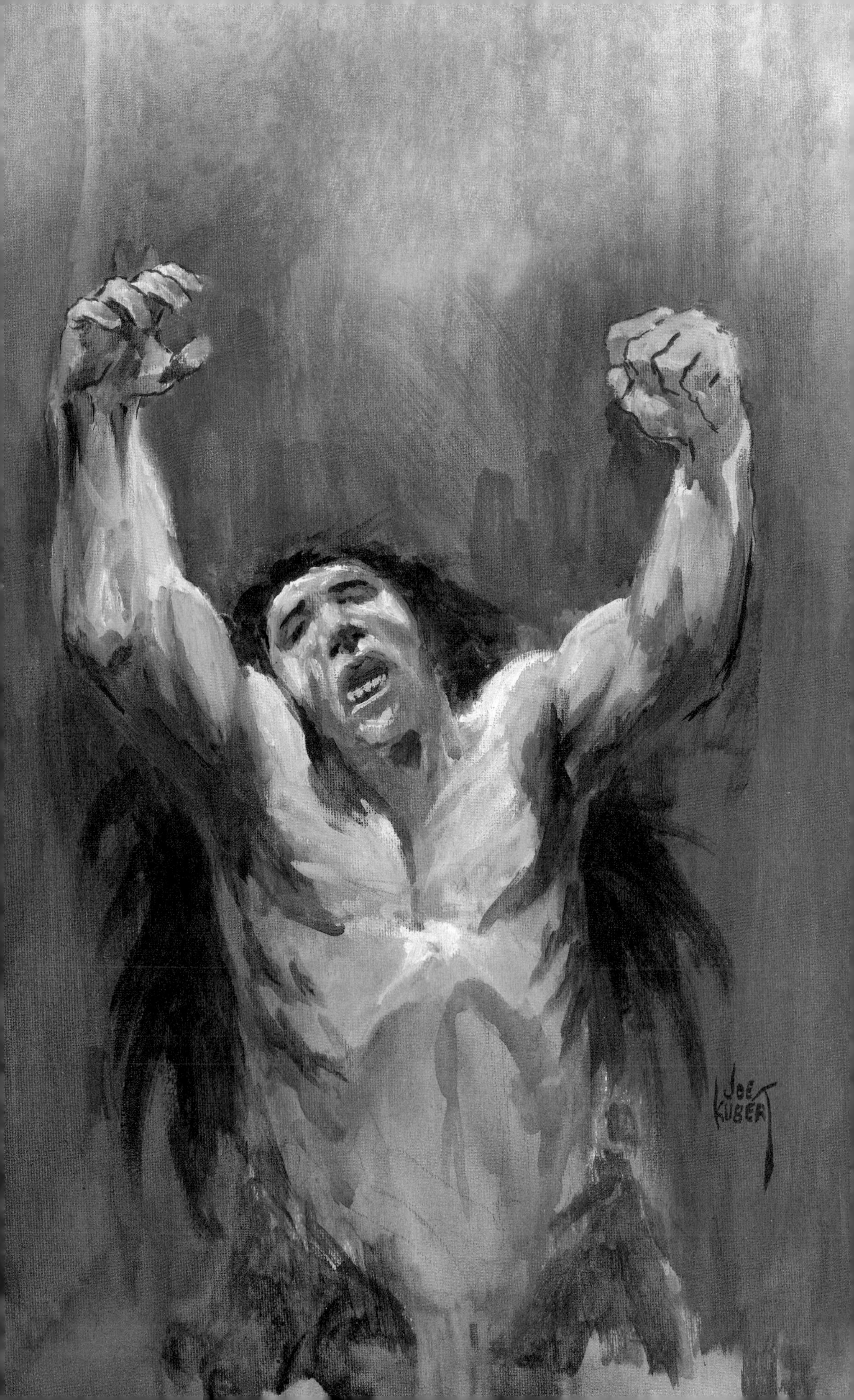
JOE
KUBERT

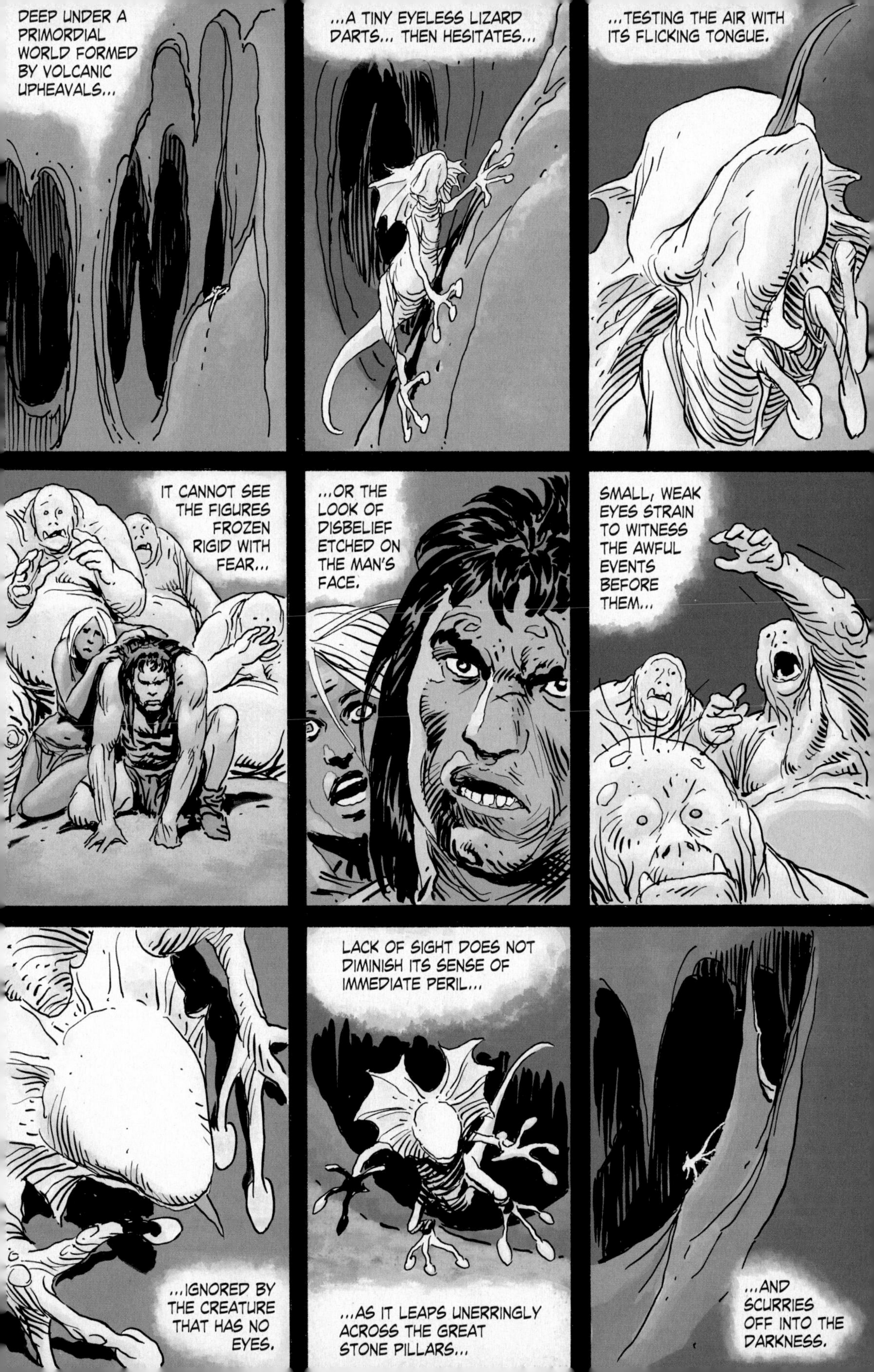
DEEP UNDER A PRIMORDIAL WORLD FORMED BY VOLCANIC UPHEAVALS...
...A TINY EYELESS LIZARD DARTS... THEN HESITATES...
...TESTING THE AIR WITH ITS FLICKING TONGUE.
IT CANNOT SEE THE FIGURES FROZEN RIGID WITH FEAR...
...OR THE LOOK OF DISBELIEF ETCHED ON THE MAN'S FACE.
SMALL, WEAK EYES STRAIN TO WITNESS THE AWFUL EVENTS BEFORE THEM...
...IGNORED BY THE CREATURE THAT HAS NO EYES.
LACK OF SIGHT DOES NOT DIMINISH ITS SENSE OF IMMEDIATE PERIL...
...AS IT LEAPS UNERRINGLY ACROSS THE GREAT STONE PILLARS...
...AND SCURRIES OFF INTO THE DARKNESS.

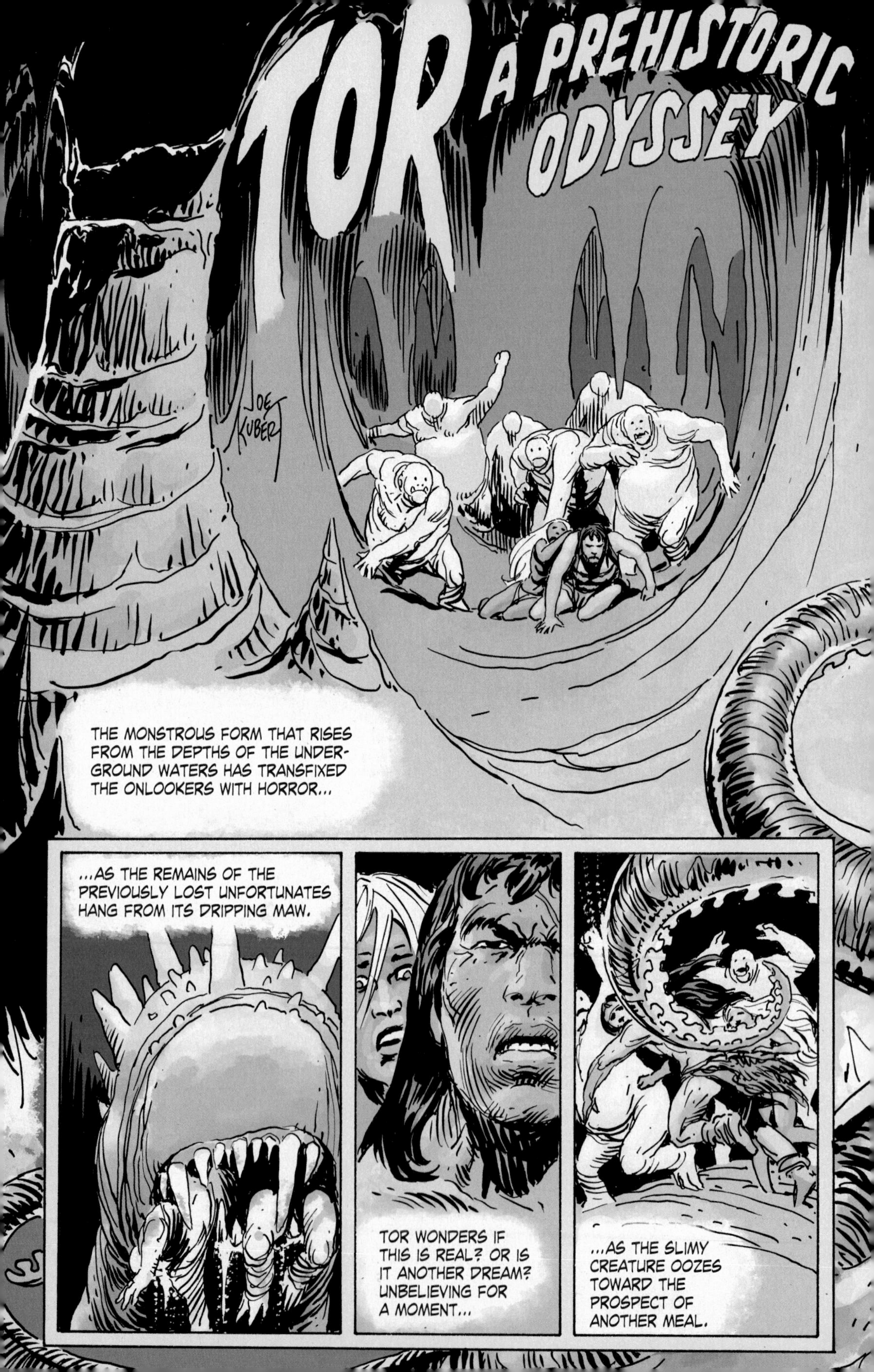
TOR
A PREHISTORIC ODYSSEY
JOE KUBERT
THE MONSTROUS FORM THAT RISES FROM THE DEPTHS OF THE UNDER-GROUND WATERS HAS TRANSFIXED THE ONLOOKERS WITH HORROR...
...AS THE REMAINS OF THE PREVIOUSLY LOST UNFORTUNATES HANG FROM ITS DRIPPING MAW.
TOR WONDERS IF THIS IS REAL? OR IS IT ANOTHER DREAM? UNBELIEVING FOR A MOMENT...
...AS THE SLIMY CREATURE OOZES TOWARD THE PROSPECT OF ANOTHER MEAL.

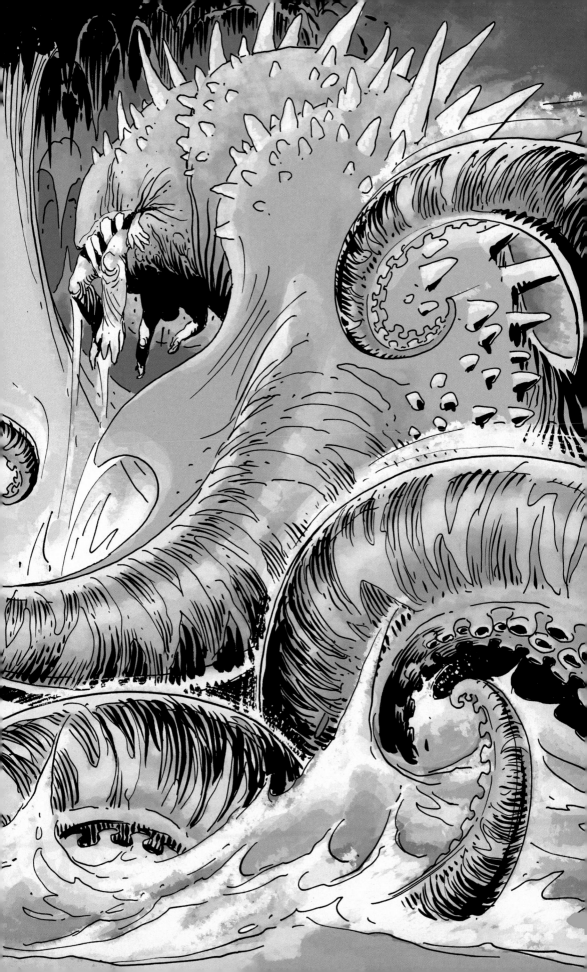

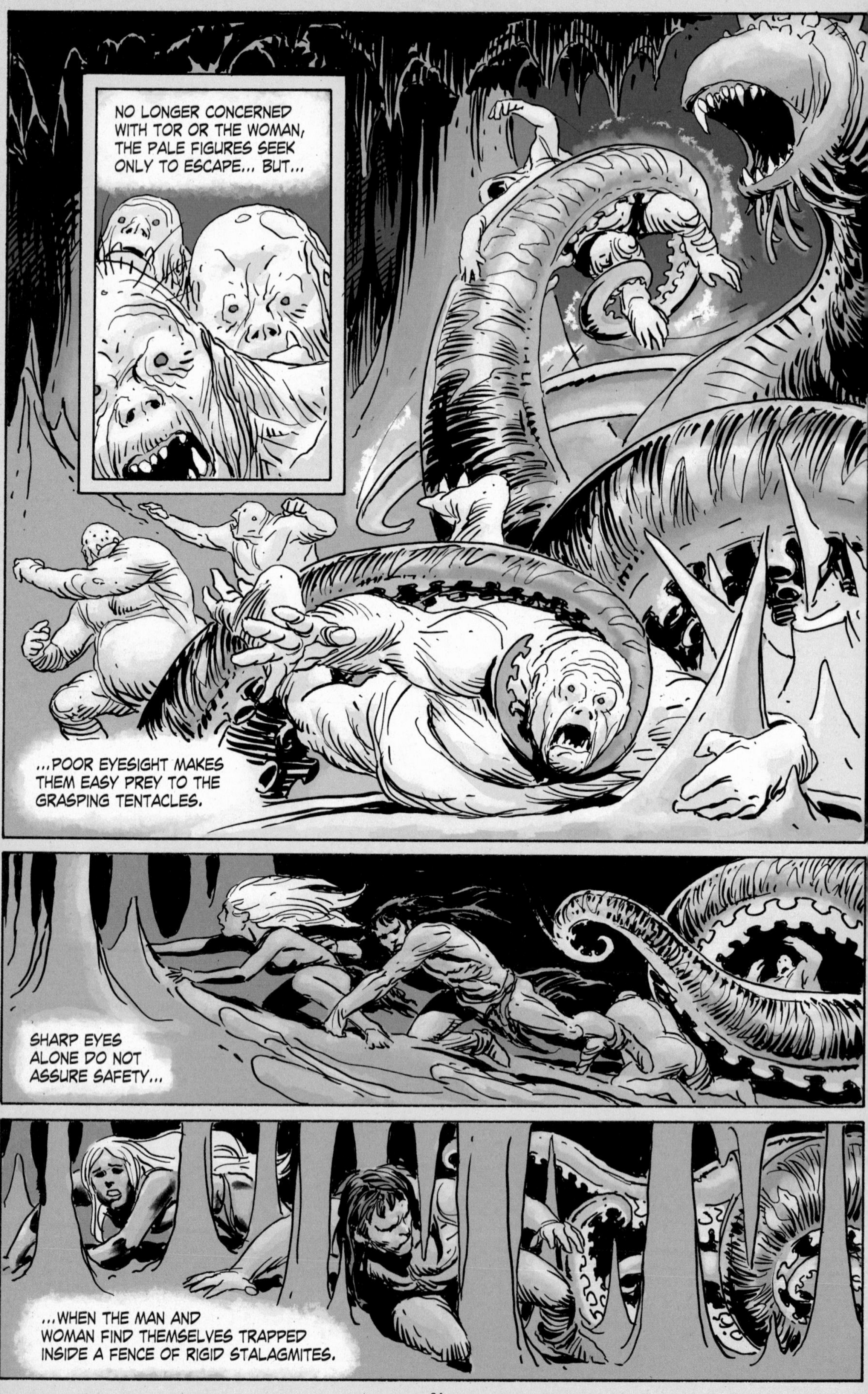
NO LONGER CONCERNED WITH TOR OR THE WOMAN, THE PALE FIGURES SEEK ONLY TO ESCAPE... BUT...
...POOR EYESIGHT MAKES THEM EASY PREY TO THE GRASPING TENTACLES.
SHARP EYES ALONE DO NOT ASSURE SAFETY...
...WHEN THE MAN AND WOMAN FIND THEMSELVES TRAPPED INSIDE A FENCE OF RIGID STALAGMITES.

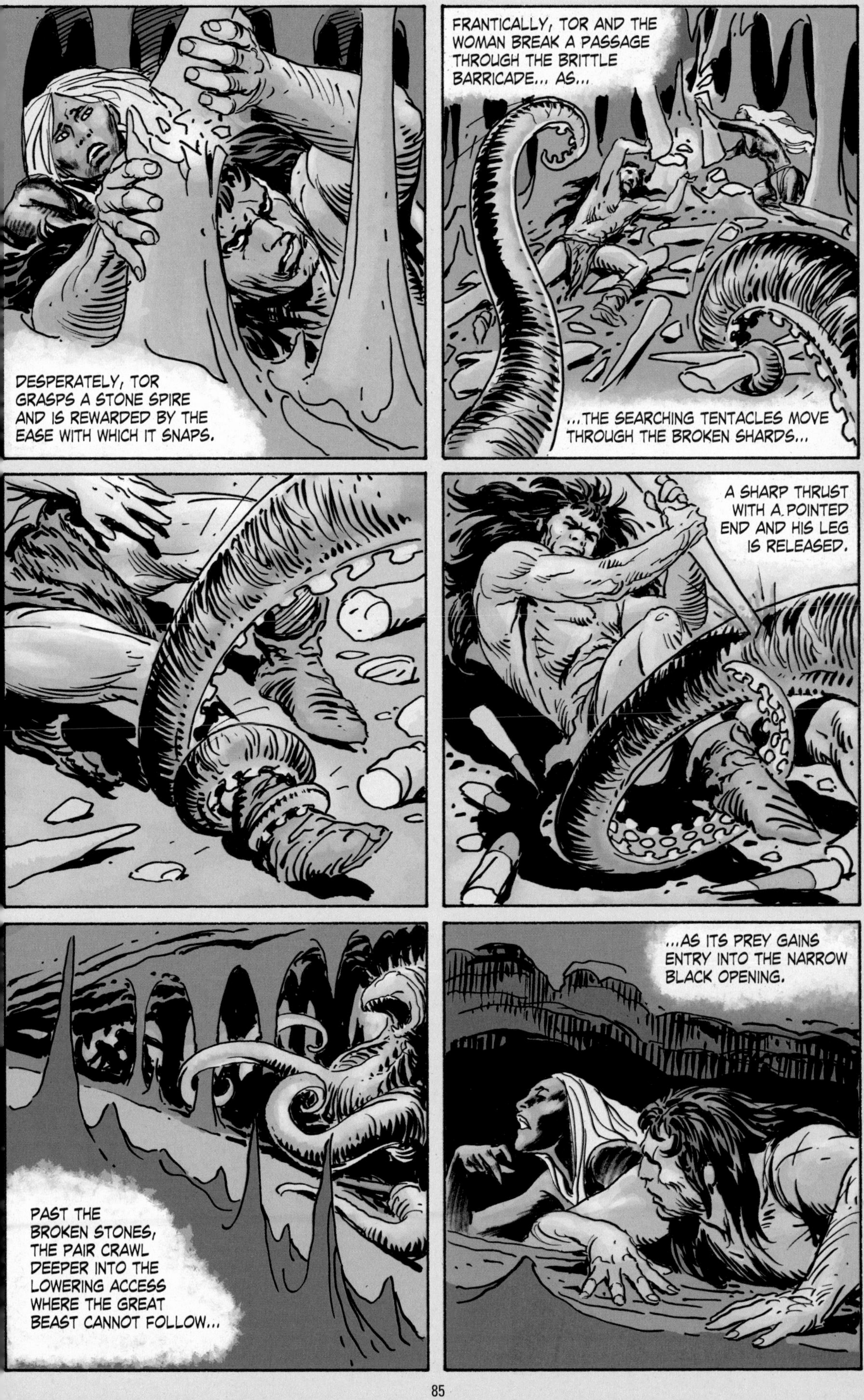
DESPERATELY, TOR GRASPS A STONE SPIRE AND IS REWARDED BY THE EASE WITH WHICH IT SNAPS.
FRANTICALLY, TOR AND THE WOMAN BREAK A PASSAGE THROUGH THE BRITTLE BARRICADE... AS...
...THE SEARCHING TENTACLES MOVE THROUGH THE BROKEN SHARDS...
A SHARP THRUST WITH A POINTED END AND HIS LEG IS RELEASED.
PAST THE BROKEN STONES, THE PAIR CRAWL DEEPER INTO THE LOWERING ACCESS WHERE THE GREAT BEAST CANNOT FOLLOW...
...AS ITS PREY GAINS ENTRY INTO THE NARROW BLACK OPENING.

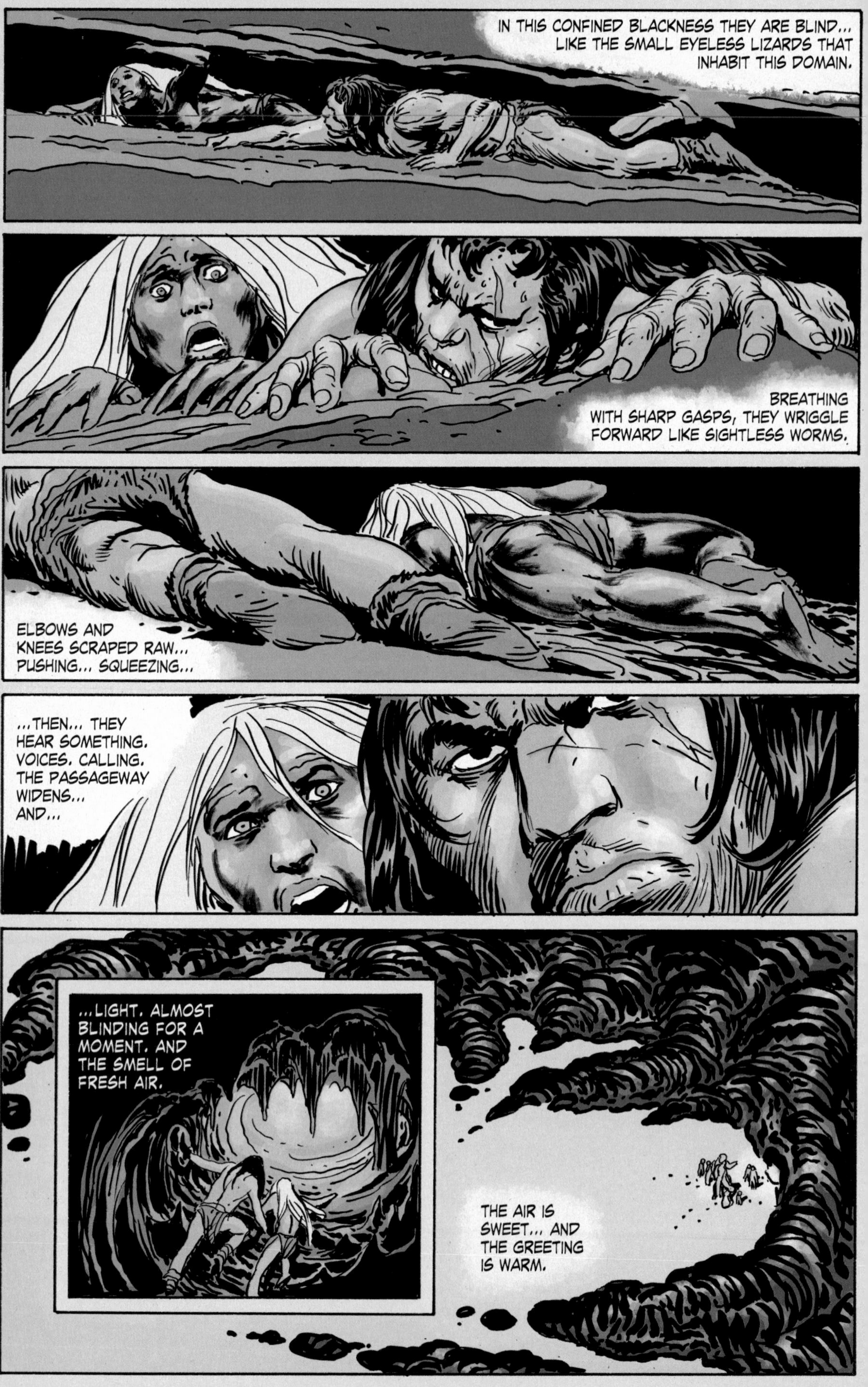
IN THIS CONFINED BLACKNESS THEY ARE BLIND... LIKE THE SMALL EYELESS LIZARDS THAT INHABIT THIS DOMAIN.
BREATHING WITH SHARP GASPS, THEY WRIGGLE FORWARD LIKE SIGHTLESS WORMS.
ELBOWS AND KNEES SCRAPED RAW... PUSHING... SQUEEZING...
...THEN... THEY HEAR SOMETHING. VOICES. CALLING. THE PASSAGEWAY WIDENS... AND...
...LIGHT. ALMOST BLINDING FOR A MOMENT. AND THE SMELL OF FRESH AIR.
THE AIR IS SWEET... AND THE GREETING IS WARM.

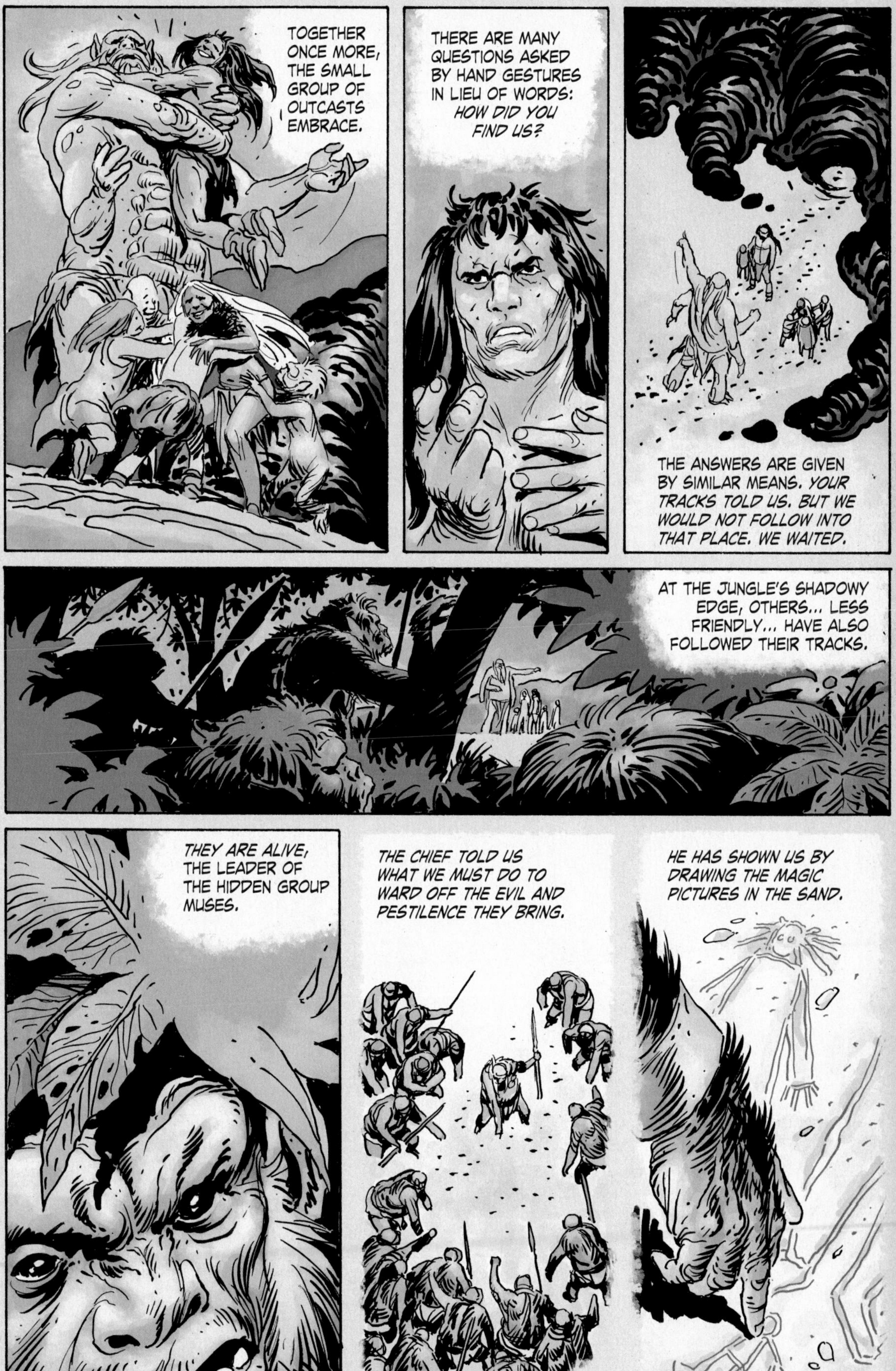
TOGETHER ONCE MORE, THE SMALL GROUP OF OUTCASTS EMBRACE.
THERE ARE MANY QUESTIONS ASKED BY HAND GESTURES IN LIEU OF WORDS: *HOW DID YOU FIND US?*
THE ANSWERS ARE GIVEN BY SIMILAR MEANS. *YOUR TRACKS TOLD US. BUT WE WOULD NOT FOLLOW INTO THAT PLACE. WE WAITED.*
AT THE JUNGLE'S SHADOWY EDGE, OTHERS... LESS FRIENDLY... HAVE ALSO FOLLOWED THEIR TRACKS.
THEY ARE ALIVE, THE LEADER OF THE HIDDEN GROUP MUSES.
THE CHIEF TOLD US WHAT WE MUST DO TO WARD OFF THE EVIL AND PESTILENCE THEY BRING.
HE HAS SHOWN US BY DRAWING THE MAGIC PICTURES IN THE SAND.

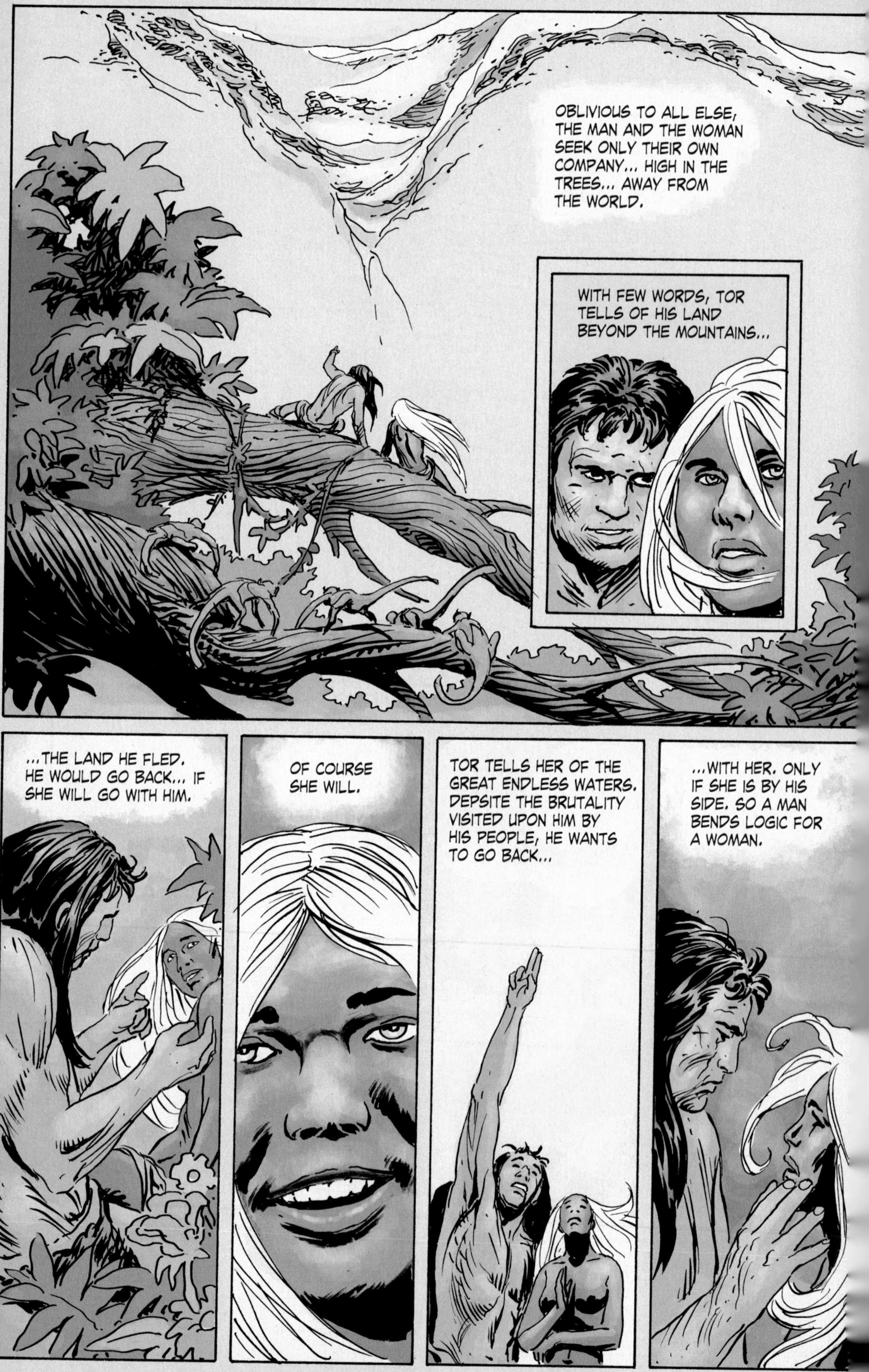
OBLIVIOUS TO ALL ELSE, THE MAN AND THE WOMAN SEEK ONLY THEIR OWN COMPANY... HIGH IN THE TREES... AWAY FROM THE WORLD.
WITH FEW WORDS, TOR TELLS OF HIS LAND BEYOND THE MOUNTAINS...
...THE LAND HE FLED. HE WOULD GO BACK... IF SHE WILL GO WITH HIM.
OF COURSE SHE WILL.
TOR TELLS HER OF THE GREAT ENDLESS WATERS. DEPSITE THE BRUTALITY VISITED UPON HIM BY HIS PEOPLE, HE WANTS TO GO BACK...
...WITH HER. ONLY IF SHE IS BY HIS SIDE. SO A MAN BENDS LOGIC FOR A WOMAN.

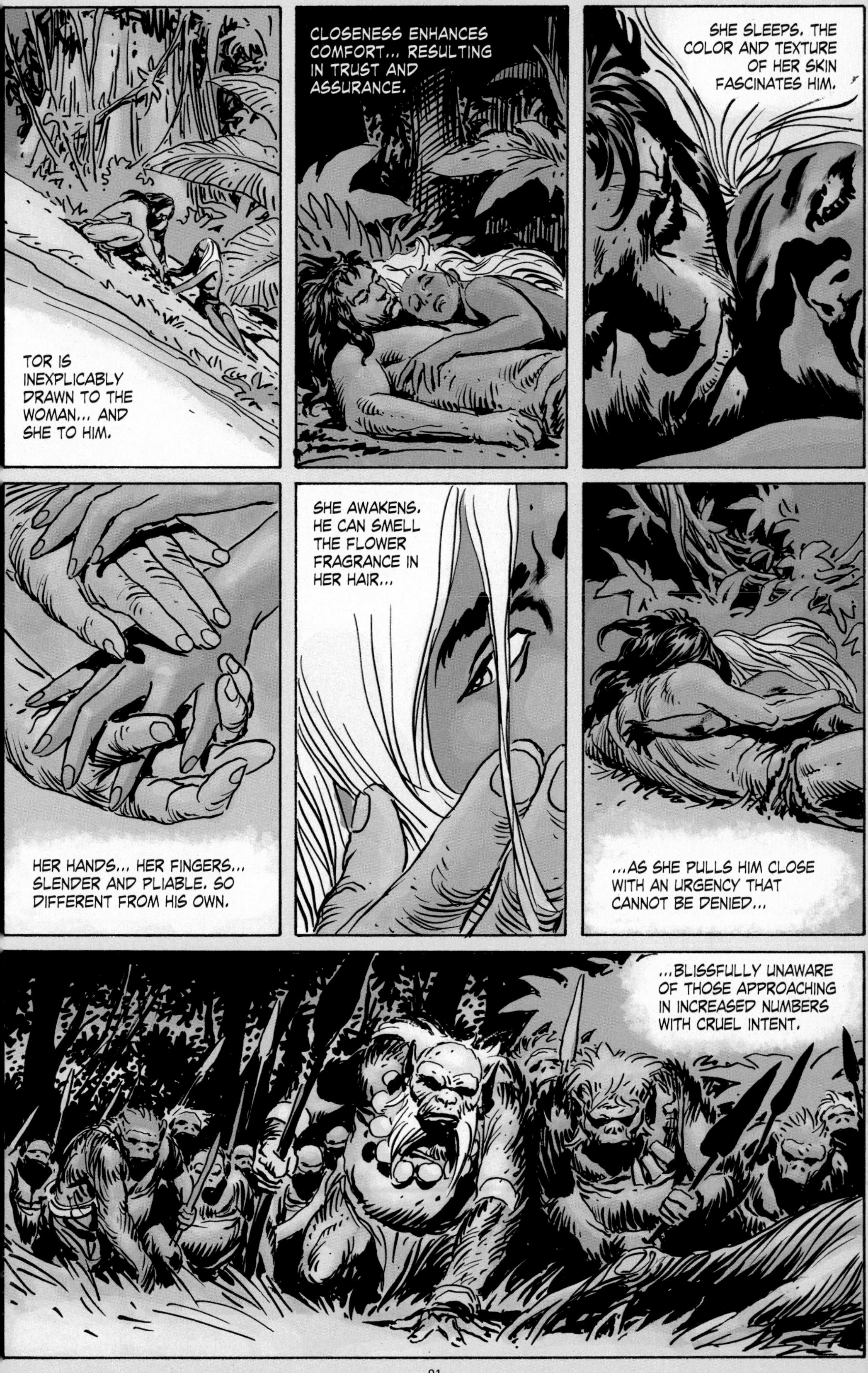
TOR IS INEXPLICABLY DRAWN TO THE WOMAN... AND SHE TO HIM.
CLOSENESS ENHANCES COMFORT... RESULTING IN TRUST AND ASSURANCE.
SHE SLEEPS. THE COLOR AND TEXTURE OF HER SKIN FASCINATES HIM.
HER HANDS... HER FINGERS... SLENDER AND PLIABLE. SO DIFFERENT FROM HIS OWN.
SHE AWAKENS. HE CAN SMELL THE FLOWER FRAGRANCE IN HER HAIR...
...AS SHE PULLS HIM CLOSE WITH AN URGENCY THAT CANNOT BE DENIED...
...BLISSFULLY UNAWARE OF THOSE APPROACHING IN INCREASED NUMBERS WITH CRUEL INTENT.

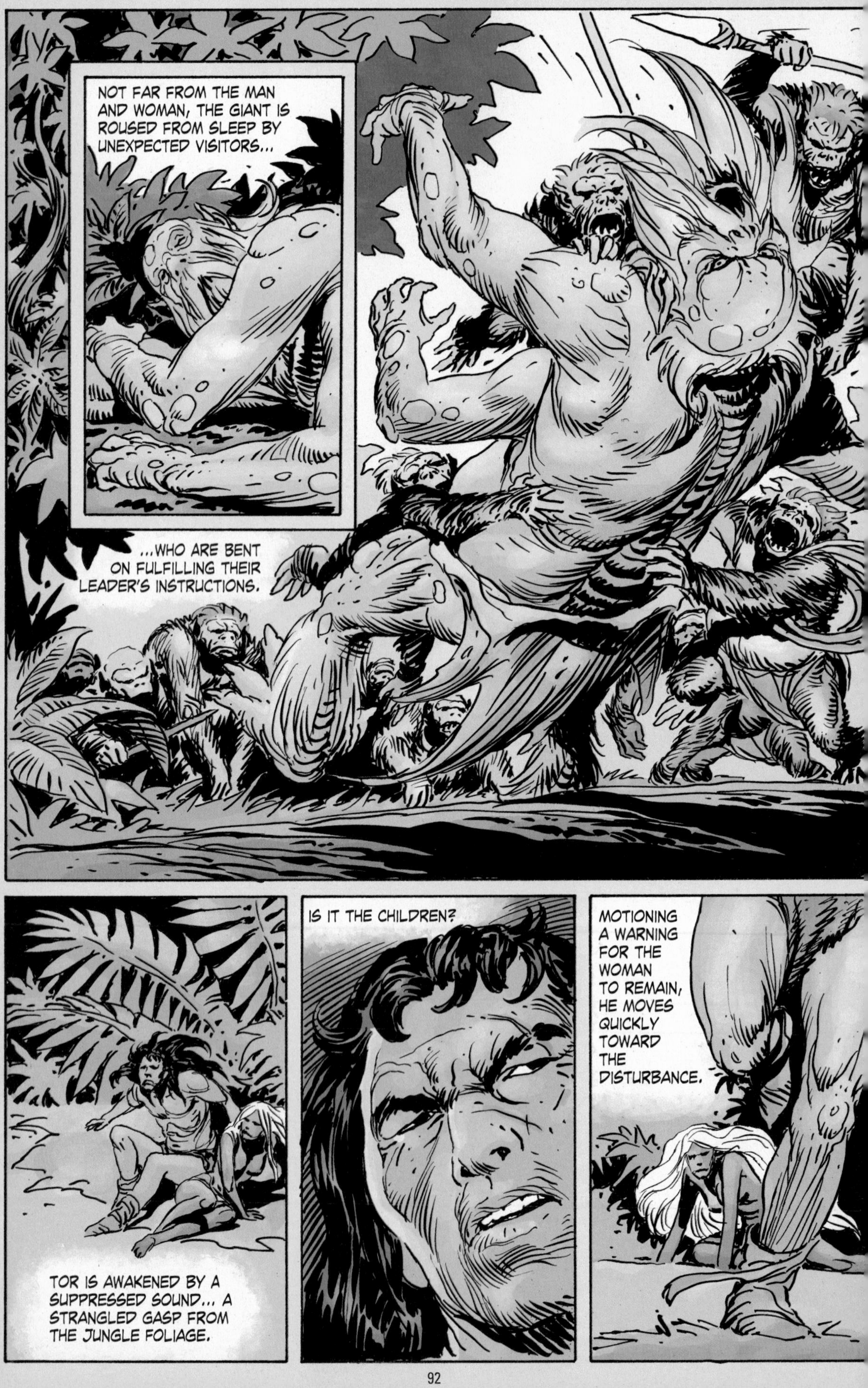
NOT FAR FROM THE MAN AND WOMAN, THE GIANT IS ROUSED FROM SLEEP BY UNEXPECTED VISITORS...
...WHO ARE BENT ON FULFILLING THEIR LEADER'S INSTRUCTIONS.
TOR IS AWAKENED BY A SUPPRESSED SOUND... A STRANGLED GASP FROM THE JUNGLE FOLIAGE.
IS IT THE CHILDREN?
MOTIONING A WARNING FOR THE WOMAN TO REMAIN, HE MOVES QUICKLY TOWARD THE DISTURBANCE.

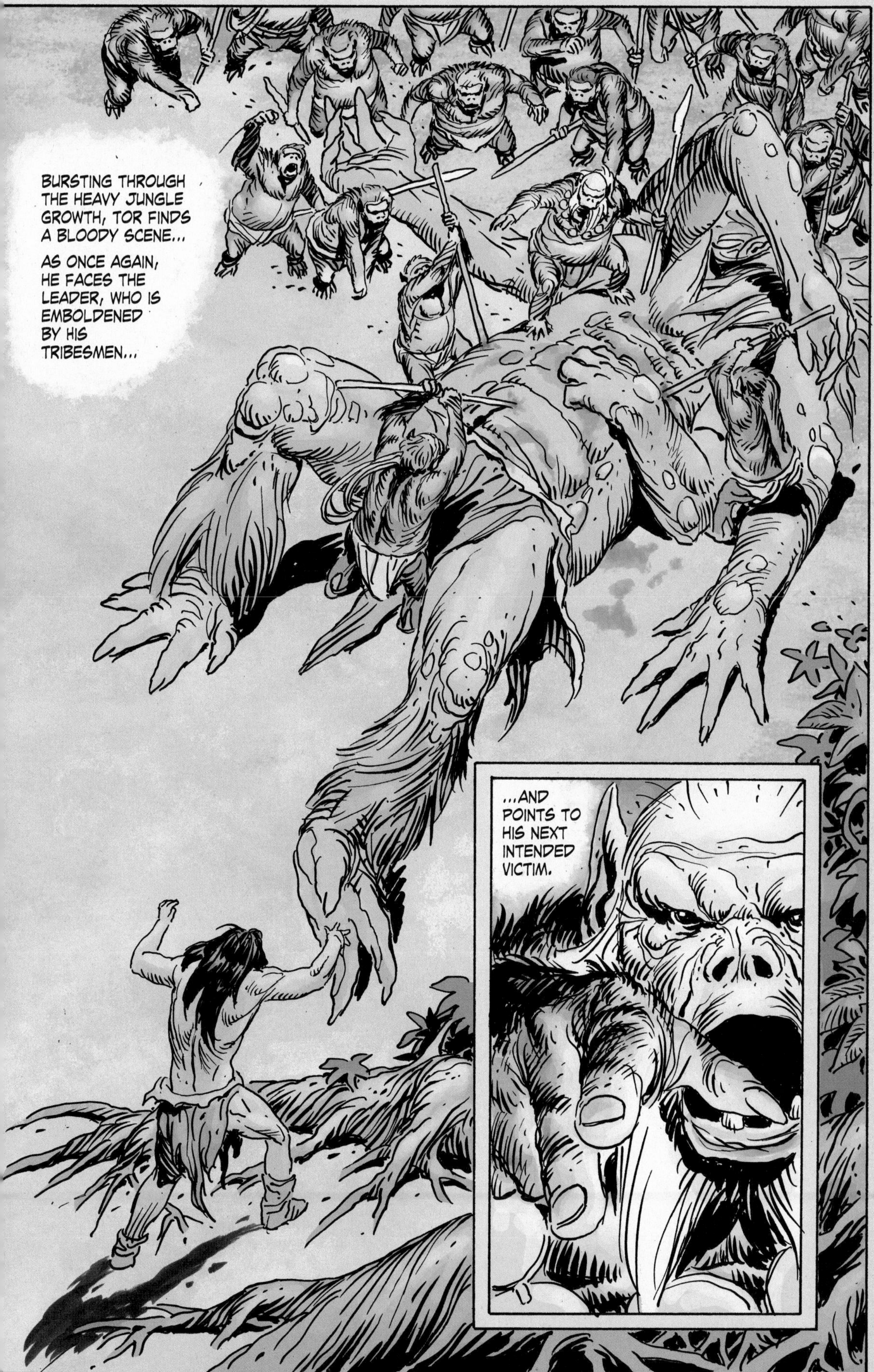
BURSTING THROUGH THE HEAVY JUNGLE GROWTH, TOR FINDS A BLOODY SCENE...
AS ONCE AGAIN, HE FACES THE LEADER, WHO IS EMBOLDENED BY HIS TRIBESMEN...
...AND POINTS TO HIS NEXT INTENDED VICTIM.

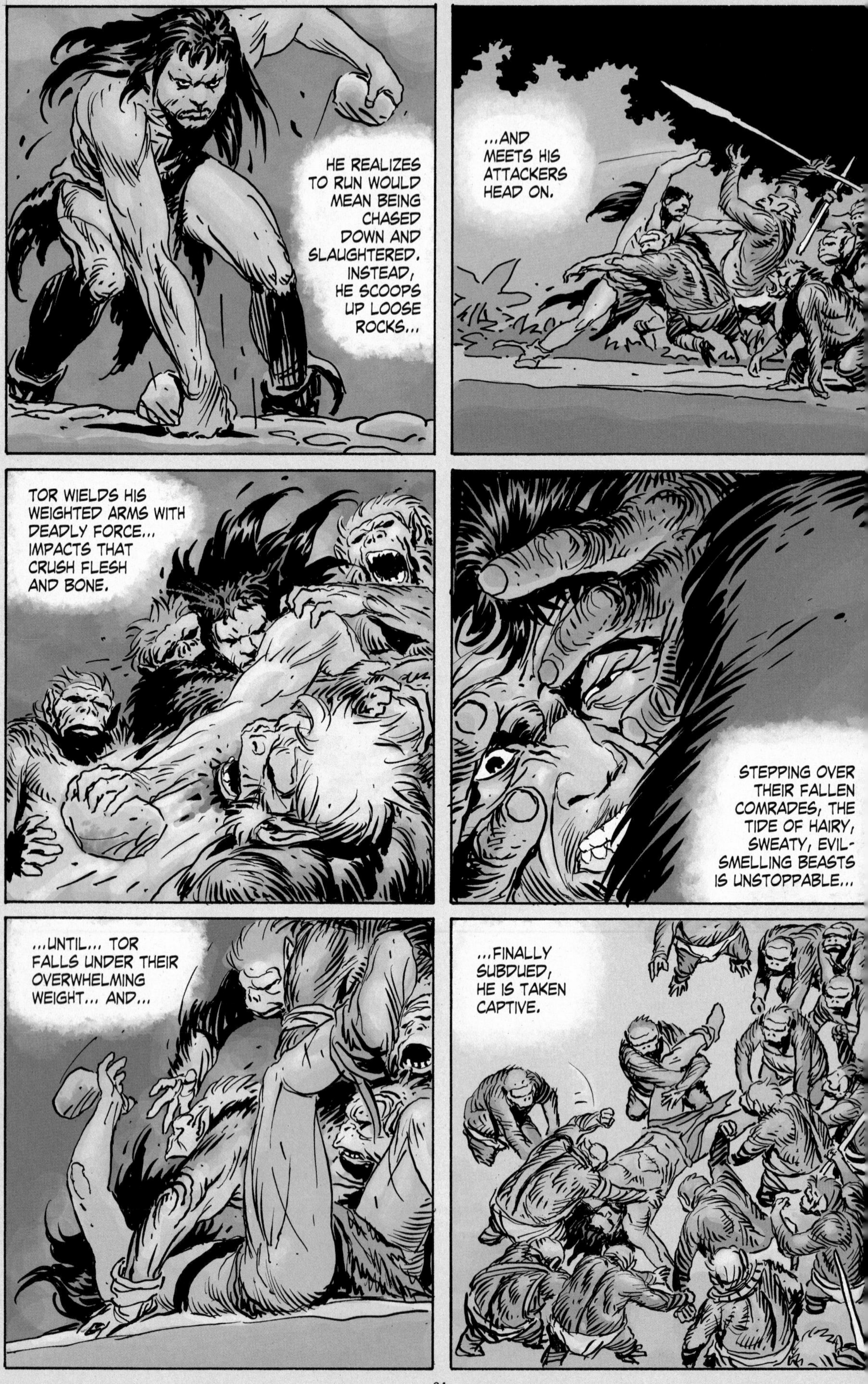
HE REALIZES TO RUN WOULD MEAN BEING CHASED DOWN AND SLAUGHTERED. INSTEAD, HE SCOOPS UP LOOSE ROCKS...
...AND MEETS HIS ATTACKERS HEAD ON.
TOR WIELDS HIS WEIGHTED ARMS WITH DEADLY FORCE... IMPACTS THAT CRUSH FLESH AND BONE.
STEPPING OVER THEIR FALLEN COMRADES, THE TIDE OF HAIRY, SWEATY, EVIL-SMELLING BEASTS IS UNSTOPPABLE...
...UNTIL... TOR FALLS UNDER THEIR OVERWHELMING WEIGHT... AND...
...FINALLY SUBDUED, HE IS TAKEN CAPTIVE.

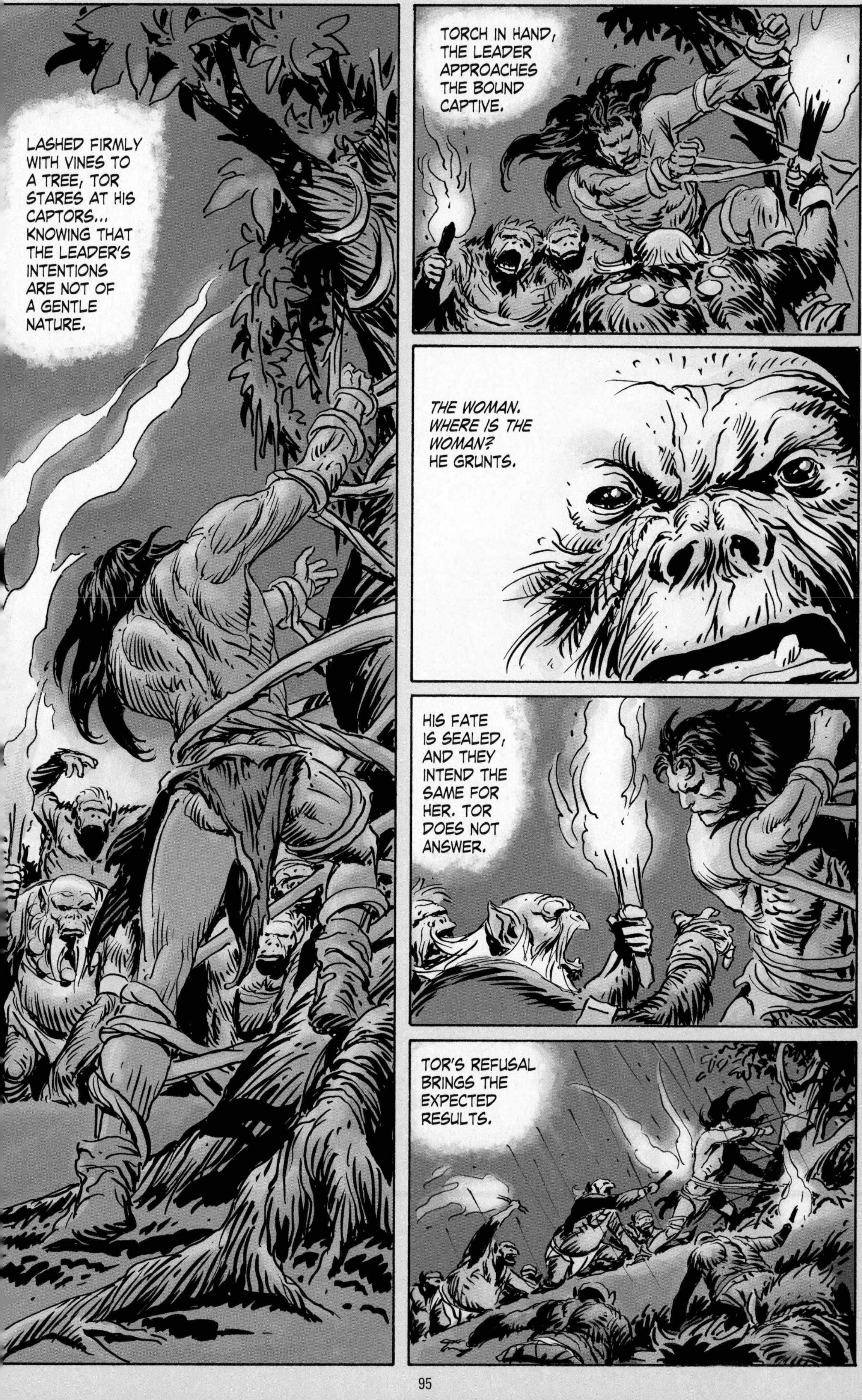
LASHED FIRMLY WITH VINES TO A TREE, TOR STARES AT HIS CAPTORS... KNOWING THAT THE LEADER'S INTENTIONS ARE NOT OF A GENTLE NATURE.
TORCH IN HAND, THE LEADER APPROACHES THE BOUND CAPTIVE.
THE WOMAN. WHERE IS THE WOMAN? HE GRUNTS.
HIS FATE IS SEALED, AND THEY INTEND THE SAME FOR HER. TOR DOES NOT ANSWER.
TOR'S REFUSAL BRINGS THE EXPECTED RESULTS.

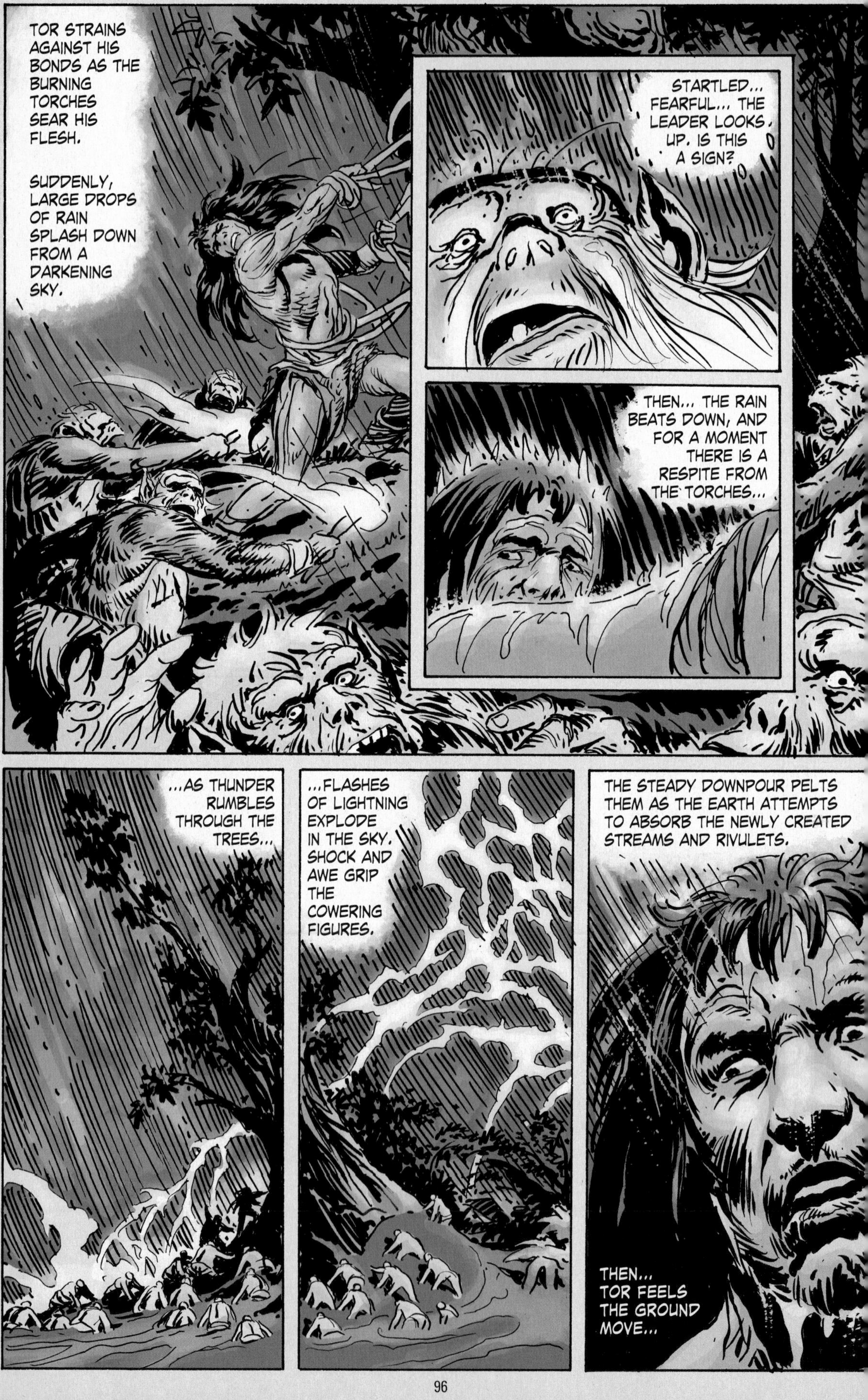
TOR STRAINS AGAINST HIS BONDS AS THE BURNING TORCHES SEAR HIS FLESH.
SUDDENLY, LARGE DROPS OF RAIN SPLASH DOWN FROM A DARKENING SKY.
STARTLED... FEARFUL... THE LEADER LOOKS UP. IS THIS A SIGN?
THEN... THE RAIN BEATS DOWN, AND FOR A MOMENT THERE IS A RESPITE FROM THE TORCHES...
...AS THUNDER RUMBLES THROUGH THE TREES...
...FLASHES OF LIGHTNING EXPLODE IN THE SKY. SHOCK AND AWE GRIP THE COWERING FIGURES.
THE STEADY DOWNPOUR PELTS THEM AS THE EARTH ATTEMPTS TO ABSORB THE NEWLY CREATED STREAMS AND RIVULETS.
THEN... TOR FEELS THE GROUND MOVE...

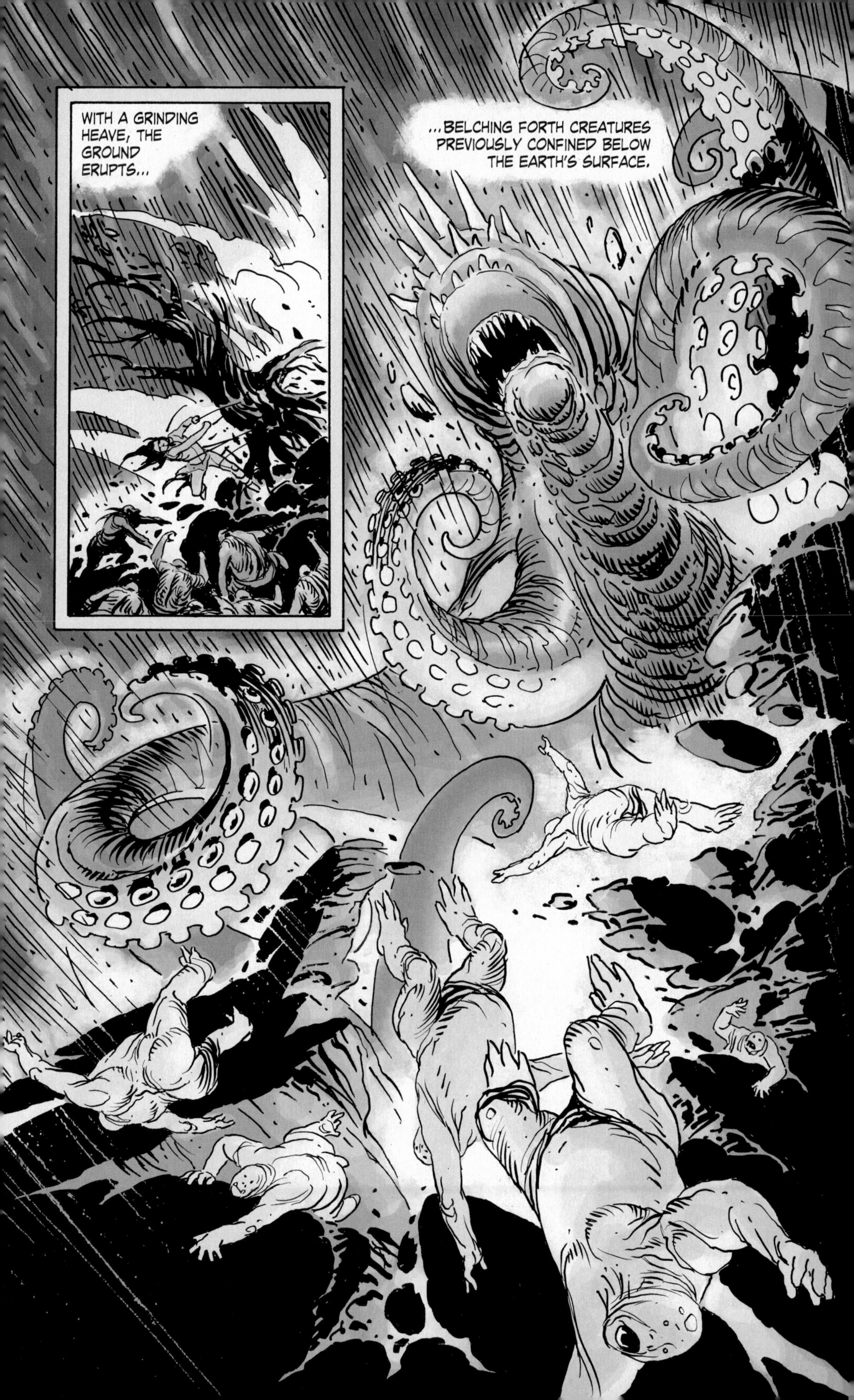
WITH A GRINDING HEAVE, THE GROUND ERUPTS...
...BELCHING FORTH CREATURES PREVIOUSLY CONFINED BELOW THE EARTH'S SURFACE.

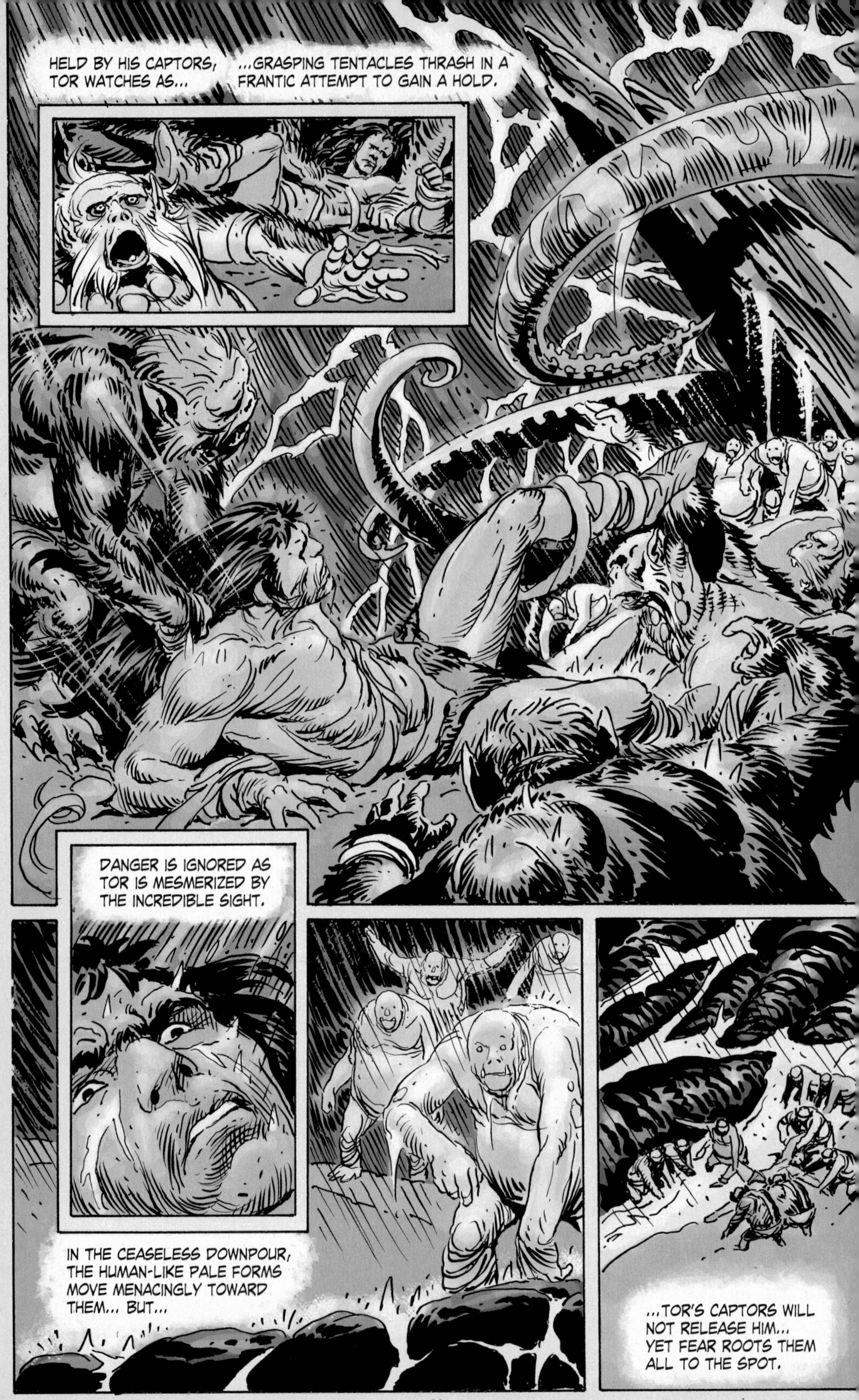
HELD BY HIS CAPTORS, TOR WATCHES AS...
...GRASPING TENTACLES THRASH IN A FRANTIC ATTEMPT TO GAIN A HOLD.
DANGER IS IGNORED AS TOR IS MESMERIZED BY THE INCREDIBLE SIGHT.
IN THE CEASELESS DOWNPOUR, THE HUMAN-LIKE PALE FORMS MOVE MENACINGLY TOWARD THEM... BUT...
...TOR'S CAPTORS WILL NOT RELEASE HIM... YET FEAR ROOTS THEM ALL TO THE SPOT.

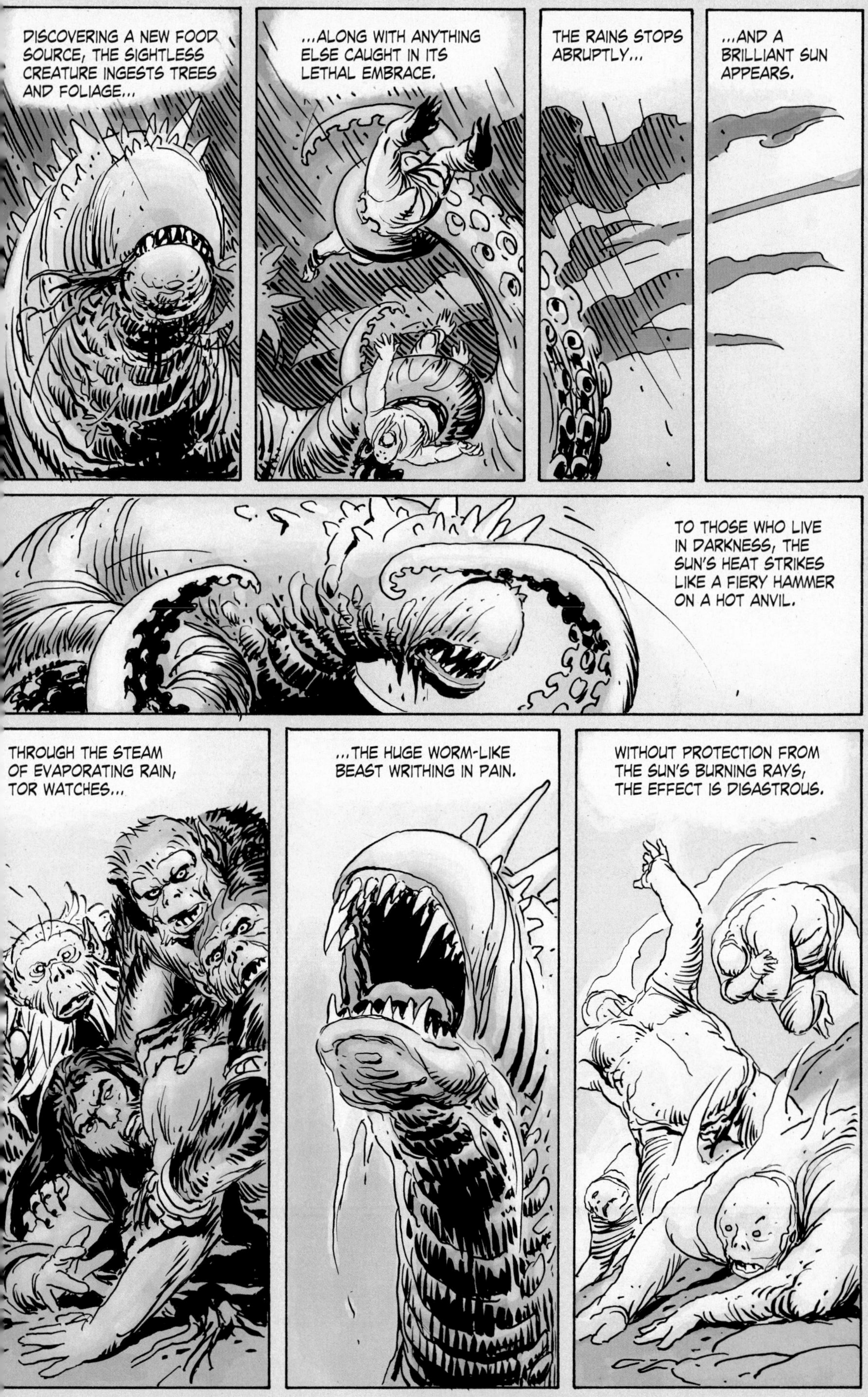
DISCOVERING A NEW FOOD SOURCE, THE SIGHTLESS CREATURE INGESTS TREES AND FOLIAGE...
...ALONG WITH ANYTHING ELSE CAUGHT IN ITS LETHAL EMBRACE.
THE RAINS STOPS ABRUPTLY...
...AND A BRILLIANT SUN APPEARS.
TO THOSE WHO LIVE IN DARKNESS, THE SUN'S HEAT STRIKES LIKE A FIERY HAMMER ON A HOT ANVIL.
THROUGH THE STEAM OF EVAPORATING RAIN, TOR WATCHES...
...THE HUGE WORM-LIKE BEAST WRITHING IN PAIN.
WITHOUT PROTECTION FROM THE SUN'S BURNING RAYS, THE EFFECT IS DISASTROUS.

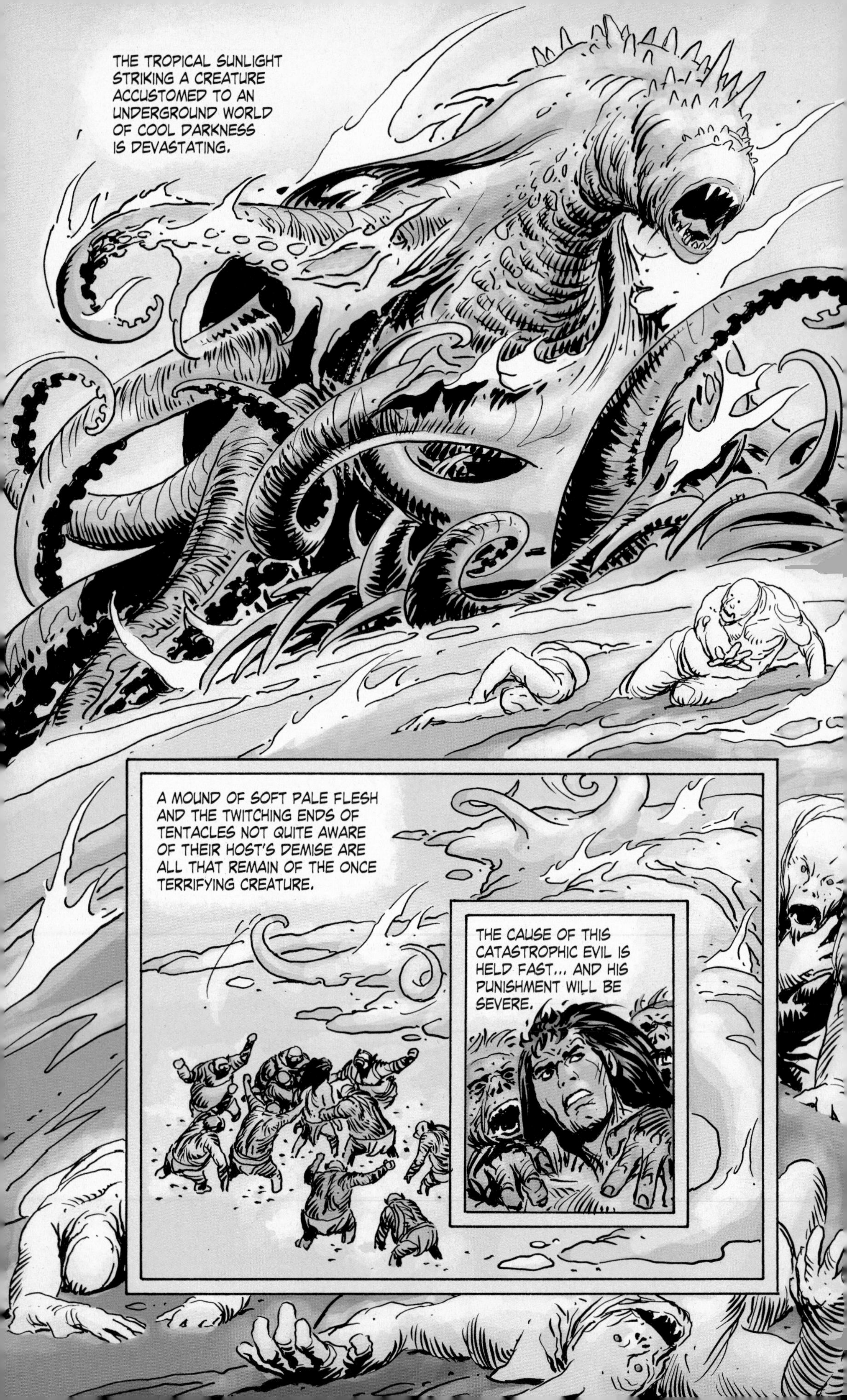
THE TROPICAL SUNLIGHT STRIKING A CREATURE ACCUSTOMED TO AN UNDERGROUND WORLD OF COOL DARKNESS IS DEVASTATING.
A MOUND OF SOFT PALE FLESH AND THE TWITCHING ENDS OF TENTACLES NOT QUITE AWARE OF THEIR HOST'S DEMISE ARE ALL THAT REMAIN OF THE ONCE TERRIFYING CREATURE.
THE CAUSE OF THIS CATASTROPHIC EVIL IS HELD FAST... AND HIS PUNISHMENT WILL BE SEVERE.

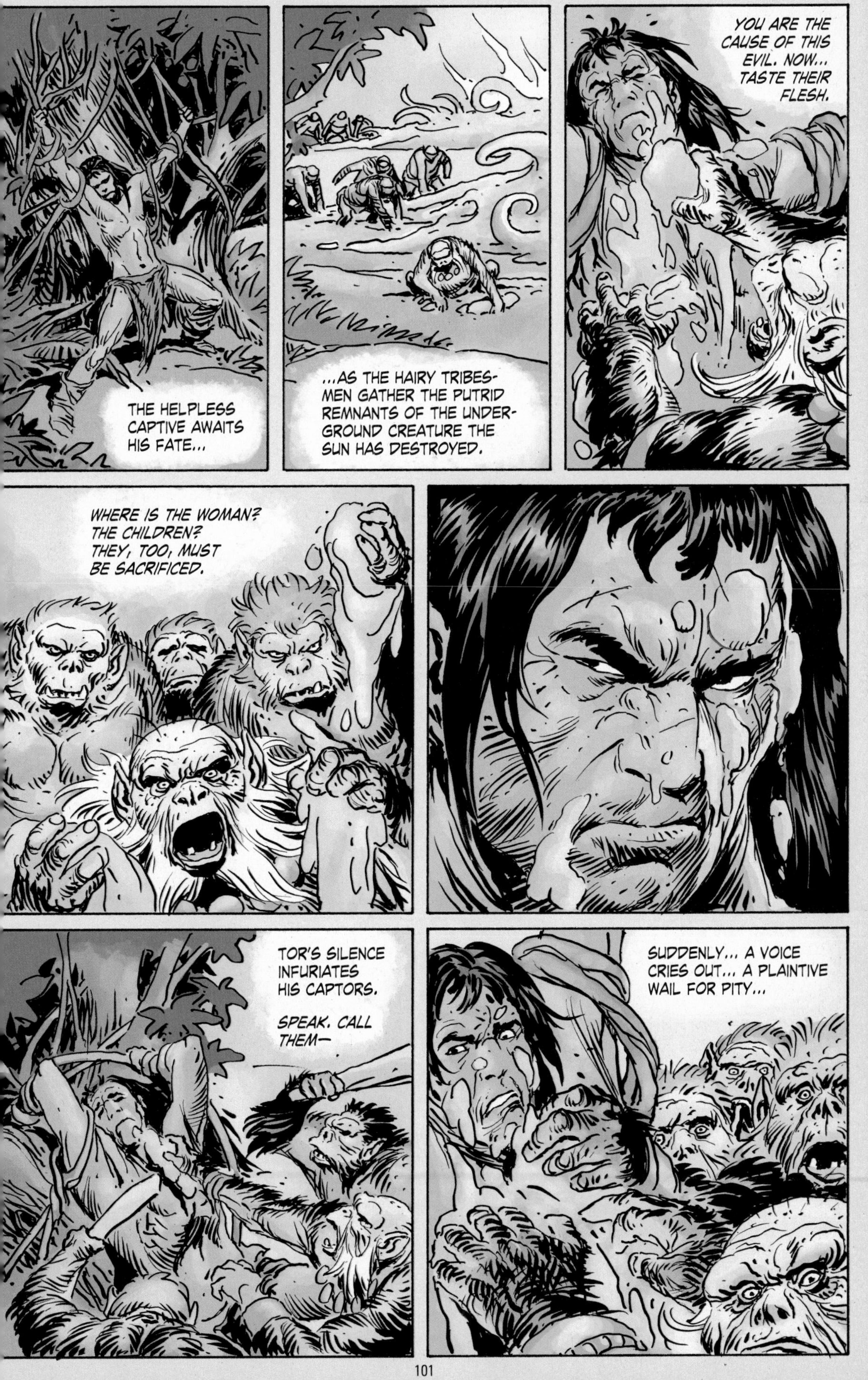
THE HELPLESS CAPTIVE AWAITS HIS FATE...
...AS THE HAIRY TRIBESMEN GATHER THE PUTRID REMNANTS OF THE UNDERGROUND CREATURE THE SUN HAS DESTROYED.
YOU ARE THE CAUSE OF THIS EVIL. NOW... TASTE THEIR FLESH.
WHERE IS THE WOMAN? THE CHILDREN? THEY, TOO, MUST BE SACRIFICED.
TOR'S SILENCE INFURIATES HIS CAPTORS.
SPEAK. CALL THEM—
SUDDENLY... A VOICE CRIES OUT... A PLAINTIVE WAIL FOR PITY...

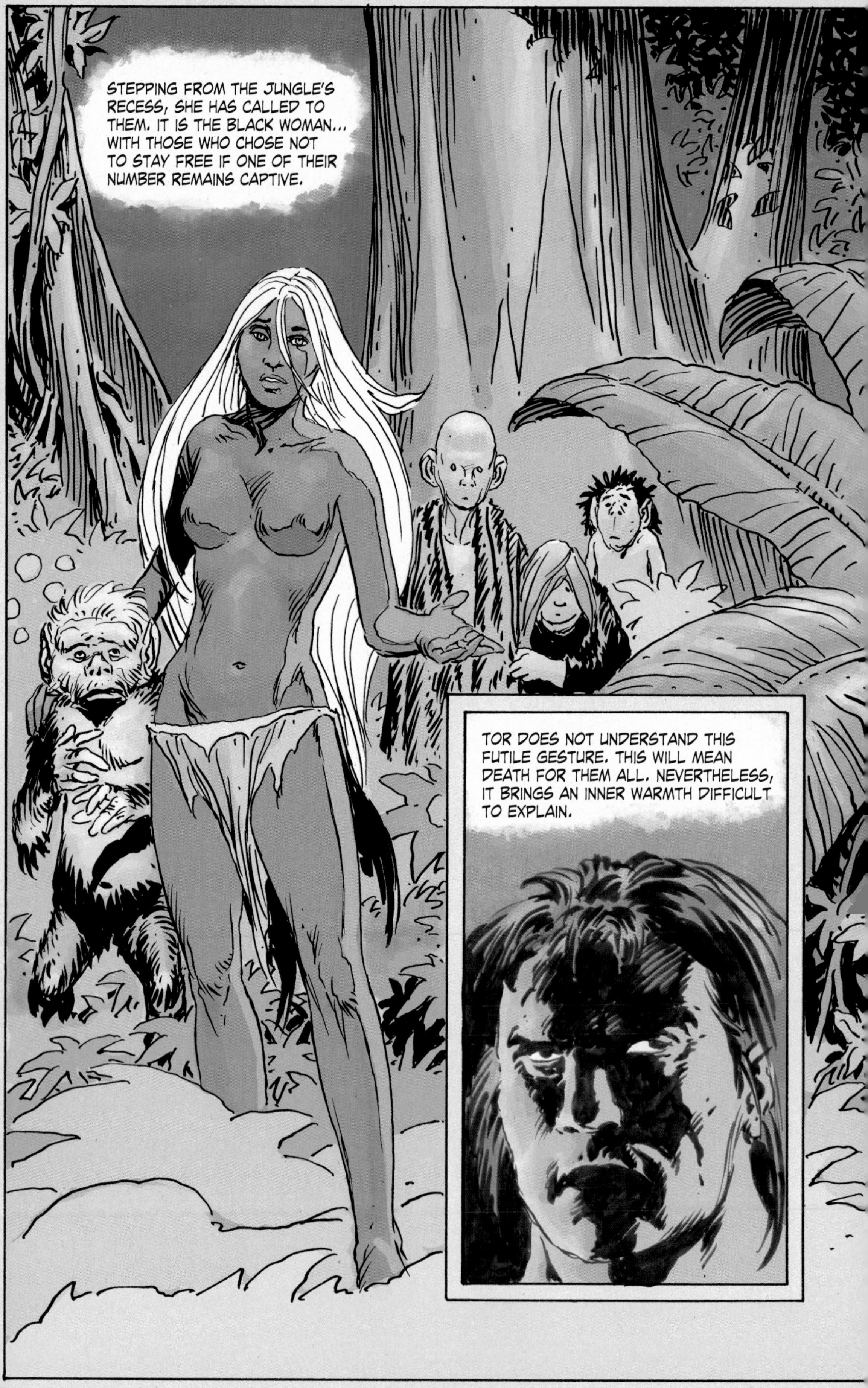
STEPPING FROM THE JUNGLE'S RECESS, SHE HAS CALLED TO THEM. IT IS THE BLACK WOMAN... WITH THOSE WHO CHOSE NOT TO STAY FREE IF ONE OF THEIR NUMBER REMAINS CAPTIVE.
TOR DOES NOT UNDERSTAND THIS FUTILE GESTURE. THIS WILL MEAN DEATH FOR THEM ALL. NEVERTHELESS, IT BRINGS AN INNER WARMTH DIFFICULT TO EXPLAIN.

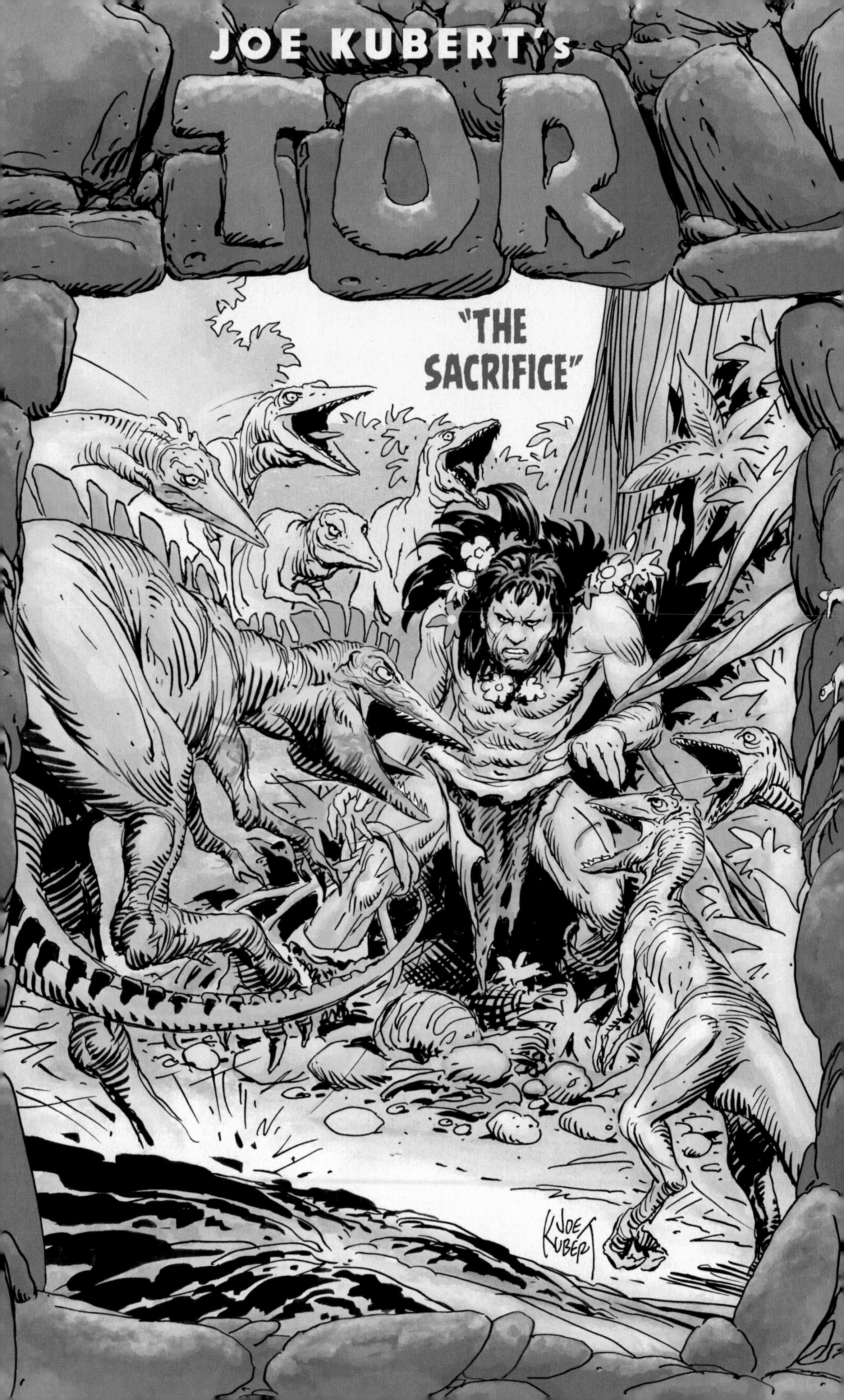
JOE KUBERT's
TOR
"THE SACRIFICE"
JOE KUBERT

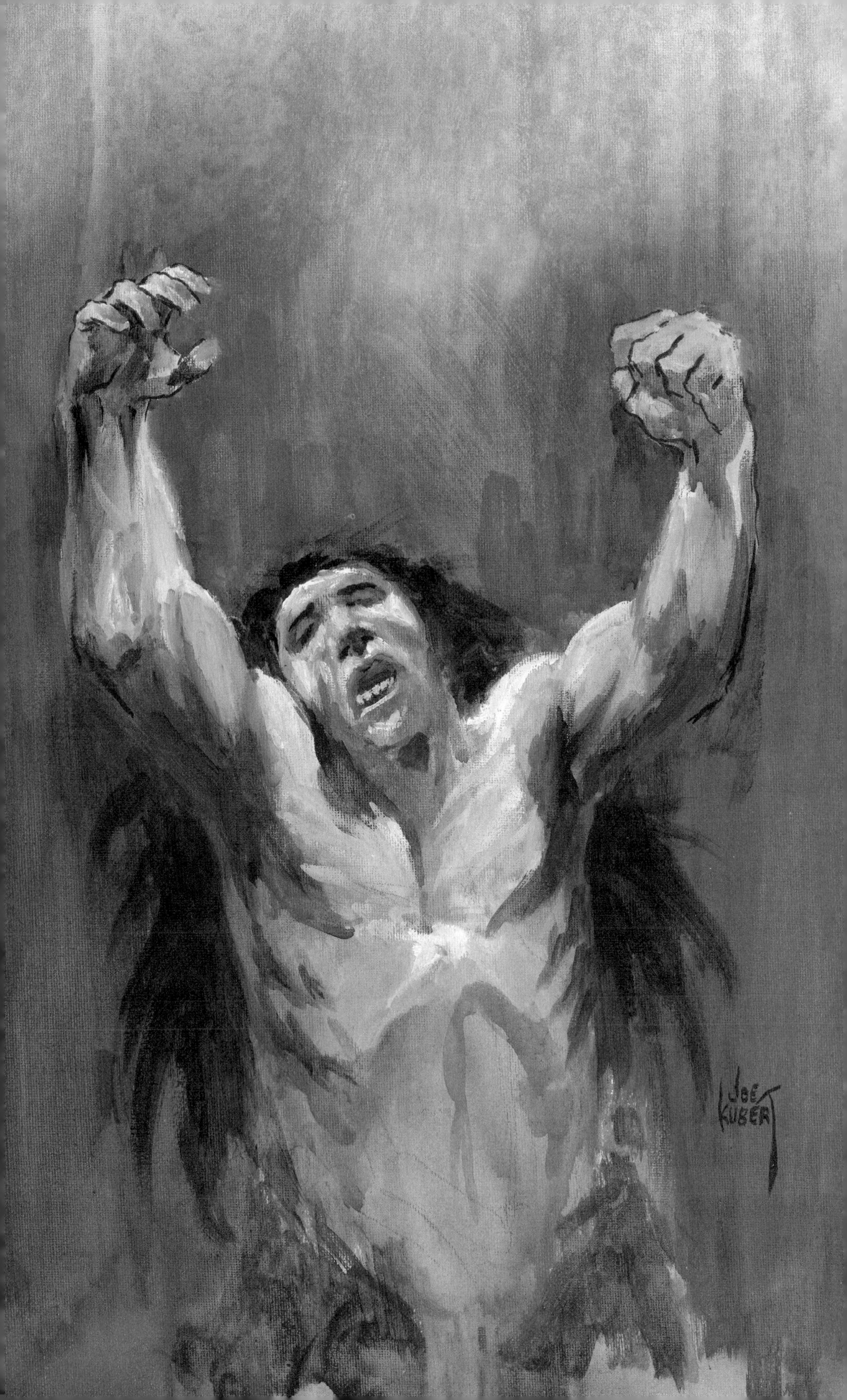
JOE KUBERT

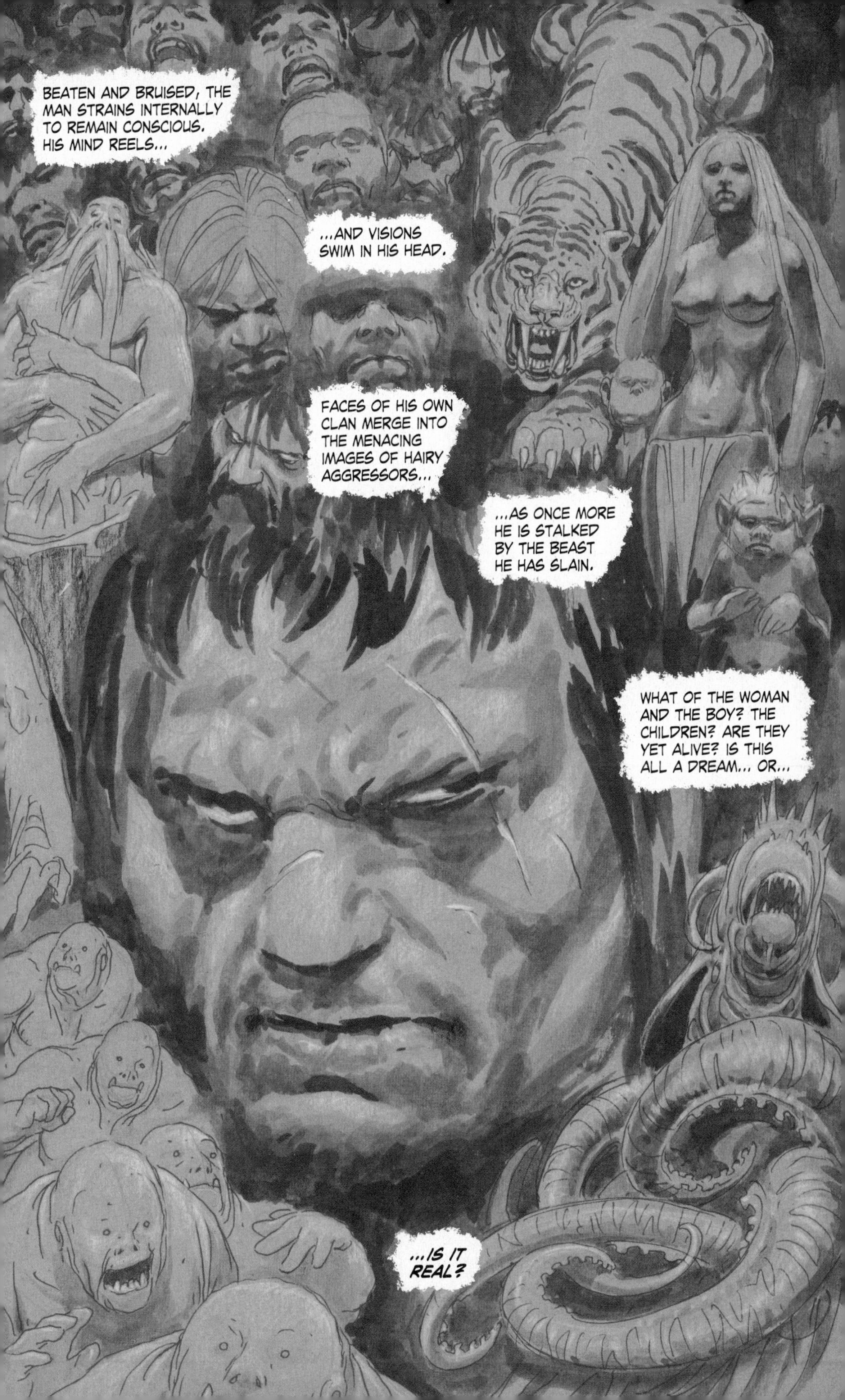
BEATEN AND BRUISED, THE MAN STRAINS INTERNALLY TO REMAIN CONSCIOUS. HIS MIND REELS...
...AND VISIONS SWIM IN HIS HEAD.
FACES OF HIS OWN CLAN MERGE INTO THE MENACING IMAGES OF HAIRY AGGRESSORS...
...AS ONCE MORE HE IS STALKED BY THE BEAST HE HAS SLAIN.
WHAT OF THE WOMAN AND THE BOY? THE CHILDREN? ARE THEY YET ALIVE? IS THIS ALL A DREAM... OR...
...IS IT REAL?

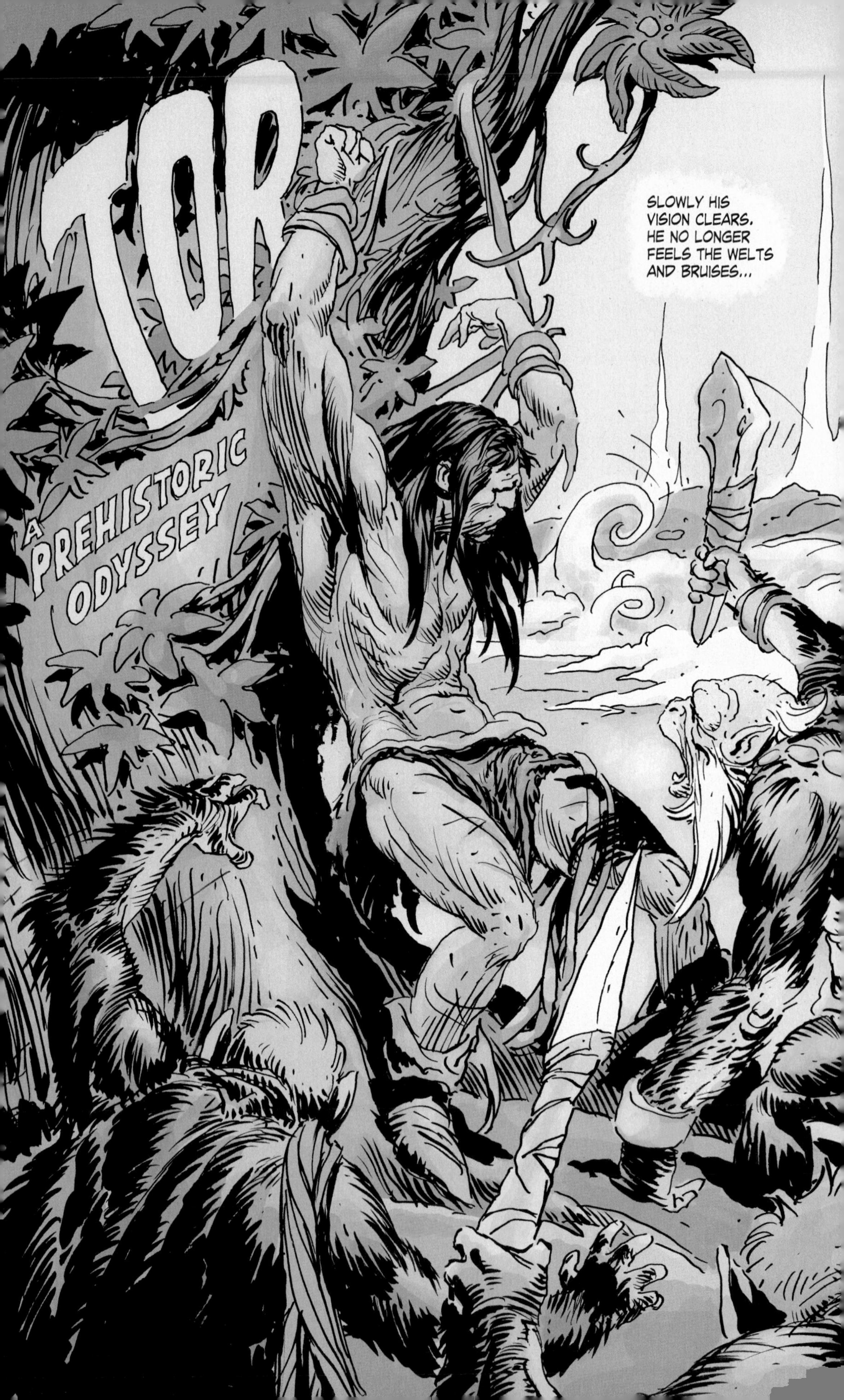
TOR
A PREHISTORIC ODYSSEY
SLOWLY HIS VISION CLEARS. HE NO LONGER FEELS THE WELTS AND BRUISES...

THE FIRE ASHES SAY THEY MUST BE OFFERED... AS GIFTS.

...AS THE WOMAN AND THE STRANGE CHILDREN COME FORWARD TO SECURE HIS RELEASE.

...ADORN FLOWERS SWEE S ACCE

THE SMELL OF FOOD FLOWERS WILL BRING SPIRITS TO US... AN WILL ACCEPT OUR O AND MAKE US SAFE

SHE IS READY TO GIVE HERSELF UP TO SAVE THE MAN WHO HAS CARED FOR HER...

...BUT THE LEADER'S SHARP MOTION DECLARES THEM ALL PRISONERS...

...AND THE GROUP IS SURROUNDED. THEIR FATES ARE SEALED.

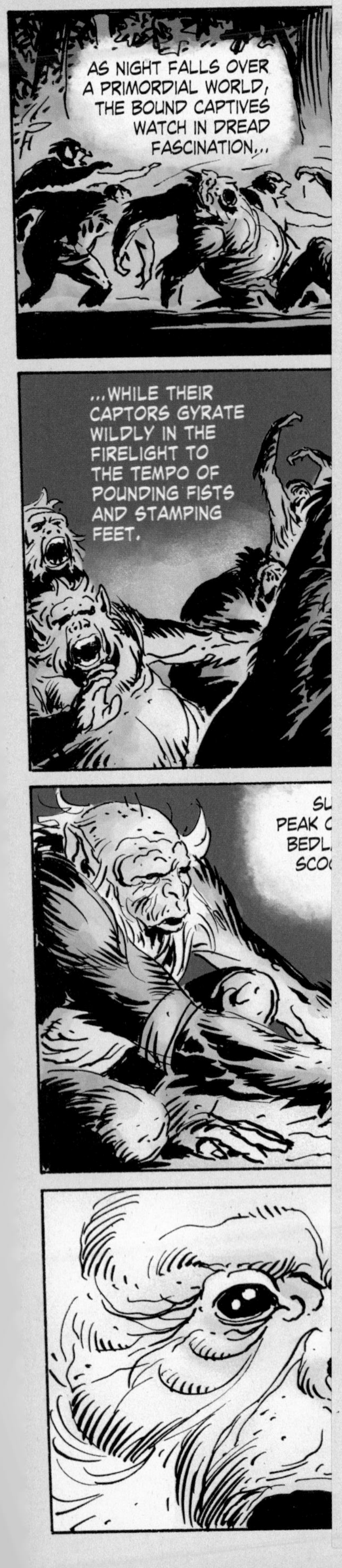
AS NIGHT FALLS OVER A PRIMORDIAL WORLD, THE BOUND CAPTIVES WATCH IN DREAD FASCINATION...
...WHILE THEIR CAPTORS GYRATE WILDLY IN THE FIRELIGHT TO THE TEMPO OF POUNDING FISTS AND STAMPING FEET.

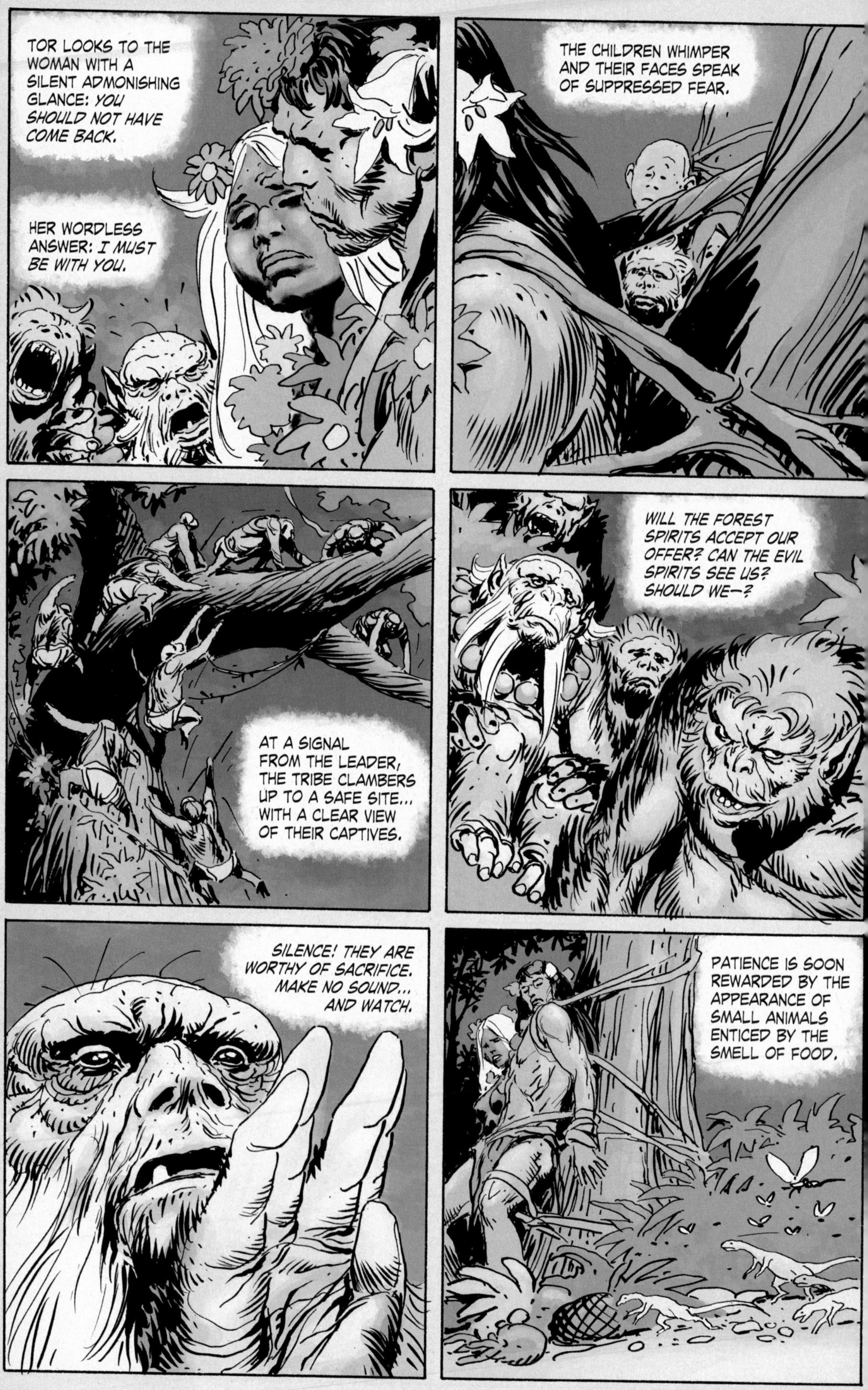
TOR LOOKS TO THE WOMAN WITH A SILENT ADMONISHING GLANCE: *YOU SHOULD NOT HAVE COME BACK.*
HER WORDLESS ANSWER: *I MUST BE WITH YOU.*
THE CHILDREN WHIMPER AND THEIR FACES SPEAK OF SUPPRESSED FEAR.
AT A SIGNAL FROM THE LEADER, THE TRIBE CLAMBERS UP TO A SAFE SITE... WITH A CLEAR VIEW OF THEIR CAPTIVES.
WILL THE FOREST SPIRITS ACCEPT OUR OFFER? CAN THE EVIL SPIRITS SEE US? SHOULD WE--?
SILENCE! THEY ARE WORTHY OF SACRIFICE. MAKE NO SOUND... AND WATCH.
PATIENCE IS SOON REWARDED BY THE APPEARANCE OF SMALL ANIMALS ENTICED BY THE SMELL OF FOOD.

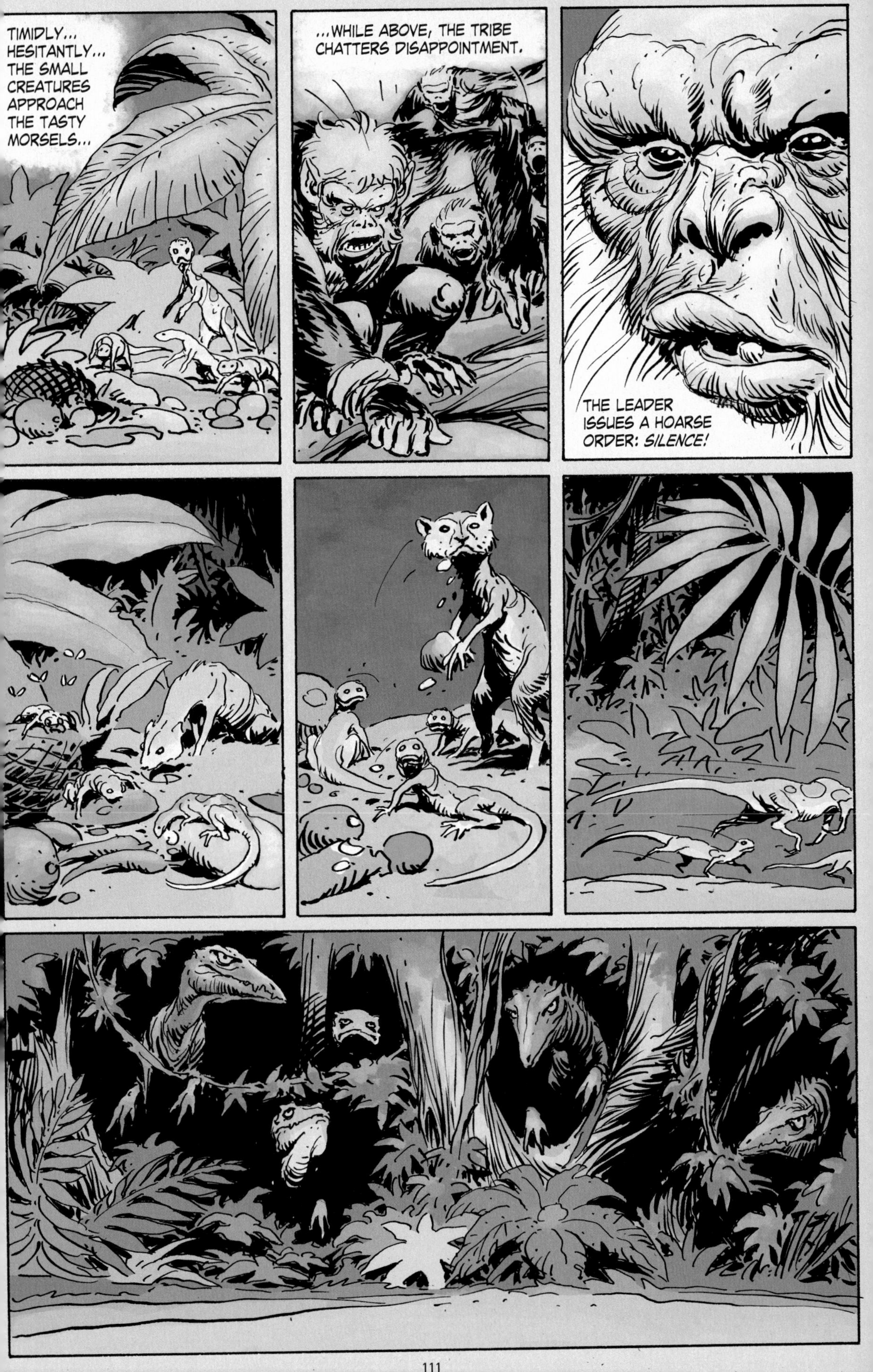
TIMIDLY... HESITANTLY... THE SMALL CREATURES APPROACH THE TASTY MORSELS...
...WHILE ABOVE, THE TRIBE CHATTERS DISAPPOINTMENT.
THE LEADER ISSUES A HOARSE ORDER: *SILENCE!*

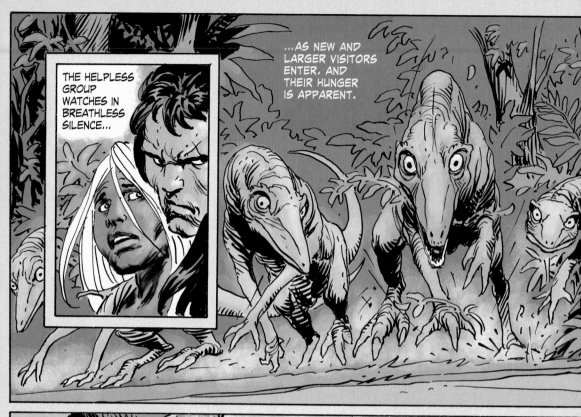

THE HELPLESS GROUP WATCHES IN BREATHLESS SILENCE...

...AS NEW AND LARGER VISITORS ENTER, AND THEIR HUNGER IS APPARENT.

FROM A SAFE PERCH OVERHEAD, AN APPROVING AUDIENCE IS WATCHING IN RAPT ANTICIPATION.

ATTRACTED BY THE OVER-RIPE FOOD, THE HUNGRY CREATURES DO NOT NOTICE THE BOUND PRISONERS...

...UNTIL ONE OF THE CHILDREN WHIMPERS.

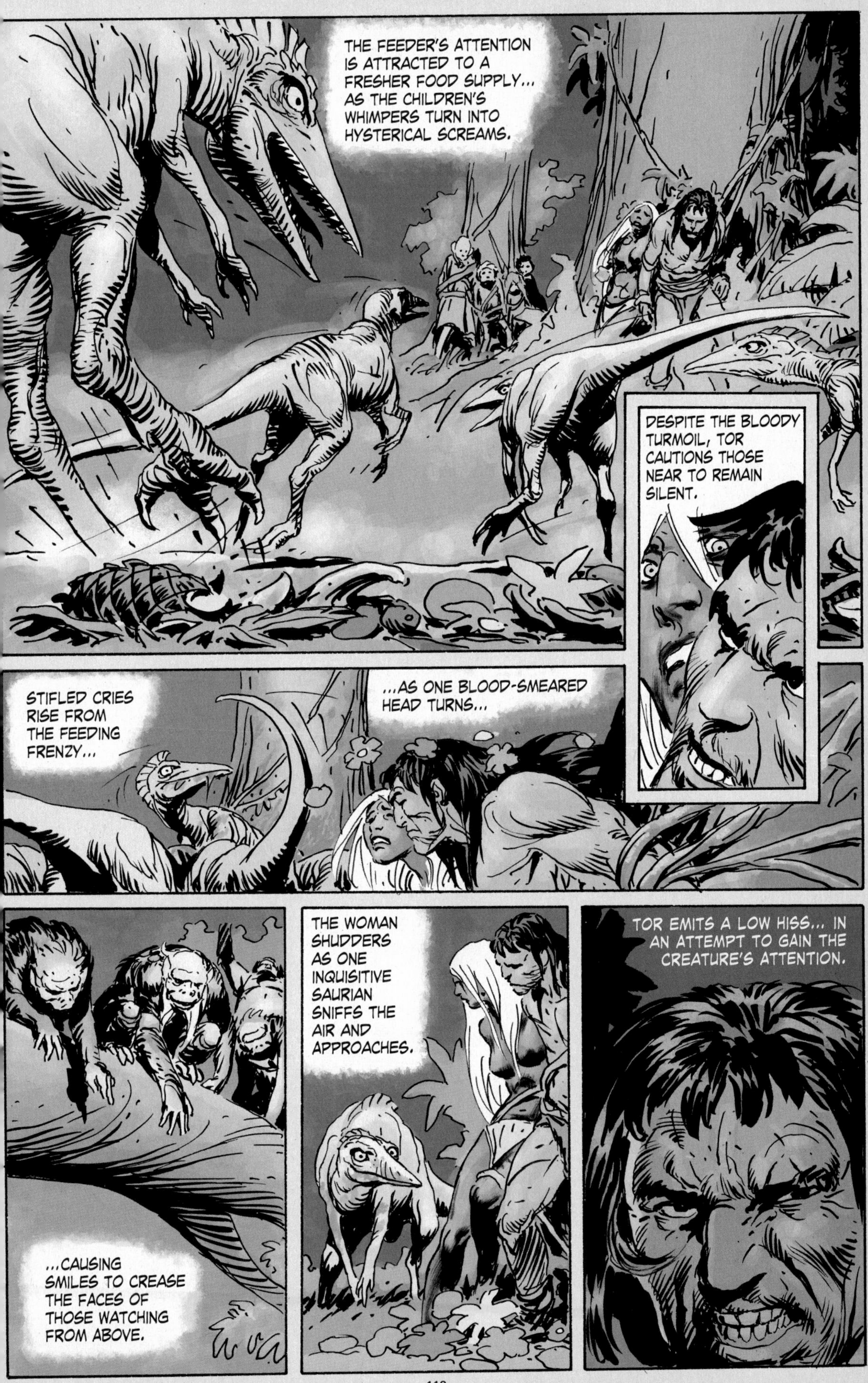
THE FEEDER'S ATTENTION IS ATTRACTED TO A FRESHER FOOD SUPPLY... AS THE CHILDREN'S WHIMPERS TURN INTO HYSTERICAL SCREAMS.
DESPITE THE BLOODY TURMOIL, TOR CAUTIONS THOSE NEAR TO REMAIN SILENT.
STIFLED CRIES RISE FROM THE FEEDING FRENZY...
...AS ONE BLOOD-SMEARED HEAD TURNS...
...CAUSING SMILES TO CREASE THE FACES OF THOSE WATCHING FROM ABOVE.
THE WOMAN SHUDDERS AS ONE INQUISITIVE SAURIAN SNIFFS THE AIR AND APPROACHES.
TOR EMITS A LOW HISS... IN AN ATTEMPT TO GAIN THE CREATURE'S ATTENTION.

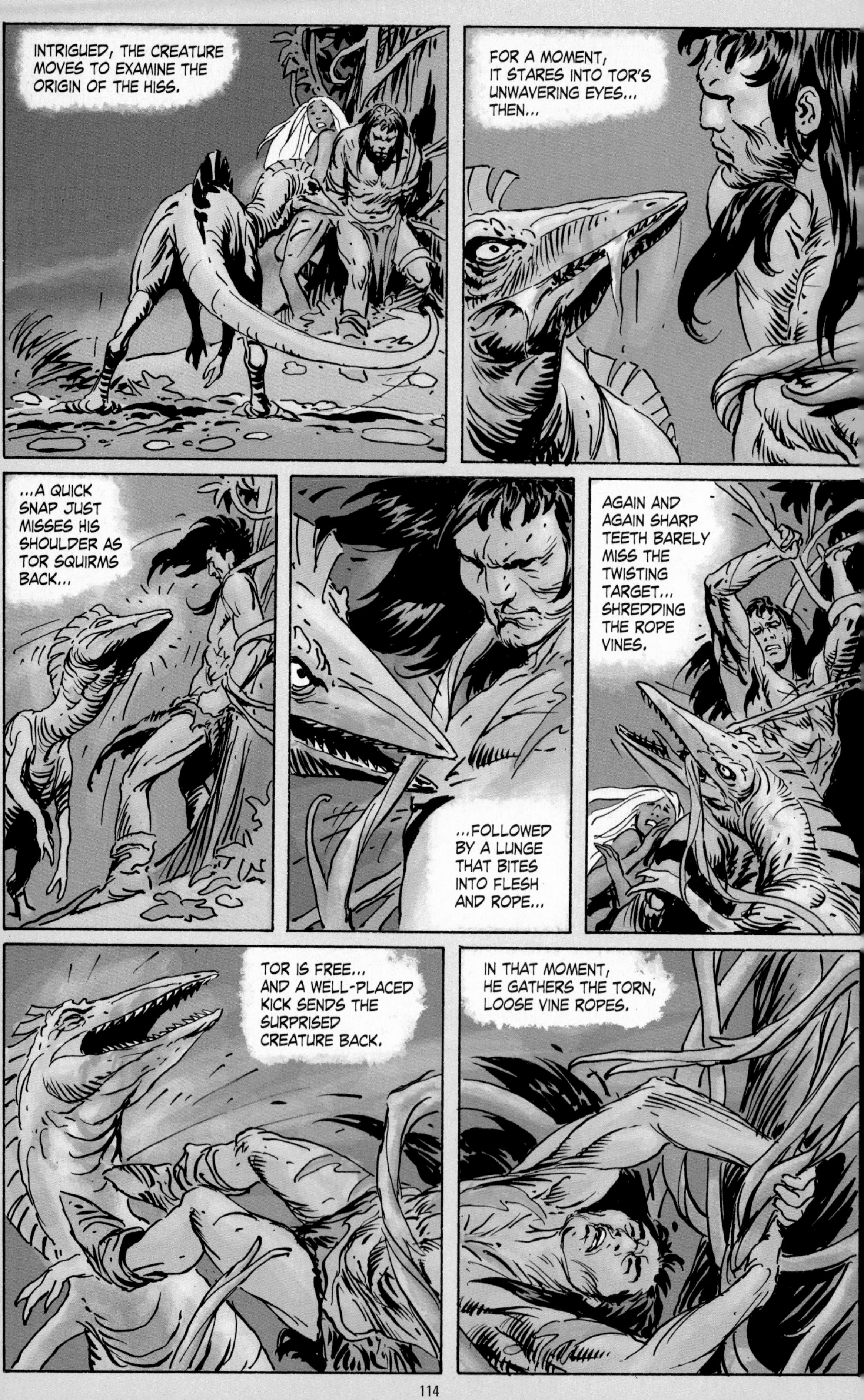
INTRIGUED, THE CREATURE MOVES TO EXAMINE THE ORIGIN OF THE HISS.
FOR A MOMENT, IT STARES INTO TOR'S UNWAVERING EYES... THEN...
...A QUICK SNAP JUST MISSES HIS SHOULDER AS TOR SQUIRMS BACK...
...FOLLOWED BY A LUNGE THAT BITES INTO FLESH AND ROPE...
AGAIN AND AGAIN SHARP TEETH BARELY MISS THE TWISTING TARGET... SHREDDING THE ROPE VINES.
TOR IS FREE... AND A WELL-PLACED KICK SENDS THE SURPRISED CREATURE BACK.
IN THAT MOMENT, HE GATHERS THE TORN, LOOSE VINE ROPES.

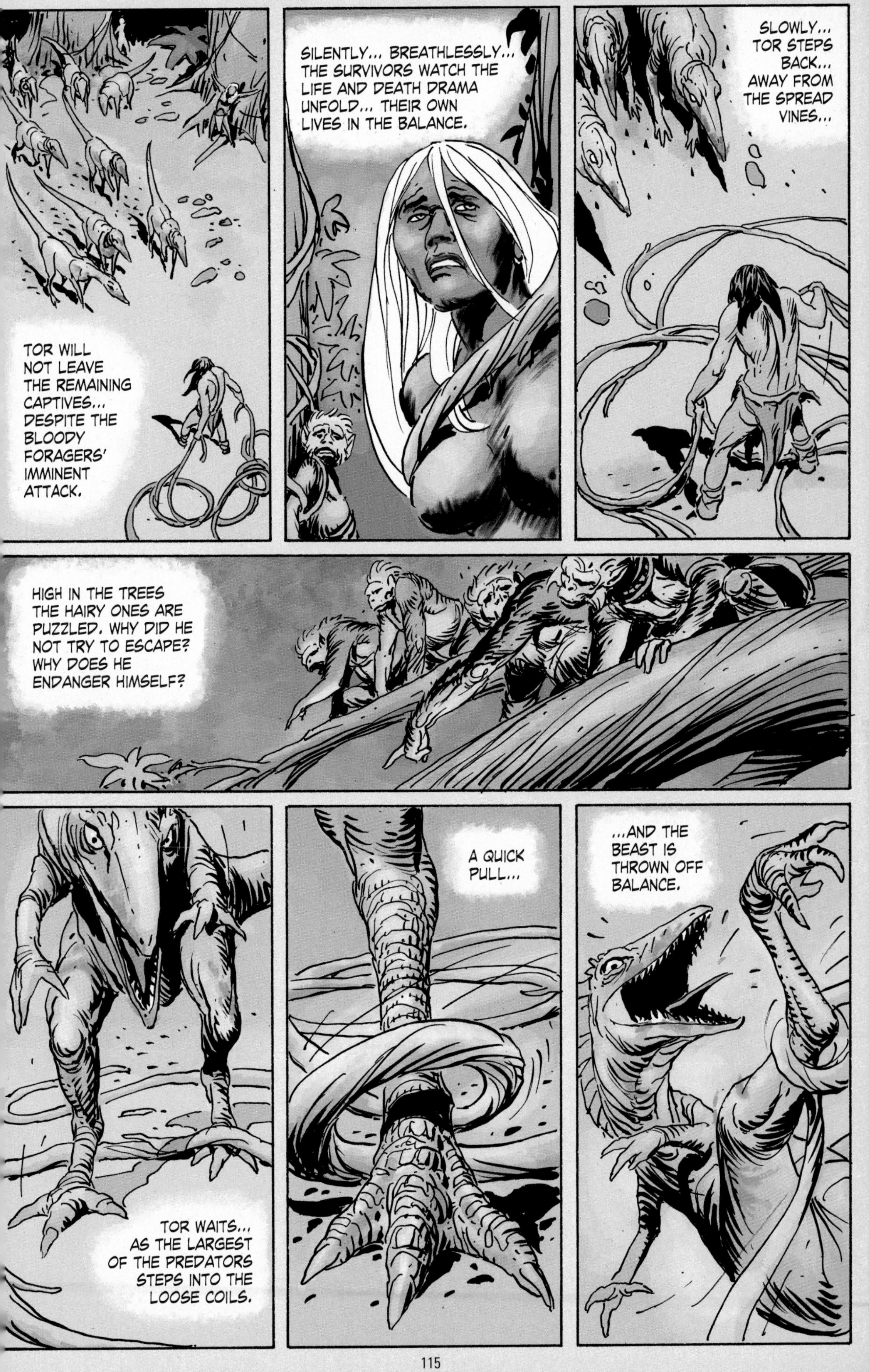
TOR WILL NOT LEAVE THE REMAINING CAPTIVES... DESPITE THE BLOODY FORAGERS' IMMINENT ATTACK.
SILENTLY... BREATHLESSLY... THE SURVIVORS WATCH THE LIFE AND DEATH DRAMA UNFOLD... THEIR OWN LIVES IN THE BALANCE.
SLOWLY... TOR STEPS BACK... AWAY FROM THE SPREAD VINES...
HIGH IN THE TREES THE HAIRY ONES ARE PUZZLED. WHY DID HE NOT TRY TO ESCAPE? WHY DOES HE ENDANGER HIMSELF?
TOR WAITS... AS THE LARGEST OF THE PREDATORS STEPS INTO THE LOOSE COILS.
A QUICK PULL...
...AND THE BEAST IS THROWN OFF BALANCE.

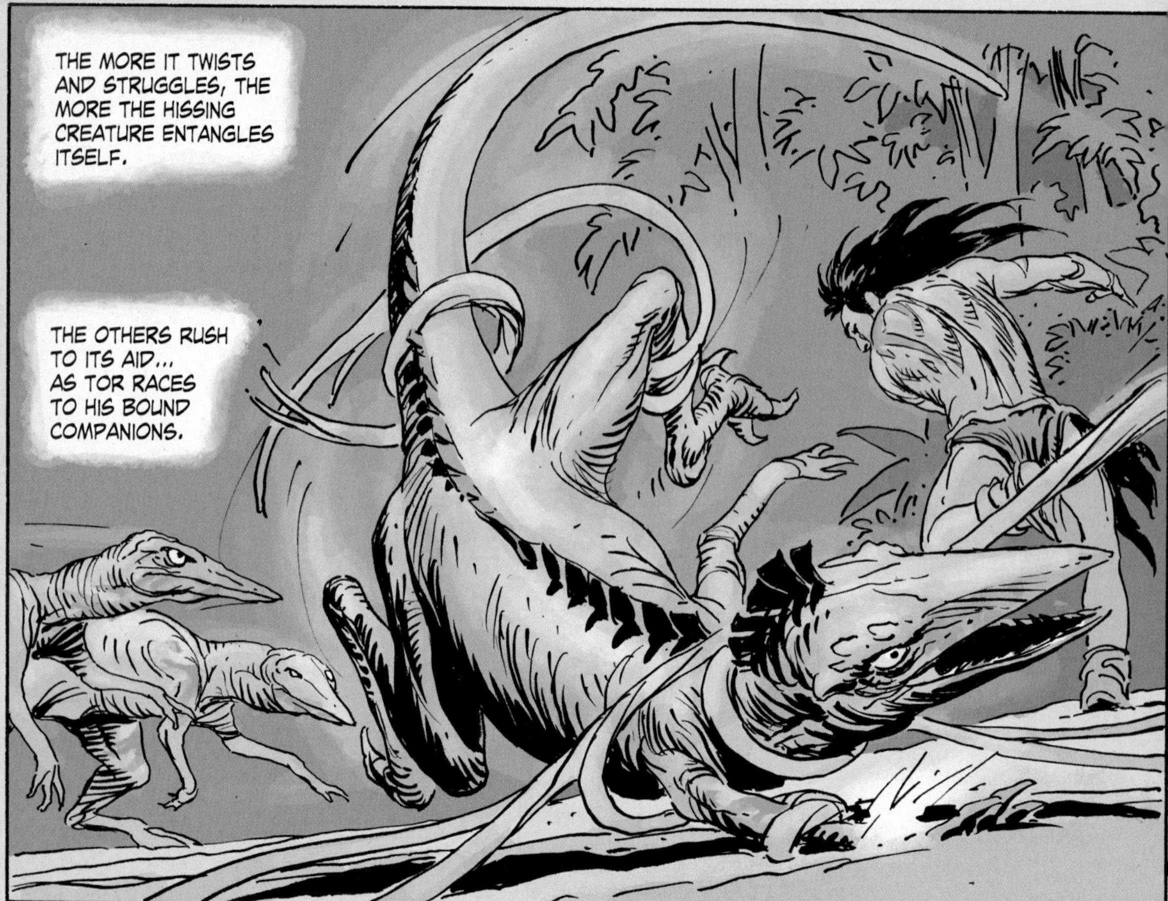
THE MORE IT TWISTS AND STRUGGLES, THE MORE THE HISSING CREATURE ENTANGLES ITSELF.
THE OTHERS RUSH TO ITS AID... AS TOR RACES TO HIS BOUND COMPANIONS.

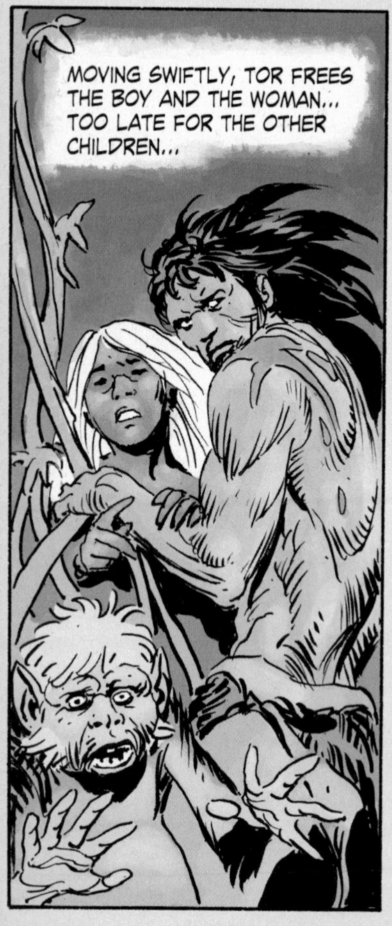
MOVING SWIFTLY, TOR FREES THE BOY AND THE WOMAN... TOO LATE FOR THE OTHER CHILDREN...

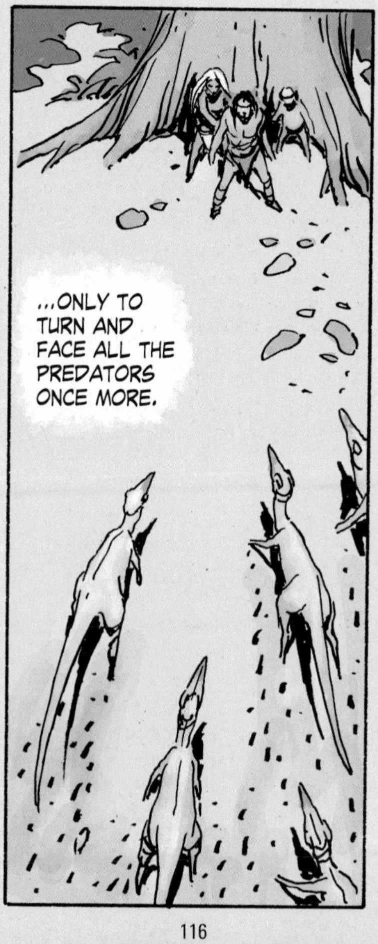
...ONLY TO TURN AND FACE ALL THE PREDATORS ONCE MORE.

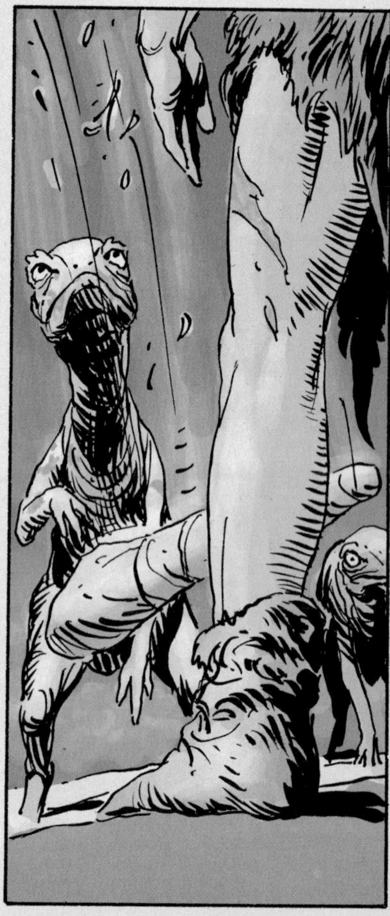

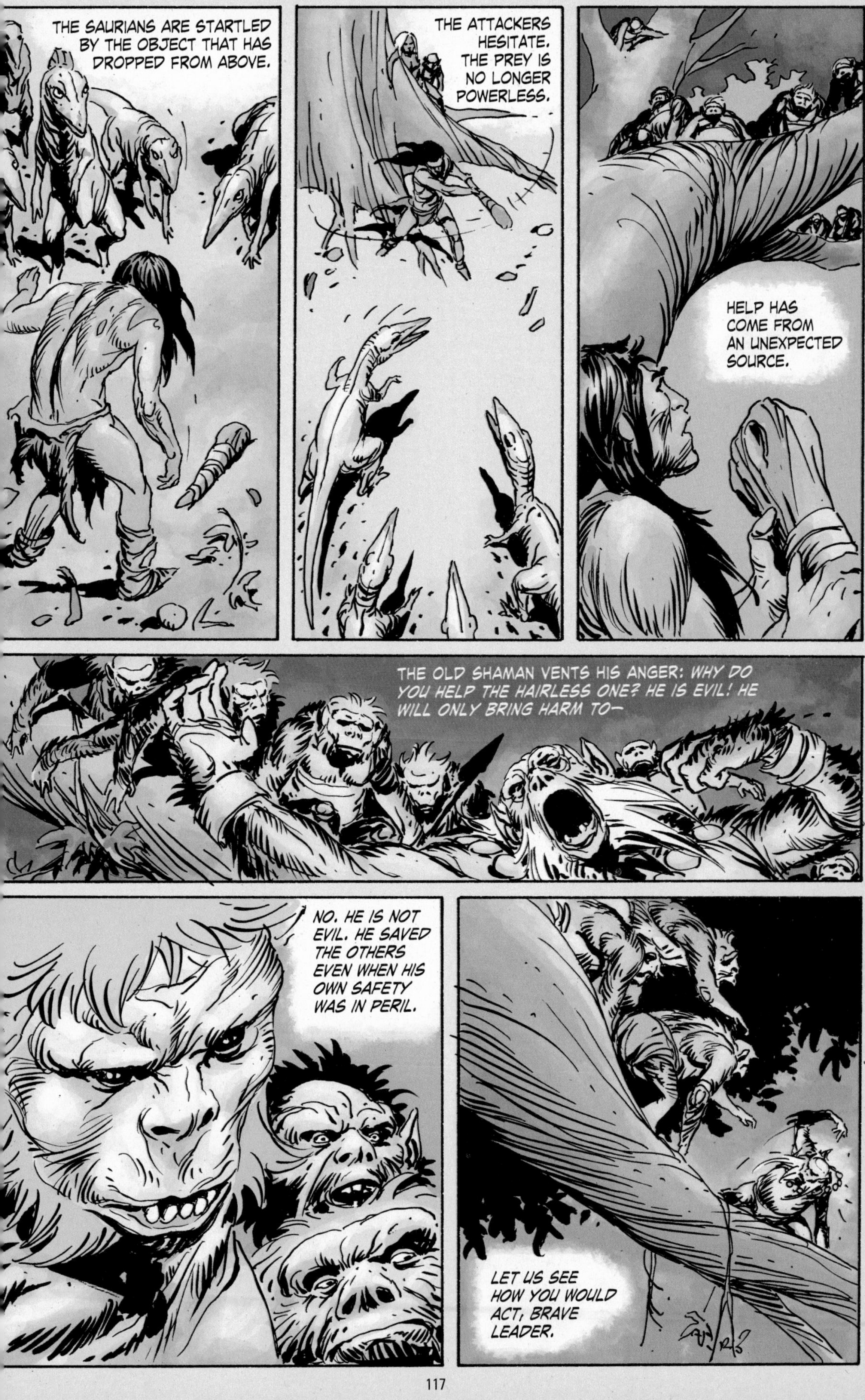
THE SAURIANS ARE STARTLED BY THE OBJECT THAT HAS DROPPED FROM ABOVE.
THE ATTACKERS HESITATE. THE PREY IS NO LONGER POWERLESS.
HELP HAS COME FROM AN UNEXPECTED SOURCE.
THE OLD SHAMAN VENTS HIS ANGER: WHY DO YOU HELP THE HAIRLESS ONE? HE IS EVIL! HE WILL ONLY BRING HARM TO—
NO. HE IS NOT EVIL. HE SAVED THE OTHERS EVEN WHEN HIS OWN SAFETY WAS IN PERIL.
LET US SEE HOW YOU WOULD ACT, BRAVE LEADER.

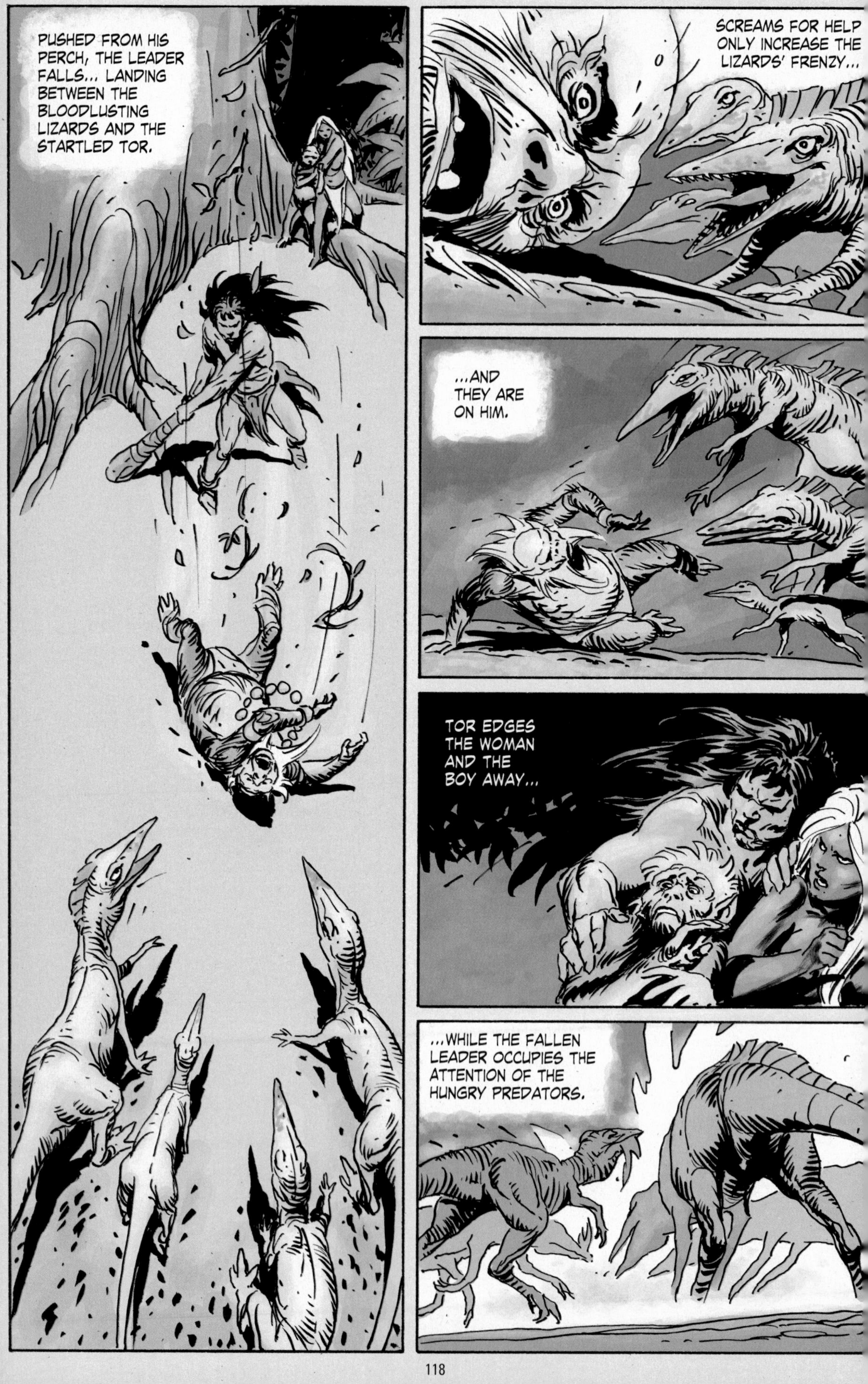
PUSHED FROM HIS PERCH, THE LEADER FALLS... LANDING BETWEEN THE BLOODLUSTING LIZARDS AND THE STARTLED TOR.
SCREAMS FOR HELP ONLY INCREASE THE LIZARDS' FRENZY...
...AND THEY ARE ON HIM.
TOR EDGES THE WOMAN AND THE BOY AWAY...
...WHILE THE FALLEN LEADER OCCUPIES THE ATTENTION OF THE HUNGRY PREDATORS.

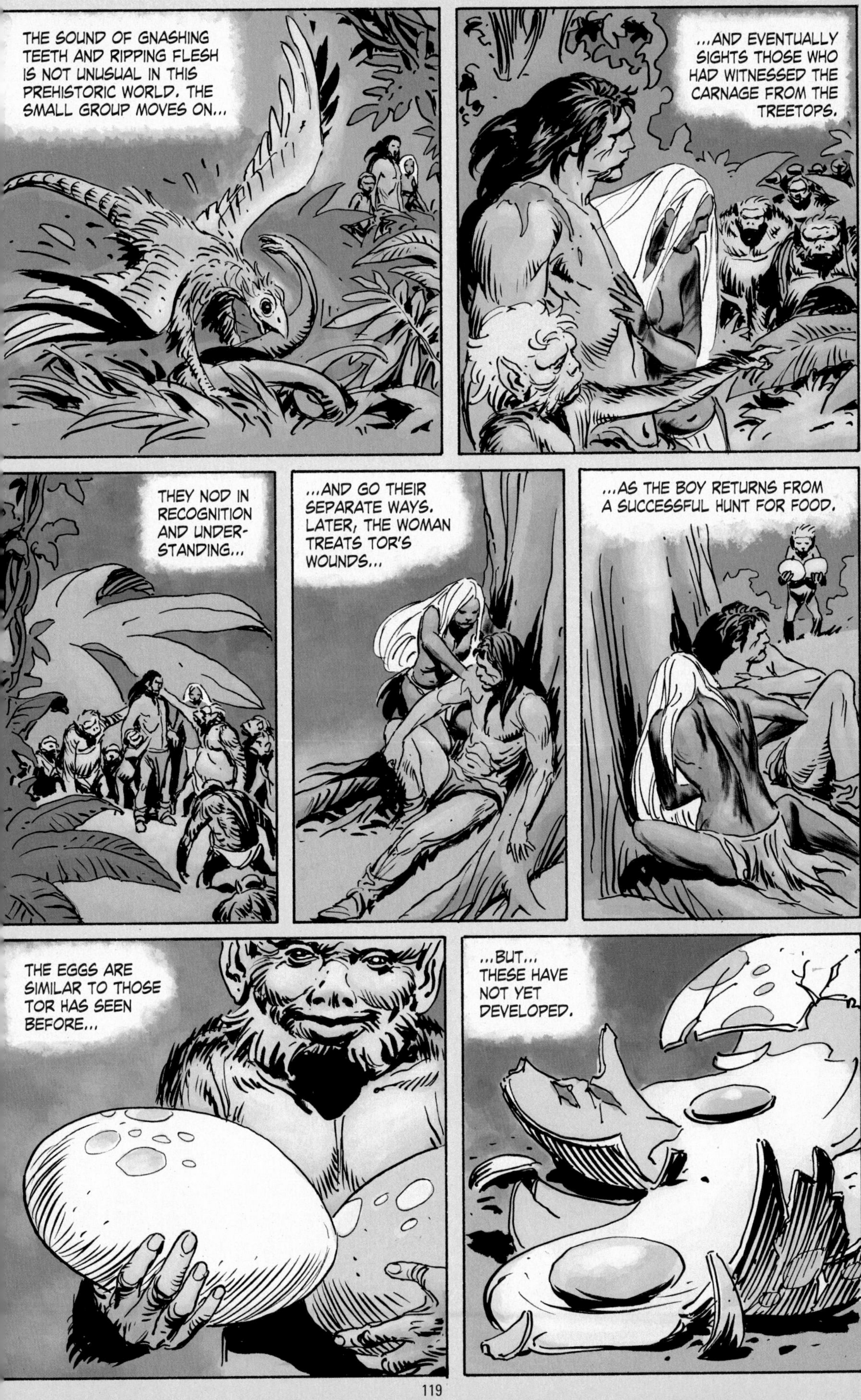
THE SOUND OF GNASHING TEETH AND RIPPING FLESH IS NOT UNUSUAL IN THIS PREHISTORIC WORLD. THE SMALL GROUP MOVES ON...
...AND EVENTUALLY SIGHTS THOSE WHO HAD WITNESSED THE CARNAGE FROM THE TREETOPS.
THEY NOD IN RECOGNITION AND UNDER-STANDING...
...AND GO THEIR SEPARATE WAYS. LATER, THE WOMAN TREATS TOR'S WOUNDS...
...AS THE BOY RETURNS FROM A SUCCESSFUL HUNT FOR FOOD.
THE EGGS ARE SIMILAR TO THOSE TOR HAS SEEN BEFORE...
...BUT... THESE HAVE NOT YET DEVELOPED.

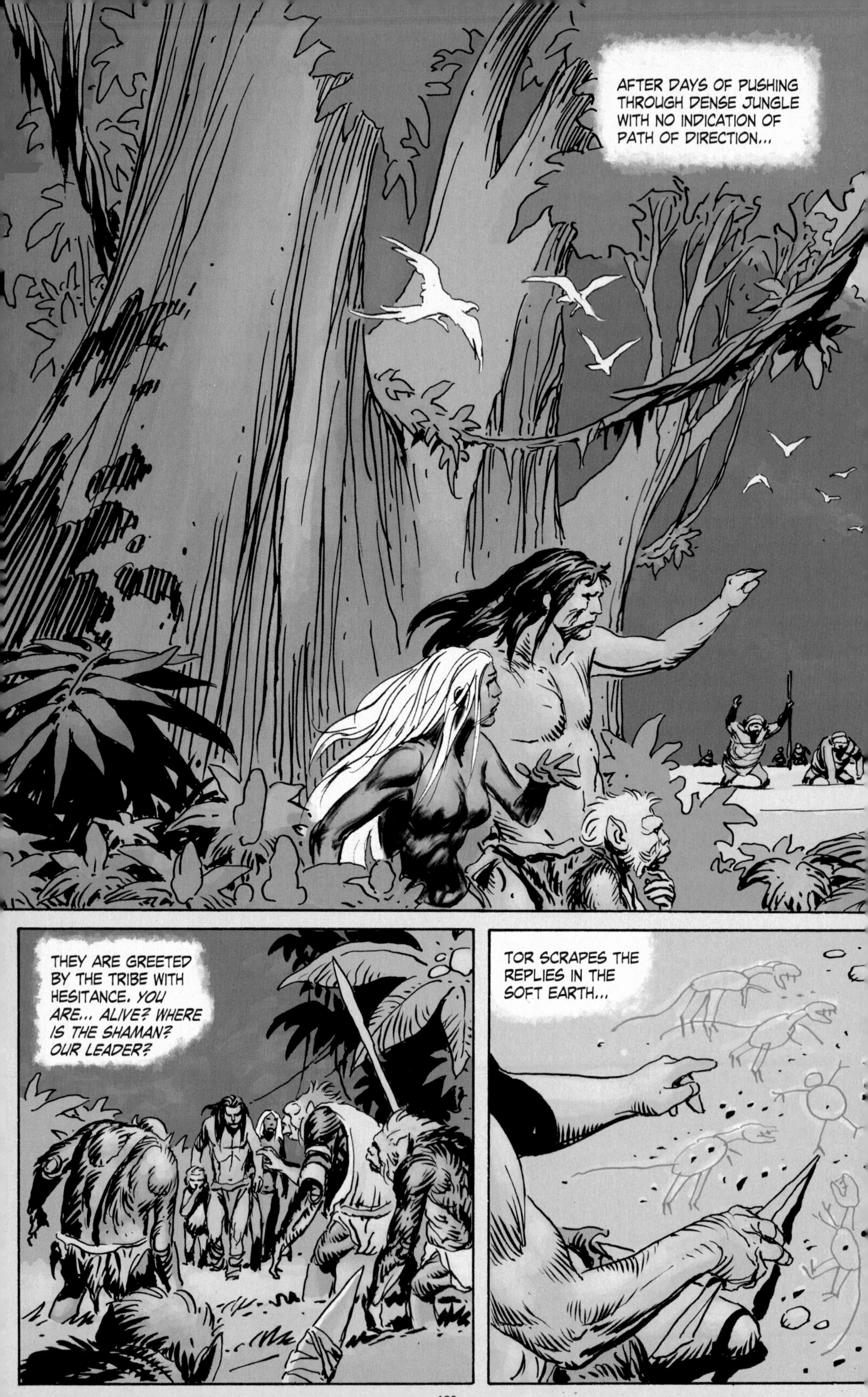
AFTER DAYS OF PUSHING THROUGH DENSE JUNGLE WITH NO INDICATION OF PATH OF DIRECTION...
THEY ARE GREETED BY THE TRIBE WITH HESITANCE. *YOU ARE... ALIVE? WHERE IS THE SHAMAN? OUR LEADER?*
TOR SCRAPES THE REPLIES IN THE SOFT EARTH...

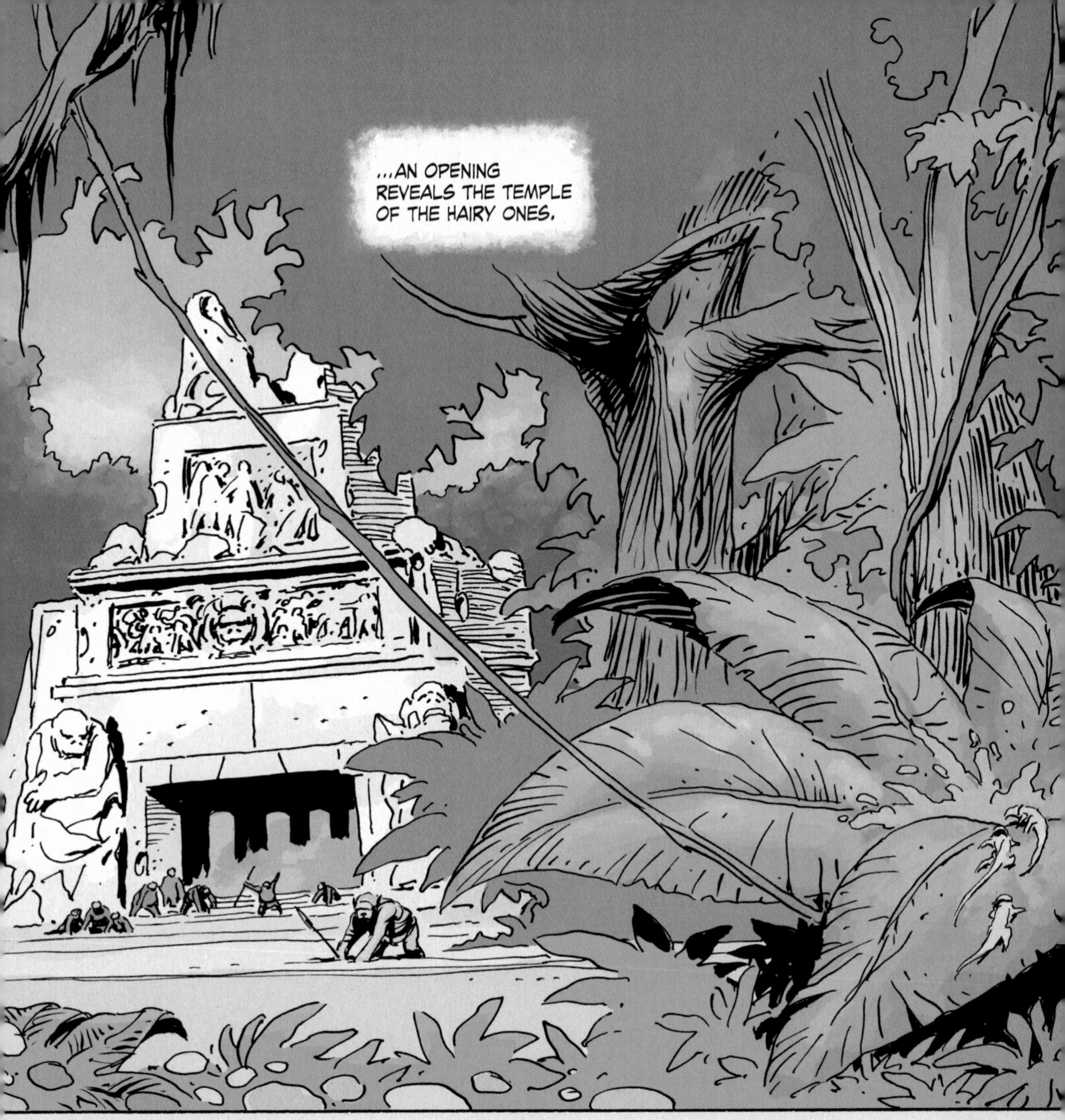
...AN OPENING
REVEALS THE TEMPLE
OF THE HAIRY ONES.

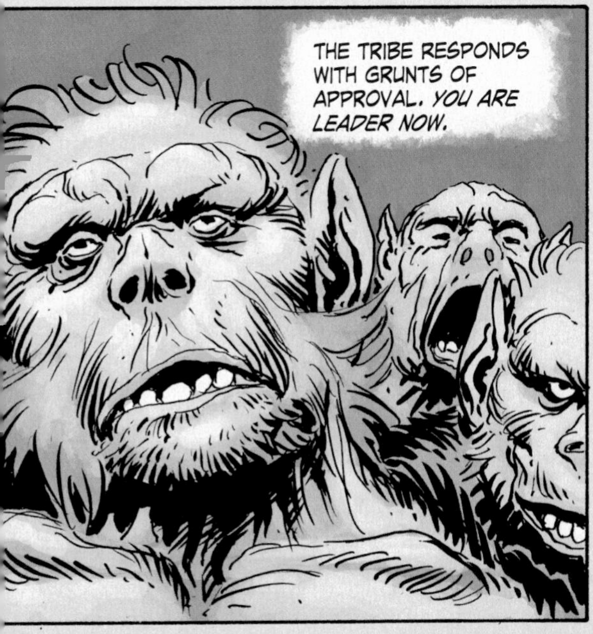
THE TRIBE RESPONDS WITH GRUNTS OF APPROVAL. *YOU ARE LEADER NOW.*

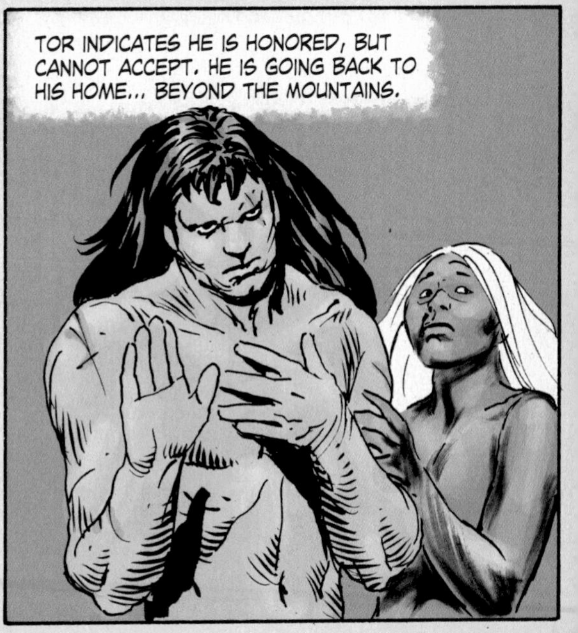
TOR INDICATES HE IS HONORED, BUT CANNOT ACCEPT. HE IS GOING BACK TO HIS HOME... BEYOND THE MOUNTAINS.

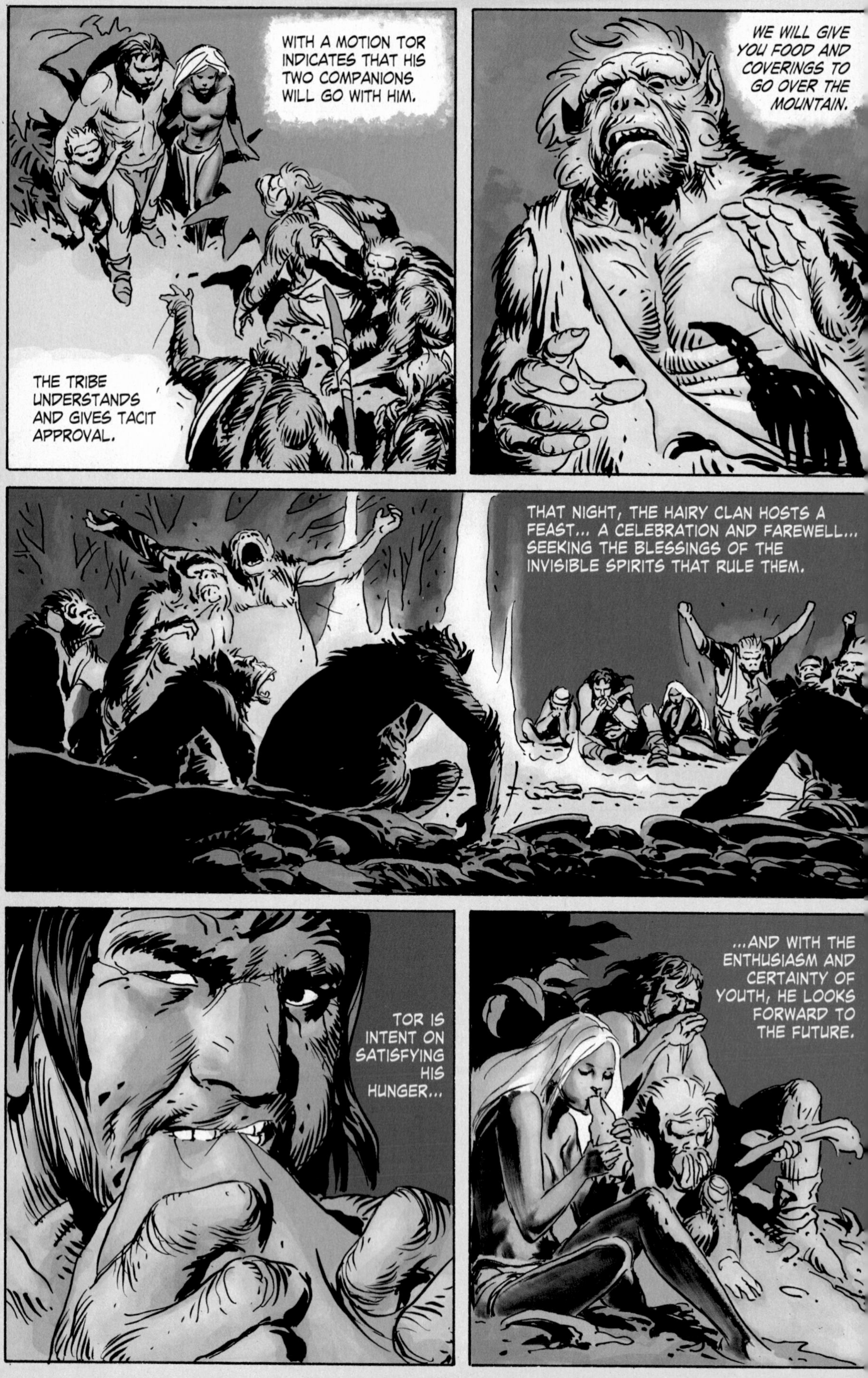
WITH A MOTION TOR INDICATES THAT HIS TWO COMPANIONS WILL GO WITH HIM.
THE TRIBE UNDERSTANDS AND GIVES TACIT APPROVAL.
WE WILL GIVE YOU FOOD AND COVERINGS TO GO OVER THE MOUNTAIN.
THAT NIGHT, THE HAIRY CLAN HOSTS A FEAST... A CELEBRATION AND FAREWELL... SEEKING THE BLESSINGS OF THE INVISIBLE SPIRITS THAT RULE THEM.
TOR IS INTENT ON SATISFYING HIS HUNGER...
...AND WITH THE ENTHUSIASM AND CERTAINTY OF YOUTH, HE LOOKS FORWARD TO THE FUTURE.

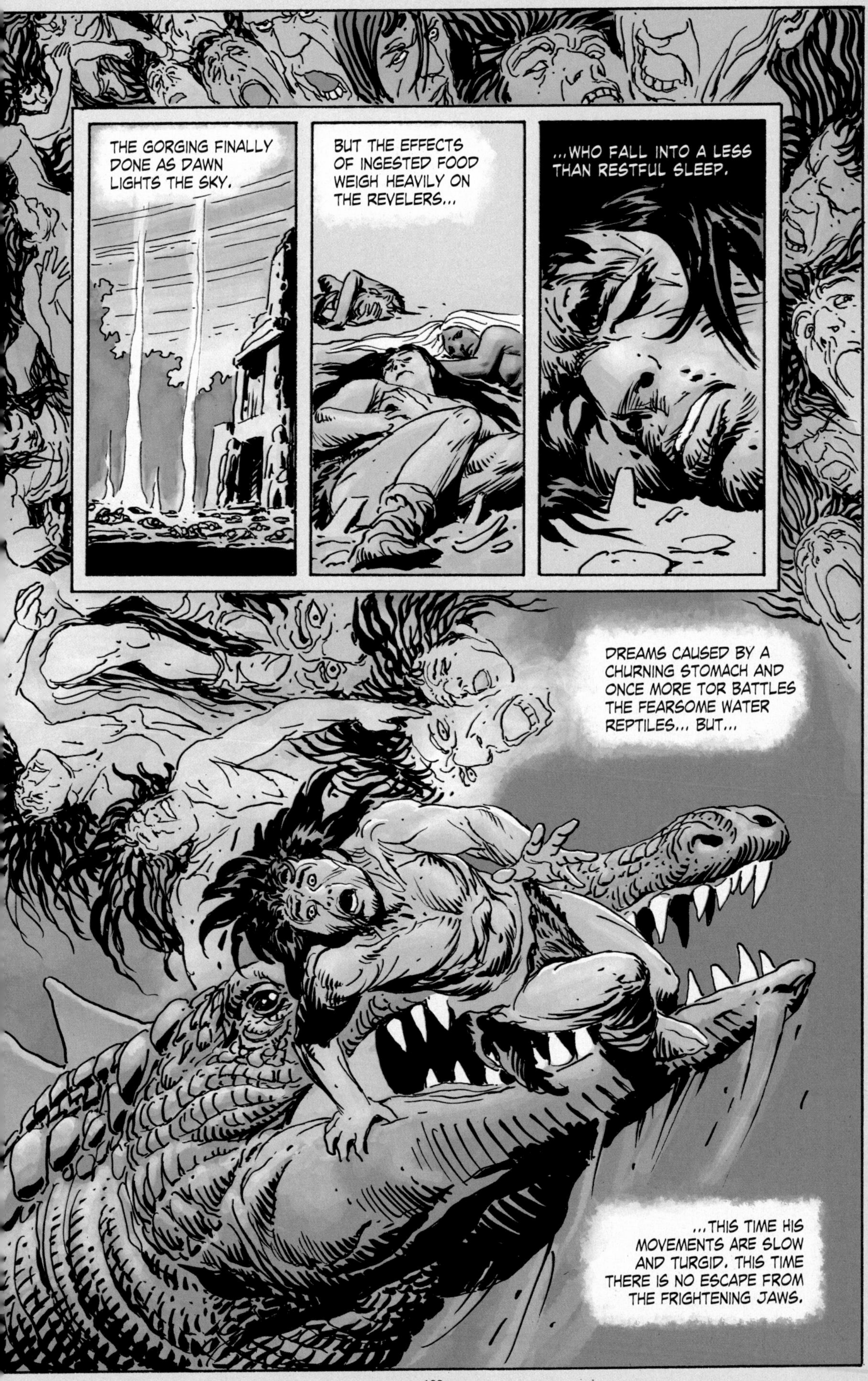
THE GORGING FINALLY DONE AS DAWN LIGHTS THE SKY.
BUT THE EFFECTS OF INGESTED FOOD WEIGH HEAVILY ON THE REVELERS...
...WHO FALL INTO A LESS THAN RESTFUL SLEEP.
DREAMS CAUSED BY A CHURNING STOMACH AND ONCE MORE TOR BATTLES THE FEARSOME WATER REPTILES... BUT...
...THIS TIME HIS MOVEMENTS ARE SLOW AND TURGID. THIS TIME THERE IS NO ESCAPE FROM THE FRIGHTENING JAWS.

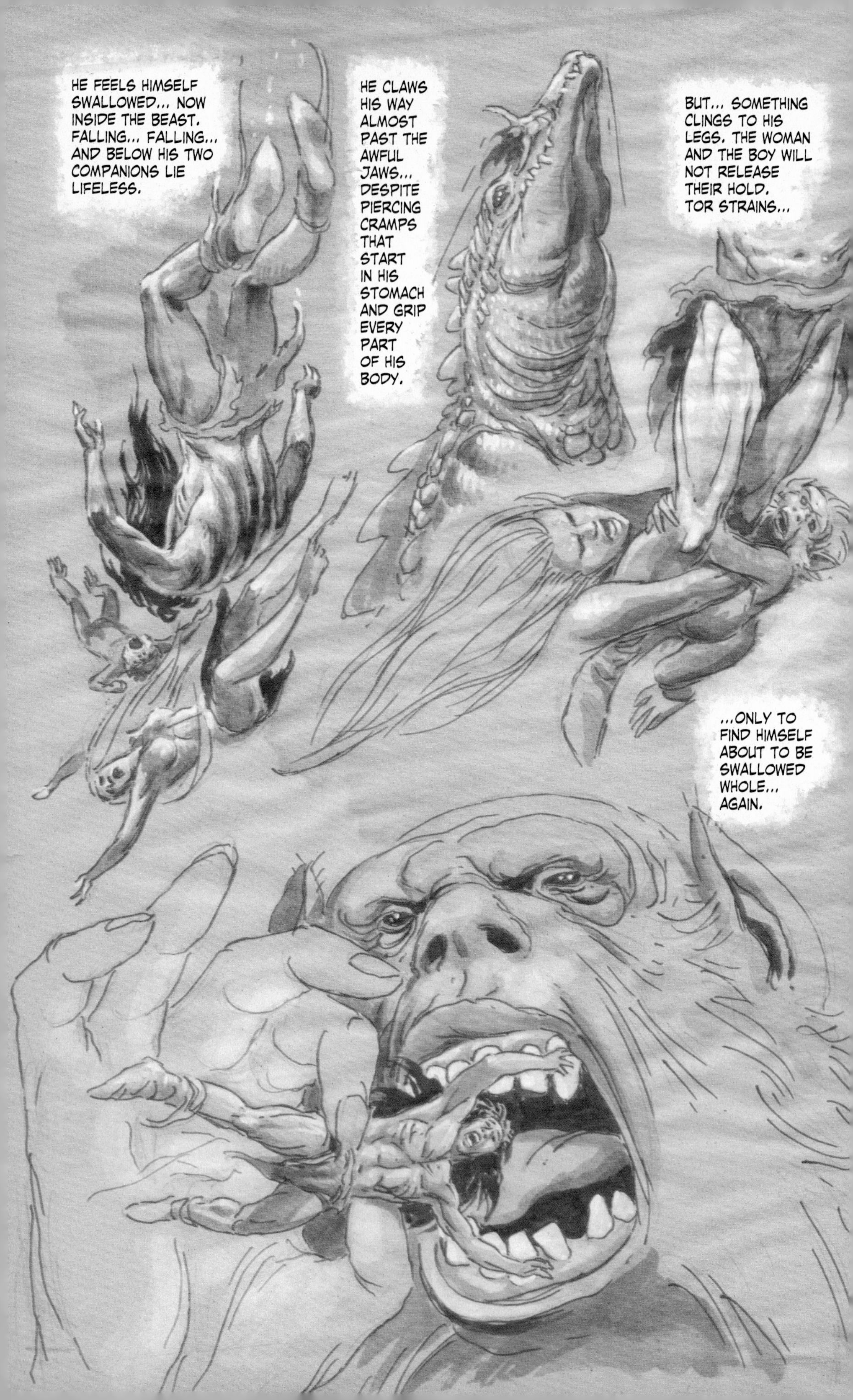
HE FEELS HIMSELF SWALLOWED... NOW INSIDE THE BEAST. FALLING... FALLING... AND BELOW HIS TWO COMPANIONS LIE LIFELESS.
HE CLAWS HIS WAY ALMOST PAST THE AWFUL JAWS... DESPITE PIERCING CRAMPS THAT START IN HIS STOMACH AND GRIP EVERY PART OF HIS BODY.
BUT... SOMETHING CLINGS TO HIS LEGS. THE WOMAN AND THE BOY WILL NOT RELEASE THEIR HOLD. TOR STRAINS...
...ONLY TO FIND HIMSELF ABOUT TO BE SWALLOWED WHOLE... AGAIN.

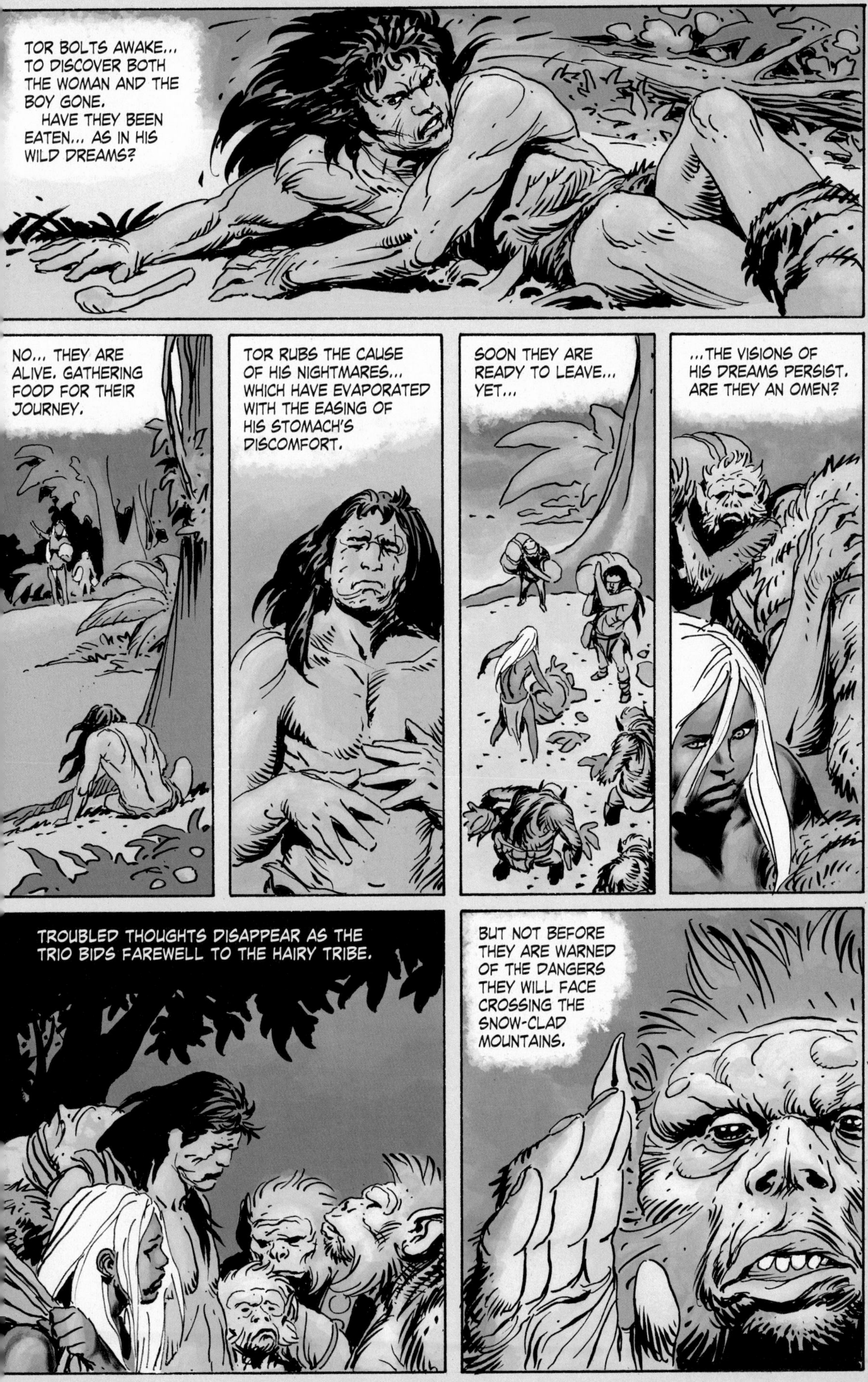
TOR BOLTS AWAKE... TO DISCOVER BOTH THE WOMAN AND THE BOY GONE.
HAVE THEY BEEN EATEN... AS IN HIS WILD DREAMS?
NO... THEY ARE ALIVE. GATHERING FOOD FOR THEIR JOURNEY.
TOR RUBS THE CAUSE OF HIS NIGHTMARES... WHICH HAVE EVAPORATED WITH THE EASING OF HIS STOMACH'S DISCOMFORT.
SOON THEY ARE READY TO LEAVE... YET...
...THE VISIONS OF HIS DREAMS PERSIST. ARE THEY AN OMEN?
TROUBLED THOUGHTS DISAPPEAR AS THE TRIO BIDS FAREWELL TO THE HAIRY TRIBE.
BUT NOT BEFORE THEY ARE WARNED OF THE DANGERS THEY WILL FACE CROSSING THE SNOW-CLAD MOUNTAINS.

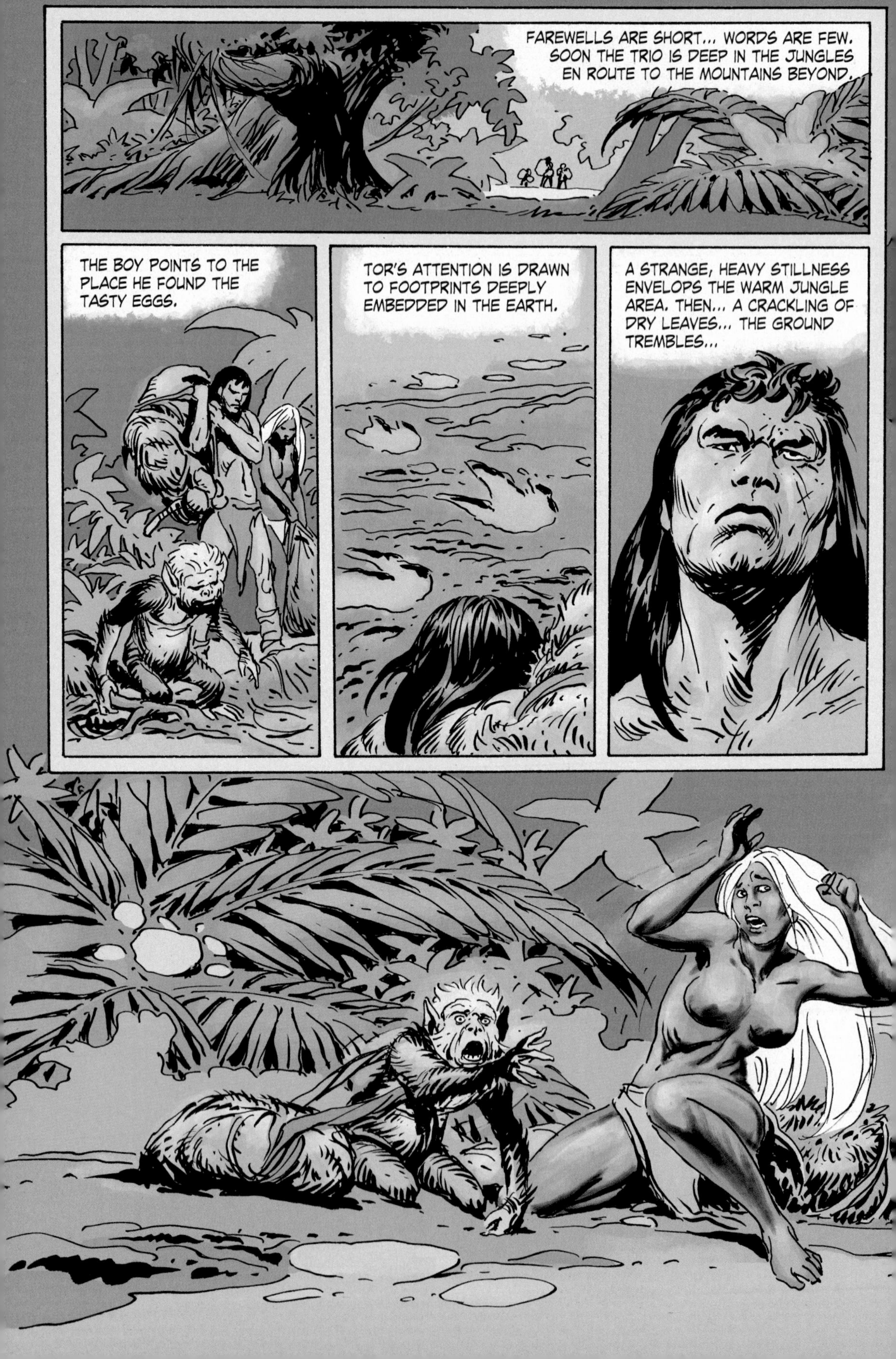
FAREWELLS ARE SHORT... WORDS ARE FEW. SOON THE TRIO IS DEEP IN THE JUNGLES EN ROUTE TO THE MOUNTAINS BEYOND.
THE BOY POINTS TO THE PLACE HE FOUND THE TASTY EGGS.
TOR'S ATTENTION IS DRAWN TO FOOTPRINTS DEEPLY EMBEDDED IN THE EARTH.
A STRANGE, HEAVY STILLNESS ENVELOPS THE WARM JUNGLE AREA. THEN... A CRACKLING OF DRY LEAVES... THE GROUND TREMBLES...

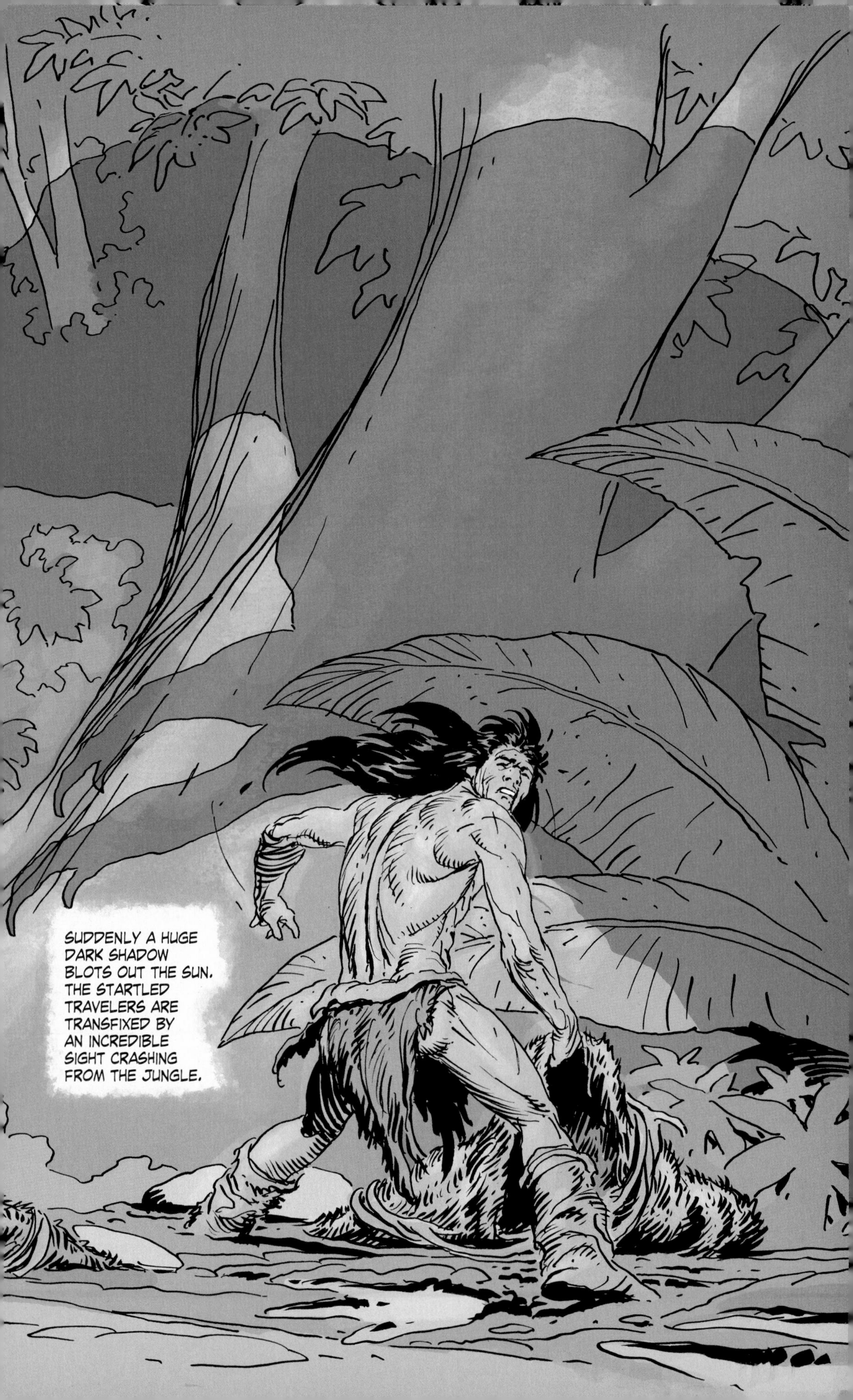
SUDDENLY A HUGE DARK SHADOW BLOTS OUT THE SUN. THE STARTLED TRAVELERS ARE TRANSFIXED BY AN INCREDIBLE SIGHT CRASHING FROM THE JUNGLE.

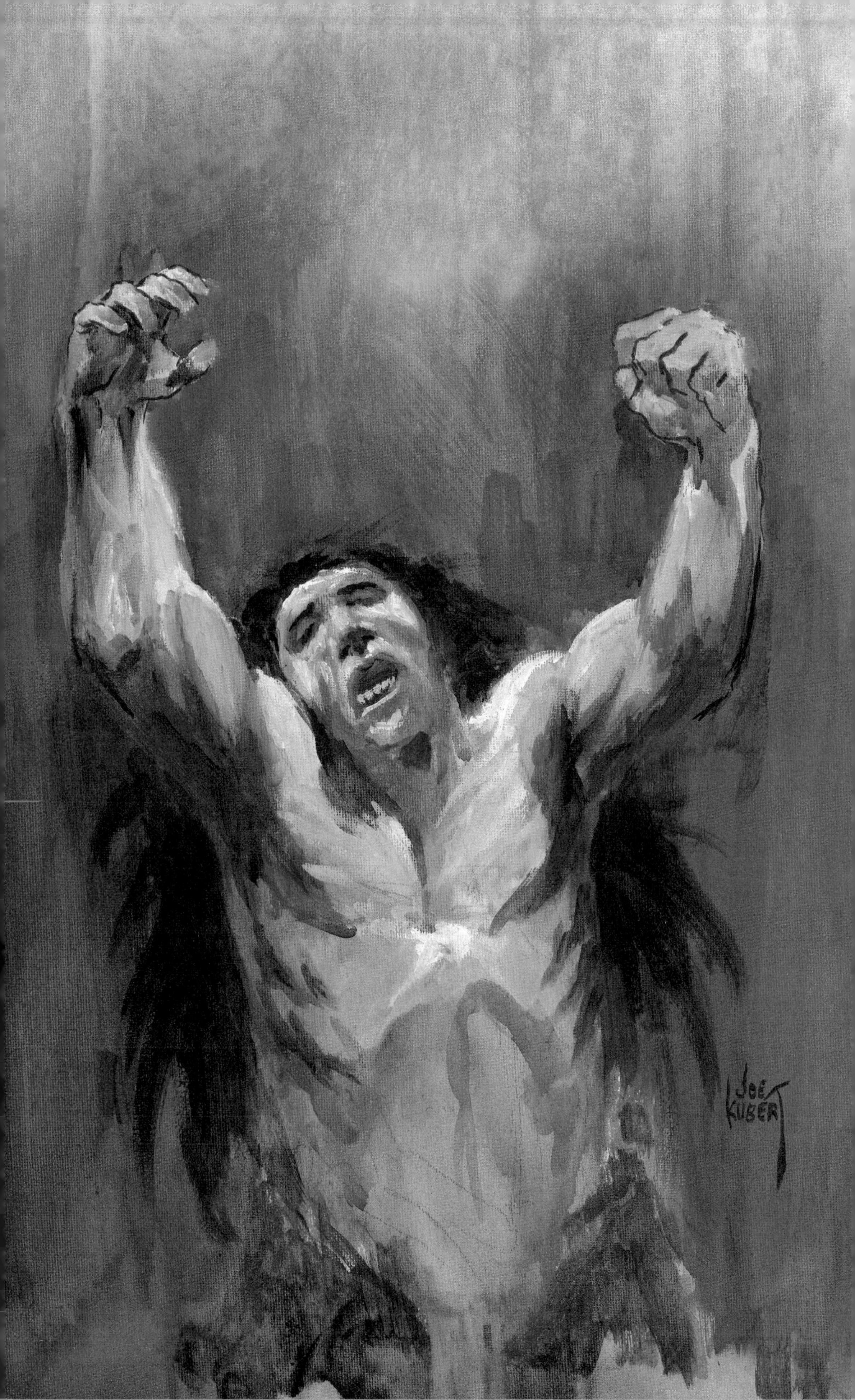
JOE KUBERT

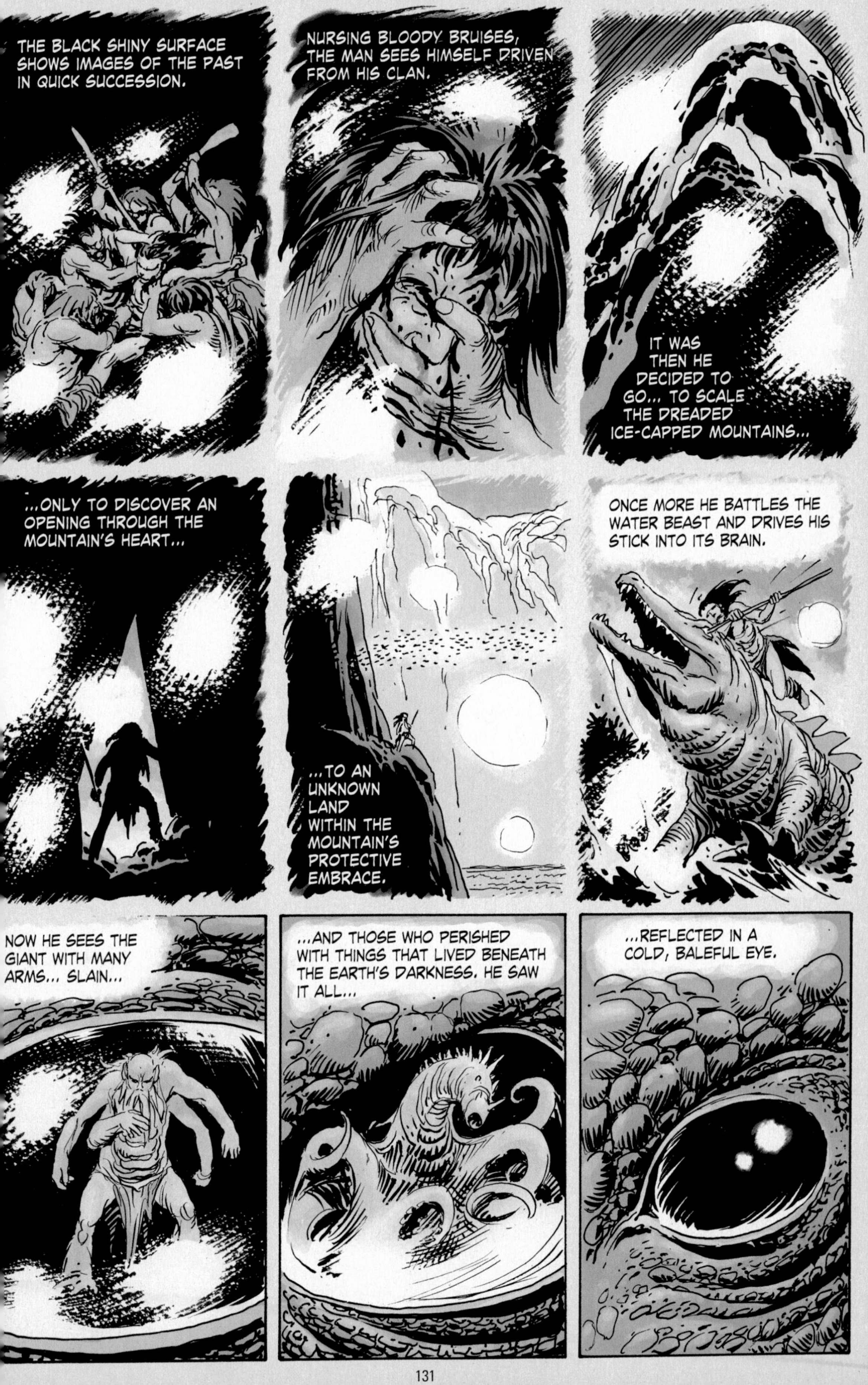
THE BLACK SHINY SURFACE SHOWS IMAGES OF THE PAST IN QUICK SUCCESSION.
NURSING BLOODY BRUISES, THE MAN SEES HIMSELF DRIVEN FROM HIS CLAN.
IT WAS THEN HE DECIDED TO GO... TO SCALE THE DREADED ICE-CAPPED MOUNTAINS...
...ONLY TO DISCOVER AN OPENING THROUGH THE MOUNTAIN'S HEART...
...TO AN UNKNOWN LAND WITHIN THE MOUNTAIN'S PROTECTIVE EMBRACE.
ONCE MORE HE BATTLES THE WATER BEAST AND DRIVES HIS STICK INTO ITS BRAIN.
NOW HE SEES THE GIANT WITH MANY ARMS... SLAIN...
...AND THOSE WHO PERISHED WITH THINGS THAT LIVED BENEATH THE EARTH'S DARKNESS. HE SAW IT ALL...
...REFLECTED IN A COLD, BALEFUL EYE.

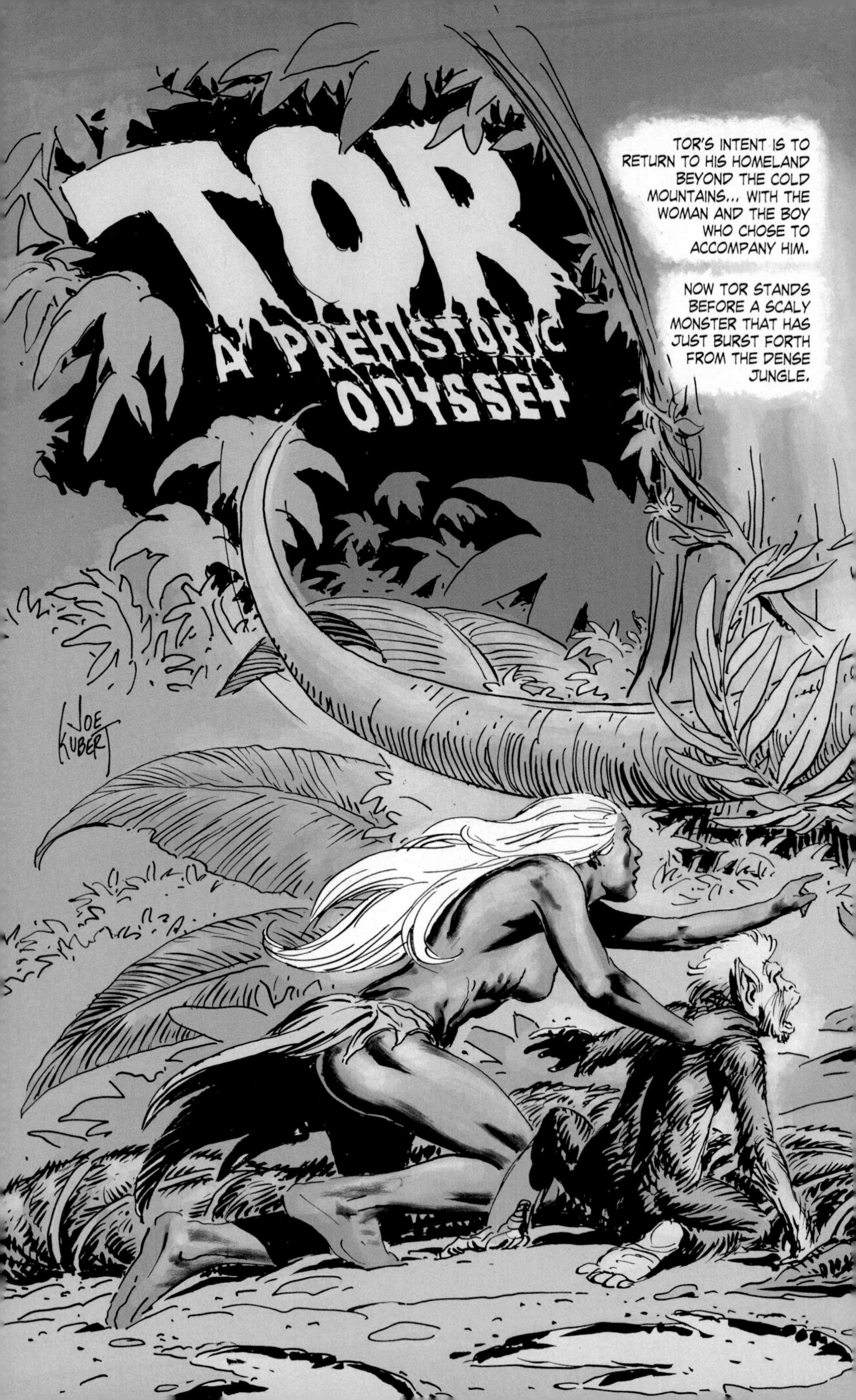
TOR
A PREHISTORIC
ODYSSEY
TOR'S INTENT IS TO RETURN TO HIS HOMELAND BEYOND THE COLD MOUNTAINS... WITH THE WOMAN AND THE BOY WHO CHOSE TO ACCOMPANY HIM.
NOW TOR STANDS BEFORE A SCALY MONSTER THAT HAS JUST BURST FORTH FROM THE DENSE JUNGLE.
JOE KUBERT

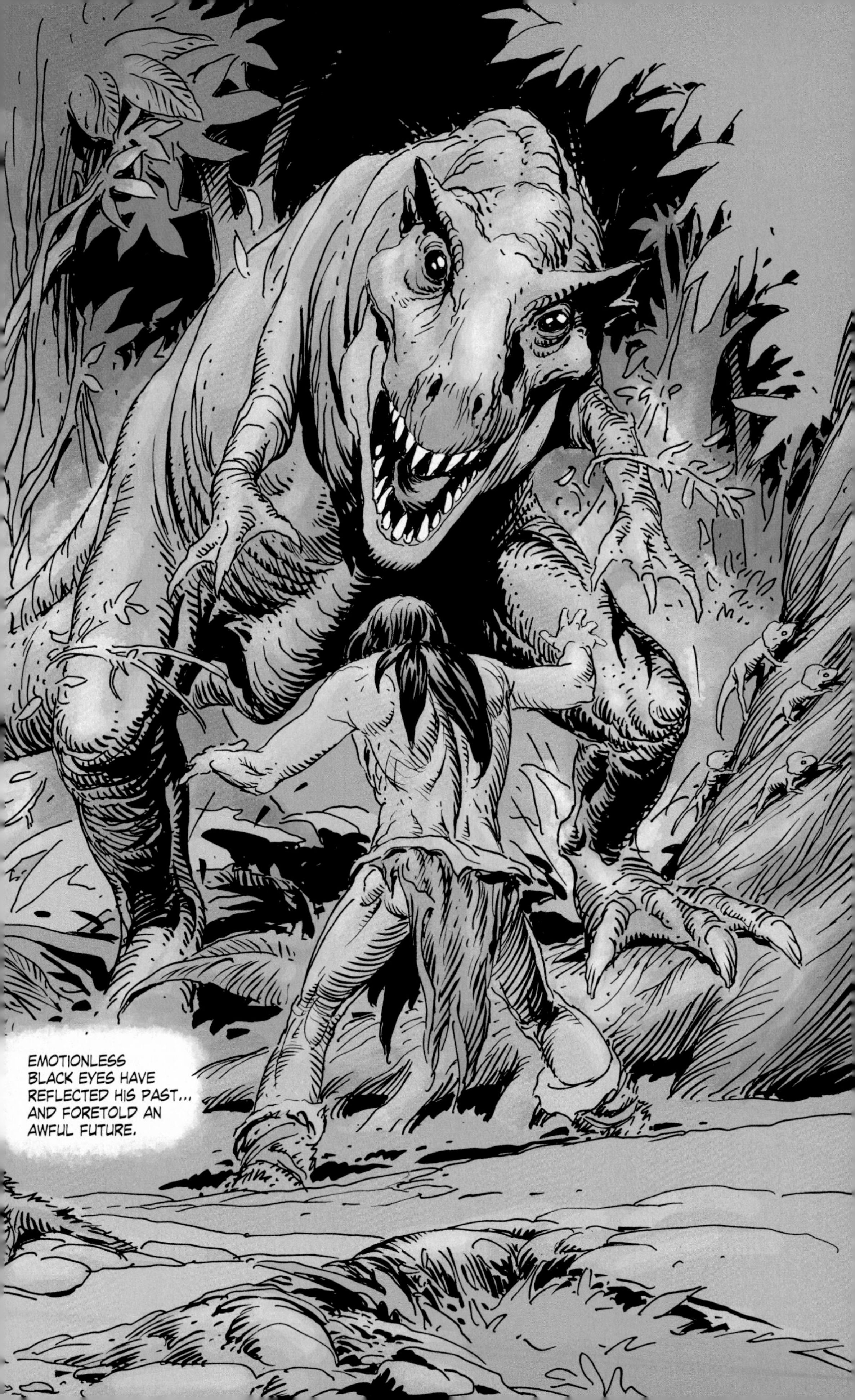
EMOTIONLESS BLACK EYES HAVE REFLECTED HIS PAST... AND FORETOLD AN AWFUL FUTURE.

THERE IS AN INSCRUTABLE MOMENT OF HESITATION... THE GREAT LIZARD TURNS...

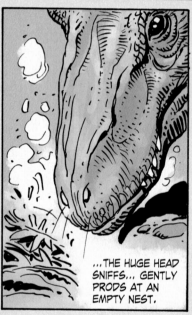

...THE HUGE HEAD SNIFFS... GENTLY PRODS AT AN EMPTY NEST.

IT-IT IS WHERE ...I FOUND... THE EGGS. THE BOY WHISPERS.

WE... HAVE EATEN... HER CHILDREN. THE WOMAN GASPS.

STRETCHED HIGH, THE FEARSOME HEAD EMITS A COUGHING ROAR THAT ECHOES THROUGH THE JUNGLE...

...AND HAS THE INTENDED EFFECT ON THE TREMBLING HUMANS.

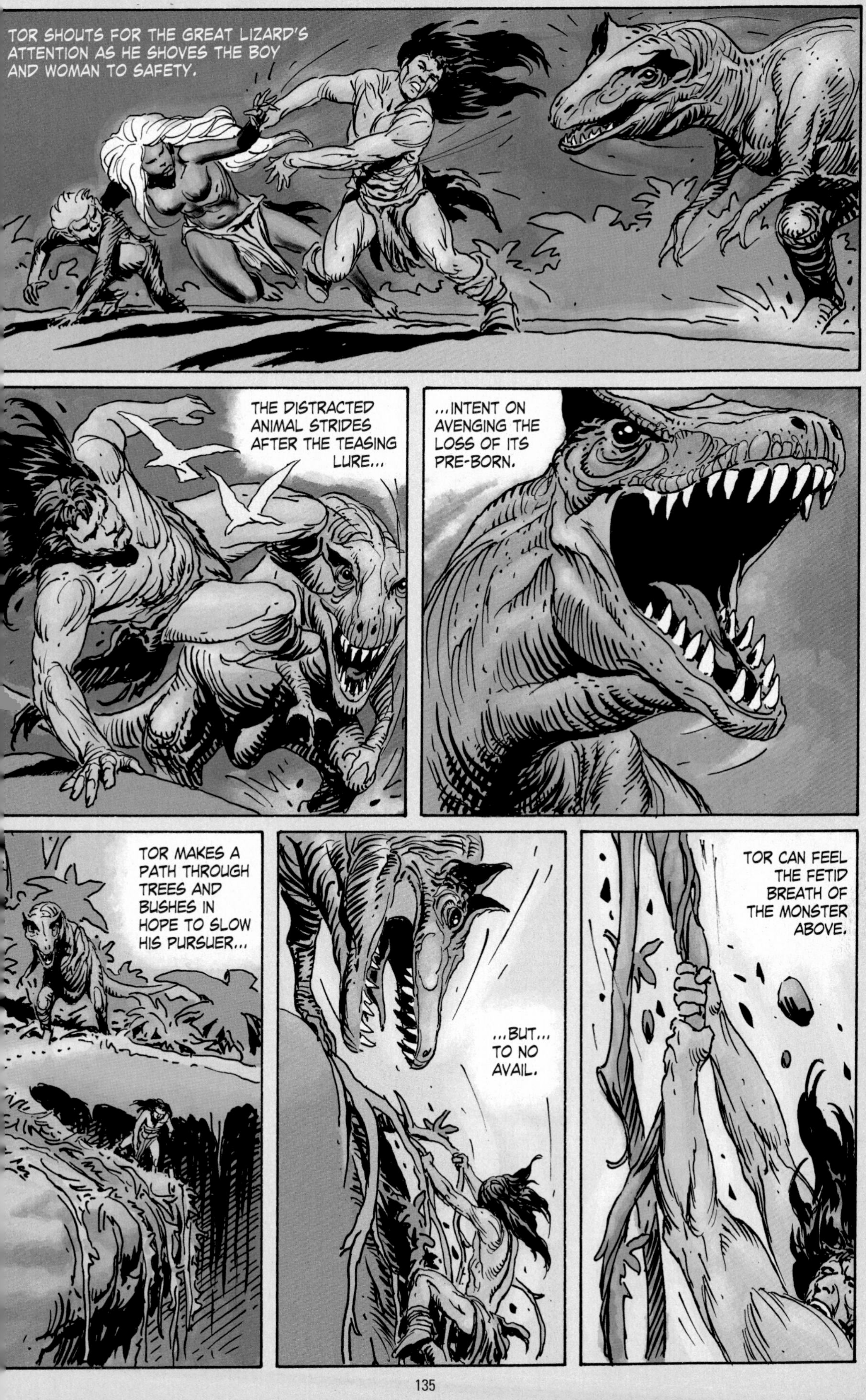
TOR SHOUTS FOR THE GREAT LIZARD'S ATTENTION AS HE SHOVES THE BOY AND WOMAN TO SAFETY.
THE DISTRACTED ANIMAL STRIDES AFTER THE TEASING LURE...
...INTENT ON AVENGING THE LOSS OF ITS PRE-BORN.
TOR MAKES A PATH THROUGH TREES AND BUSHES IN HOPE TO SLOW HIS PURSUER...
...BUT... TO NO AVAIL.
TOR CAN FEEL THE FETID BREATH OF THE MONSTER ABOVE.

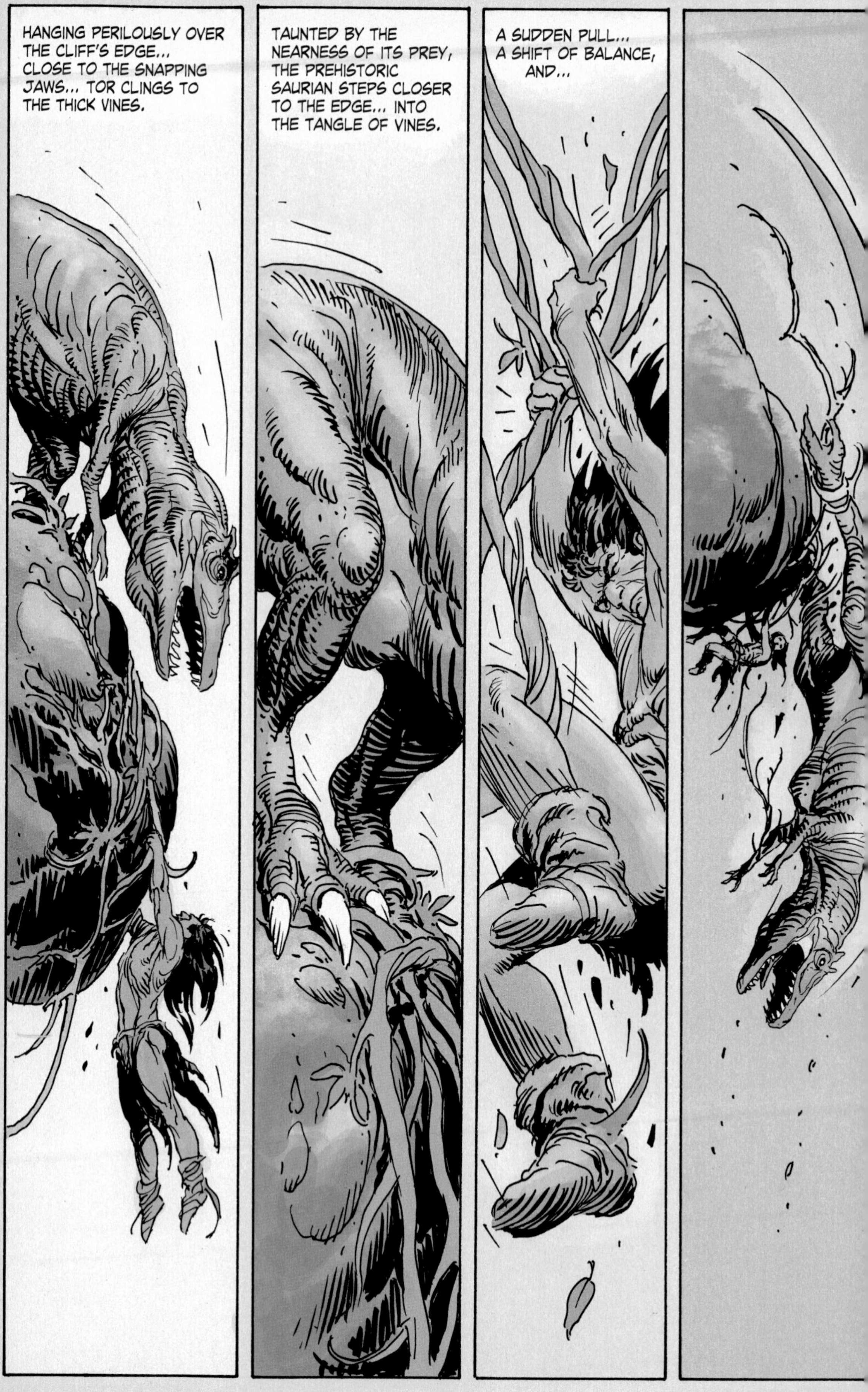
HANGING PERILOUSLY OVER THE CLIFF'S EDGE... CLOSE TO THE SNAPPING JAWS... TOR CLINGS TO THE THICK VINES.
TAUNTED BY THE NEARNESS OF ITS PREY, THE PREHISTORIC SAURIAN STEPS CLOSER TO THE EDGE... INTO THE TANGLE OF VINES.
A SUDDEN PULL... A SHIFT OF BALANCE, AND...

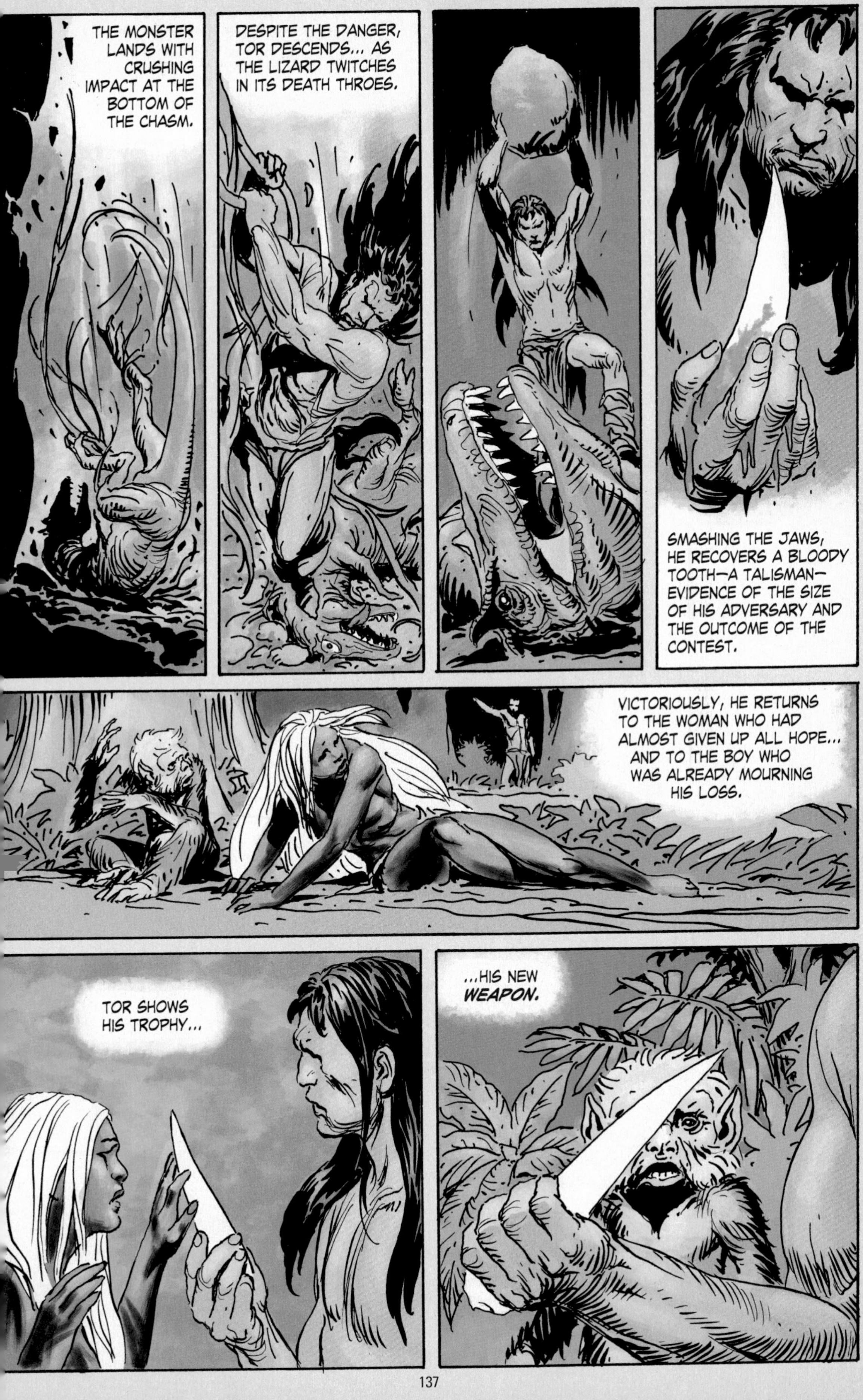
THE MONSTER LANDS WITH CRUSHING IMPACT AT THE BOTTOM OF THE CHASM.
DESPITE THE DANGER, TOR DESCENDS... AS THE LIZARD TWITCHES IN ITS DEATH THROES.
SMASHING THE JAWS, HE RECOVERS A BLOODY TOOTH—A TALISMAN—EVIDENCE OF THE SIZE OF HIS ADVERSARY AND THE OUTCOME OF THE CONTEST.
VICTORIOUSLY, HE RETURNS TO THE WOMAN WHO HAD ALMOST GIVEN UP ALL HOPE... AND TO THE BOY WHO WAS ALREADY MOURNING HIS LOSS.
TOR SHOWS HIS TROPHY...
...HIS NEW ***WEAPON.***

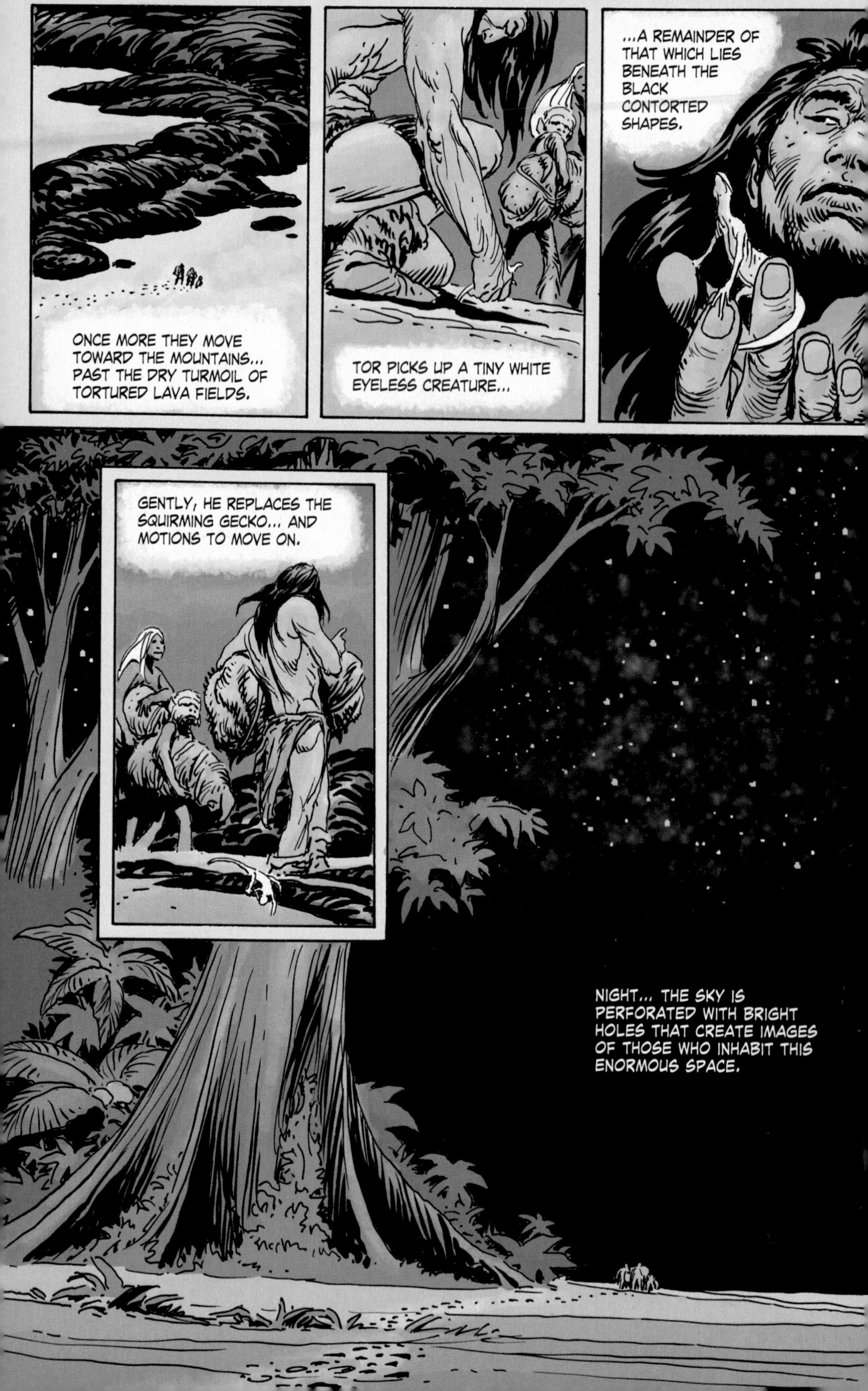
ONCE MORE THEY MOVE TOWARD THE MOUNTAINS... PAST THE DRY TURMOIL OF TORTURED LAVA FIELDS.
TOR PICKS UP A TINY WHITE EYELESS CREATURE...
...A REMAINDER OF THAT WHICH LIES BENEATH THE BLACK CONTORTED SHAPES.
GENTLY, HE REPLACES THE SQUIRMING GECKO... AND MOTIONS TO MOVE ON.
NIGHT... THE SKY IS PERFORATED WITH BRIGHT HOLES THAT CREATE IMAGES OF THOSE WHO INHABIT THIS ENORMOUS SPACE.

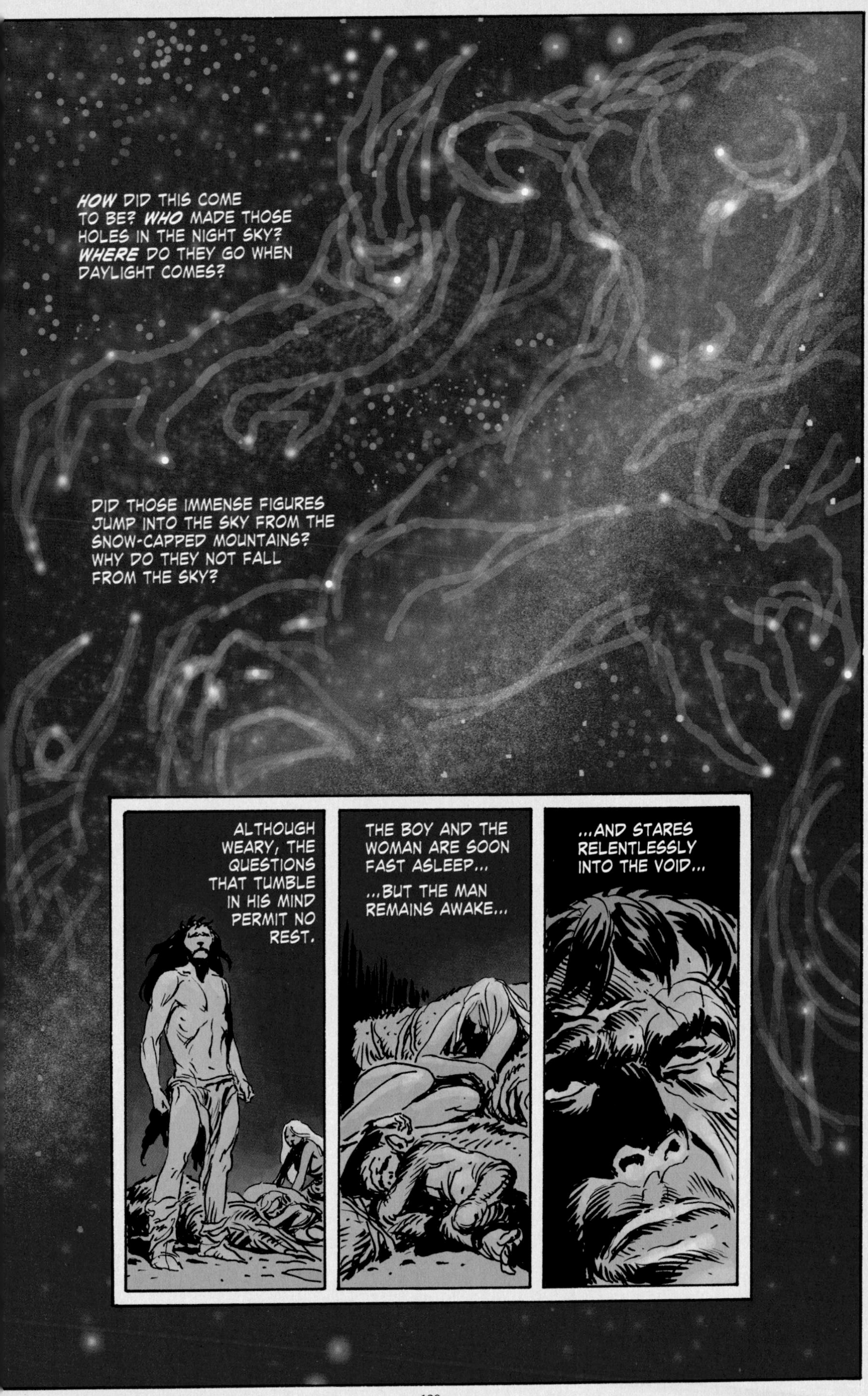
HOW DID THIS COME TO BE? WHO MADE THOSE HOLES IN THE NIGHT SKY? WHERE DO THEY GO WHEN DAYLIGHT COMES?
DID THOSE IMMENSE FIGURES JUMP INTO THE SKY FROM THE SNOW-CAPPED MOUNTAINS? WHY DO THEY NOT FALL FROM THE SKY?
ALTHOUGH WEARY, THE QUESTIONS THAT TUMBLE IN HIS MIND PERMIT NO REST.
THE BOY AND THE WOMAN ARE SOON FAST ASLEEP...
...BUT THE MAN REMAINS AWAKE...
...AND STARES RELENTLESSLY INTO THE VOID...

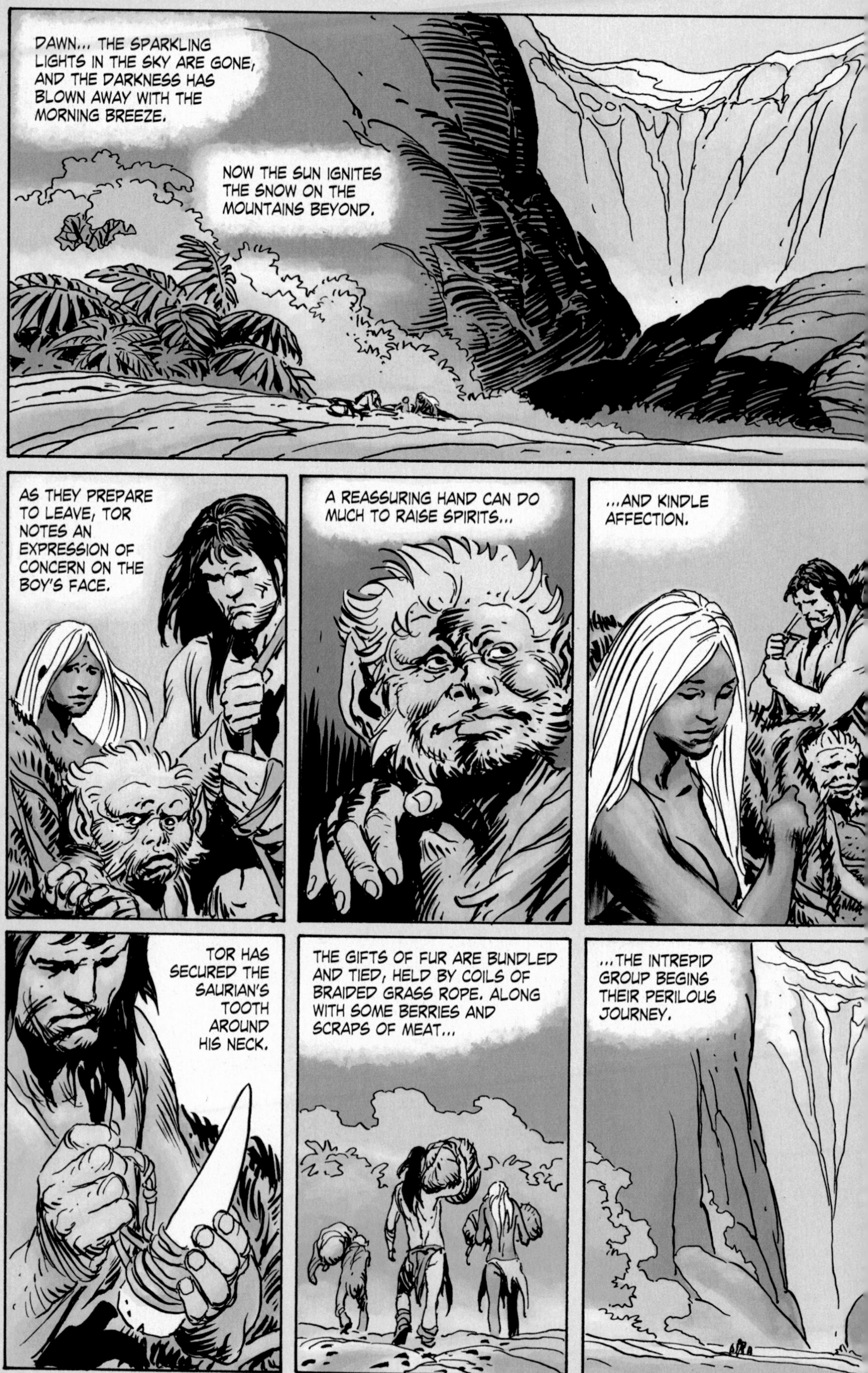

DAWN... THE SPARKLING LIGHTS IN THE SKY ARE GONE, AND THE DARKNESS HAS BLOWN AWAY WITH THE MORNING BREEZE.
NOW THE SUN IGNITES THE SNOW ON THE MOUNTAINS BEYOND.
AS THEY PREPARE TO LEAVE, TOR NOTES AN EXPRESSION OF CONCERN ON THE BOY'S FACE.
A REASSURING HAND CAN DO MUCH TO RAISE SPIRITS...
...AND KINDLE AFFECTION.
TOR HAS SECURED THE SAURIAN'S TOOTH AROUND HIS NECK.
THE GIFTS OF FUR ARE BUNDLED AND TIED, HELD BY COILS OF BRAIDED GRASS ROPE. ALONG WITH SOME BERRIES AND SCRAPS OF MEAT...
...THE INTREPID GROUP BEGINS THEIR PERILOUS JOURNEY.

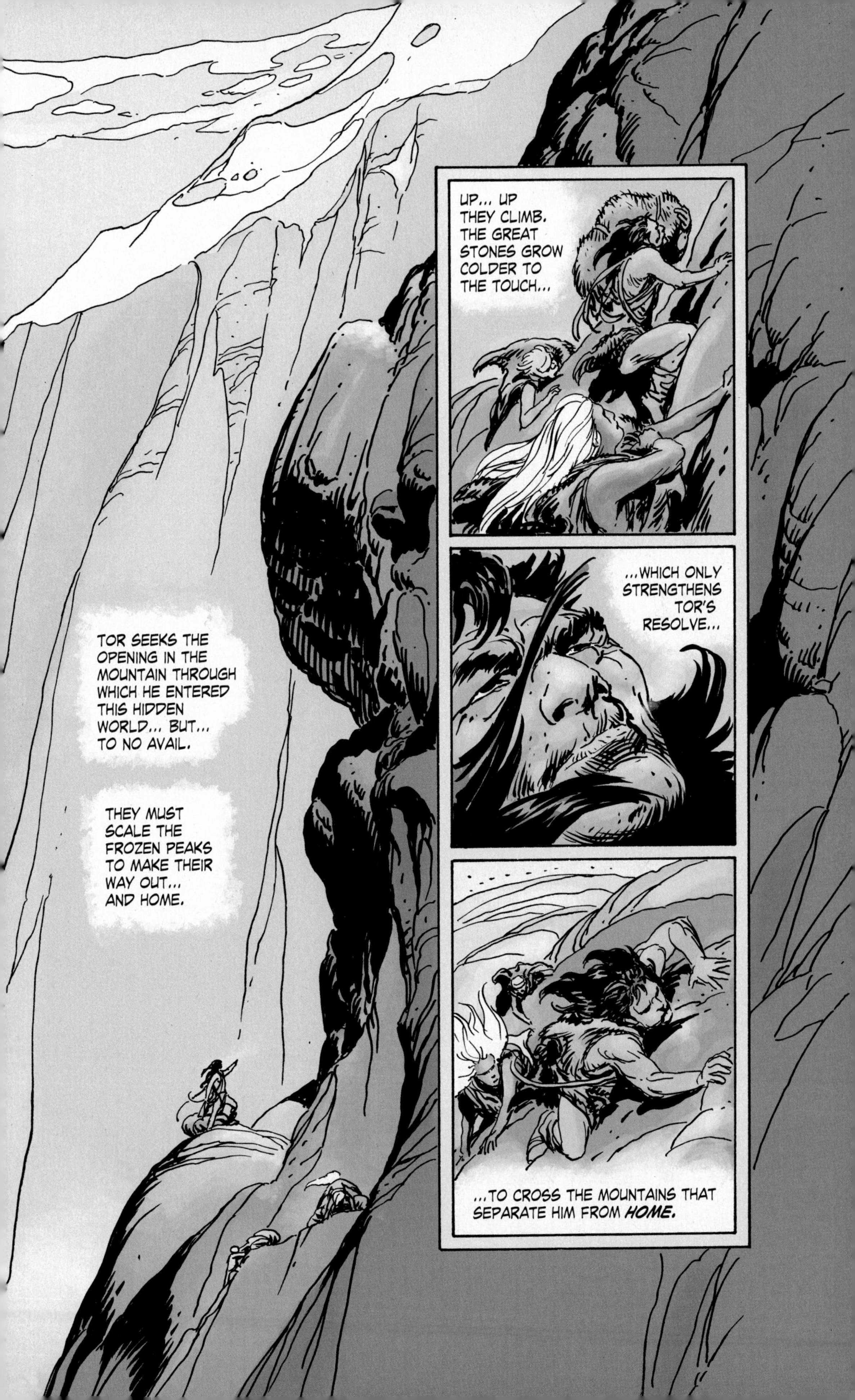
TOR SEEKS THE OPENING IN THE MOUNTAIN THROUGH WHICH HE ENTERED THIS HIDDEN WORLD... BUT... TO NO AVAIL.
THEY MUST SCALE THE FROZEN PEAKS TO MAKE THEIR WAY OUT... AND HOME.
UP... UP THEY CLIMB. THE GREAT STONES GROW COLDER TO THE TOUCH...
...WHICH ONLY STRENGTHENS TOR'S RESOLVE...
...TO CROSS THE MOUNTAINS THAT SEPARATE HIM FROM *HOME.*

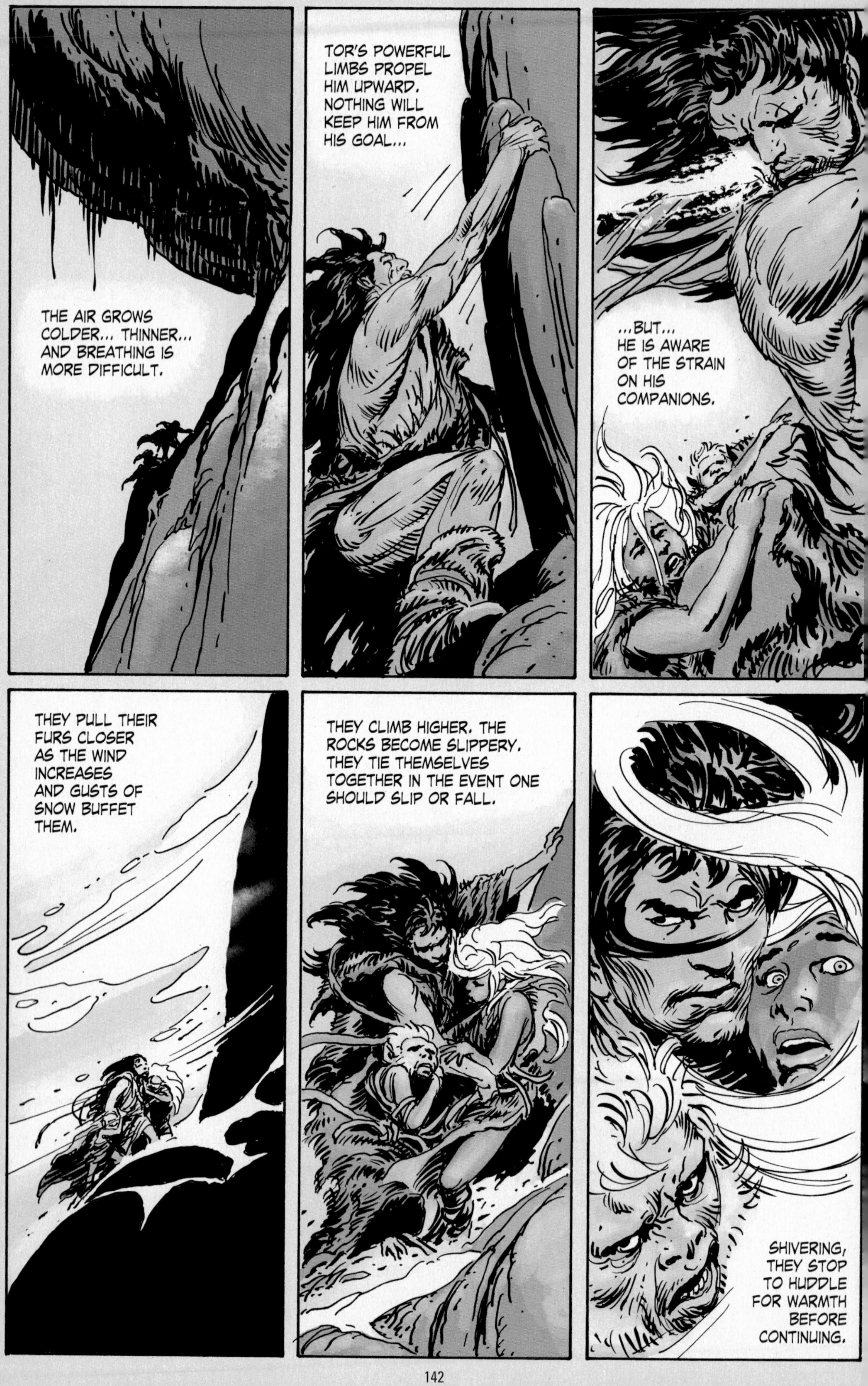
THE AIR GROWS COLDER... THINNER... AND BREATHING IS MORE DIFFICULT.
TOR'S POWERFUL LIMBS PROPEL HIM UPWARD. NOTHING WILL KEEP HIM FROM HIS GOAL...
...BUT... HE IS AWARE OF THE STRAIN ON HIS COMPANIONS.
THEY PULL THEIR FURS CLOSER AS THE WIND INCREASES AND GUSTS OF SNOW BUFFET THEM.
THEY CLIMB HIGHER. THE ROCKS BECOME SLIPPERY. THEY TIE THEMSELVES TOGETHER IN THE EVENT ONE SHOULD SLIP OR FALL.
SHIVERING, THEY STOP TO HUDDLE FOR WARMTH BEFORE CONTINUING.

...THE MOUNTAIN DID NOT LOOK SO HIGH... FROM THE GROUND BELOW.

AFTER A MOMENT TO REST THEY RESUME THEIR CLIMB. TOR WONDERS IN SILENCE, I– DID NOT KNOW...

IT SEEMED... NOT... SO COLD FROM THE WARM JUNGLE.

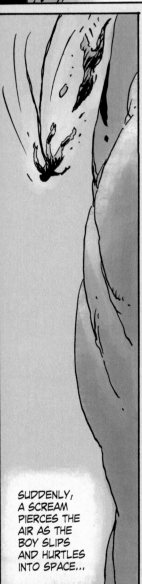

...HELD BY THE ROPE IN TOR'S TIGHT GRIP.

SUDDENLY, A SCREAM PIERCES THE AIR AS THE BOY SLIPS AND HURTLES INTO SPACE...

...AND IS SLAMMED WITH GREAT FORCE AGAINST THE FRIGID GRANITE...

...AGAIN AND AGAIN... LIKE A LIVING PENDULUM...

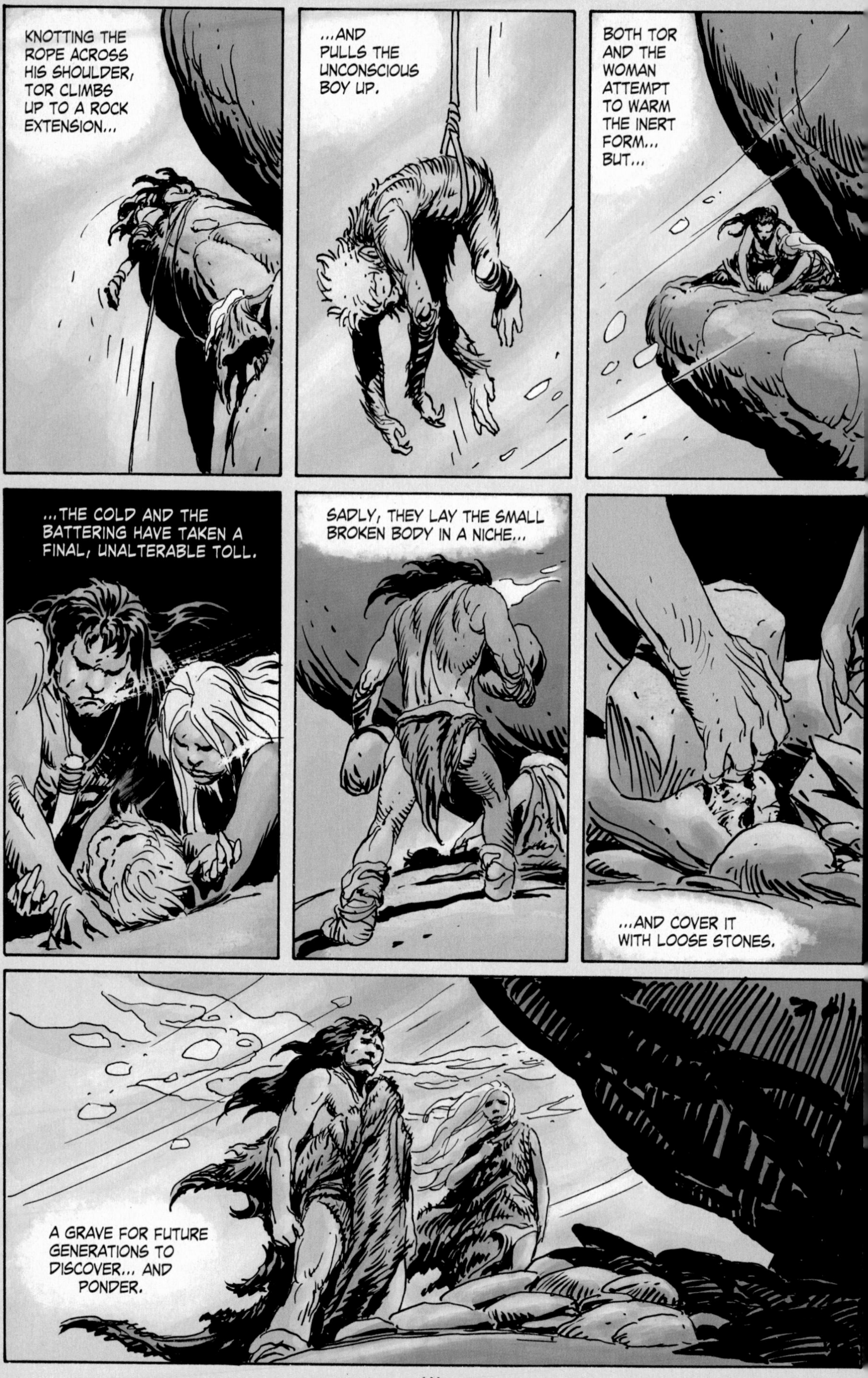
KNOTTING THE ROPE ACROSS HIS SHOULDER, TOR CLIMBS UP TO A ROCK EXTENSION...
...AND PULLS THE UNCONSCIOUS BOY UP.
BOTH TOR AND THE WOMAN ATTEMPT TO WARM THE INERT FORM... BUT...
...THE COLD AND THE BATTERING HAVE TAKEN A FINAL, UNALTERABLE TOLL.
SADLY, THEY LAY THE SMALL BROKEN BODY IN A NICHE...
...AND COVER IT WITH LOOSE STONES.
A GRAVE FOR FUTURE GENERATIONS TO DISCOVER... AND PONDER.

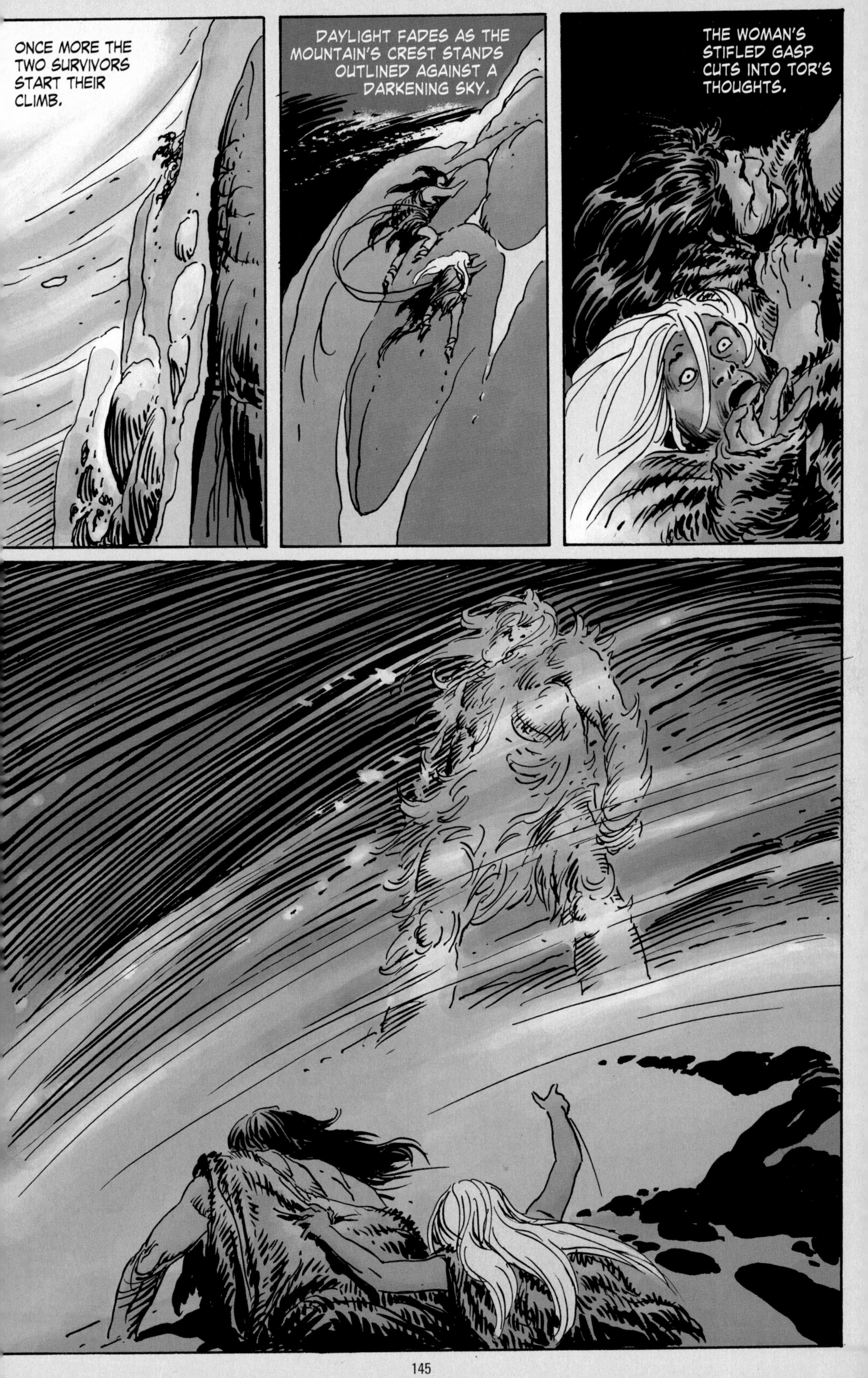
ONCE MORE THE TWO SURVIVORS START THEIR CLIMB.
DAYLIGHT FADES AS THE MOUNTAIN'S CREST STANDS OUTLINED AGAINST A DARKENING SKY.
THE WOMAN'S STIFLED GASP CUTS INTO TOR'S THOUGHTS.

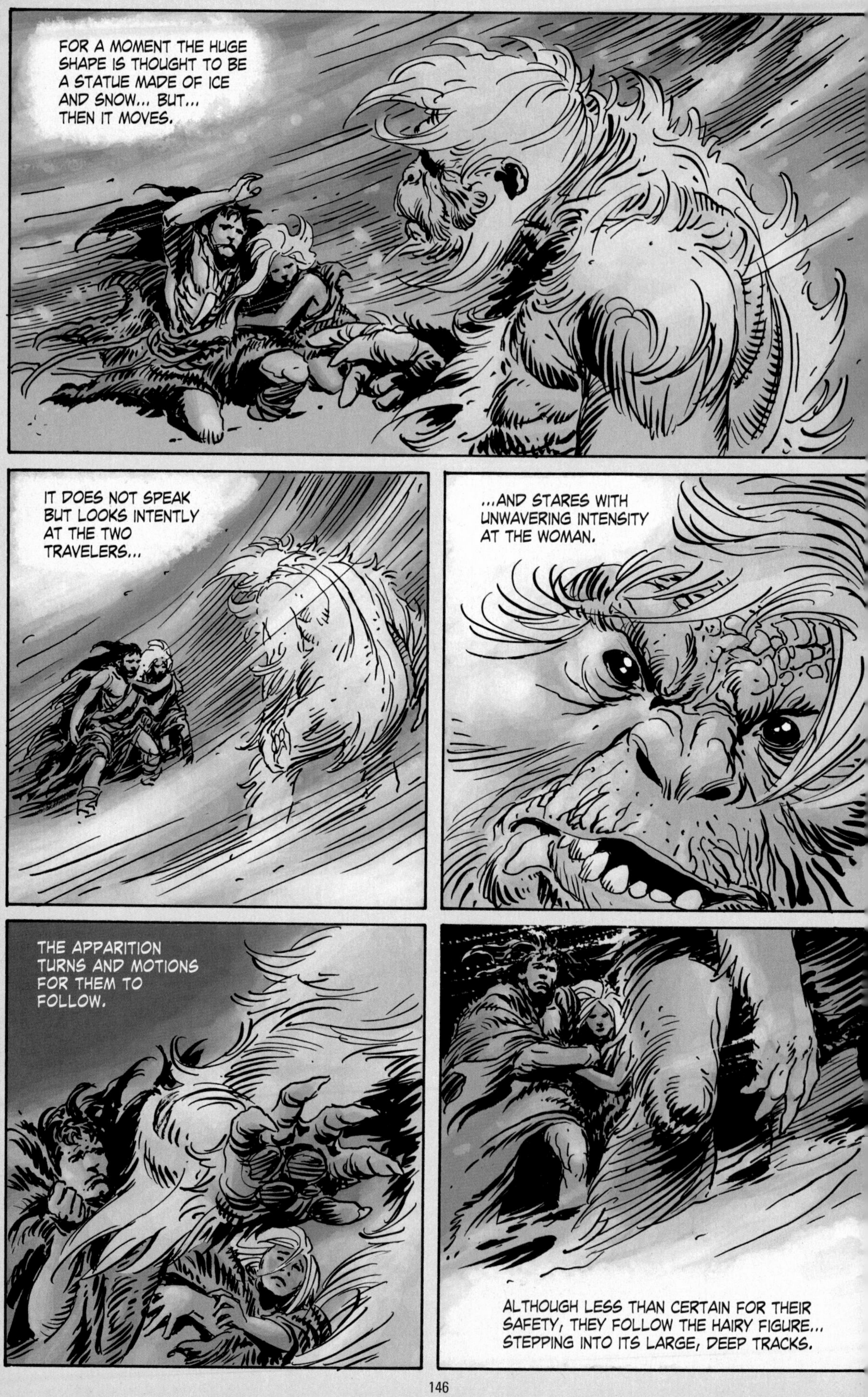
FOR A MOMENT THE HUGE SHAPE IS THOUGHT TO BE A STATUE MADE OF ICE AND SNOW... BUT... THEN IT MOVES.
IT DOES NOT SPEAK BUT LOOKS INTENTLY AT THE TWO TRAVELERS...
...AND STARES WITH UNWAVERING INTENSITY AT THE WOMAN.
THE APPARITION TURNS AND MOTIONS FOR THEM TO FOLLOW.
ALTHOUGH LESS THAN CERTAIN FOR THEIR SAFETY, THEY FOLLOW THE HAIRY FIGURE... STEPPING INTO ITS LARGE, DEEP TRACKS.

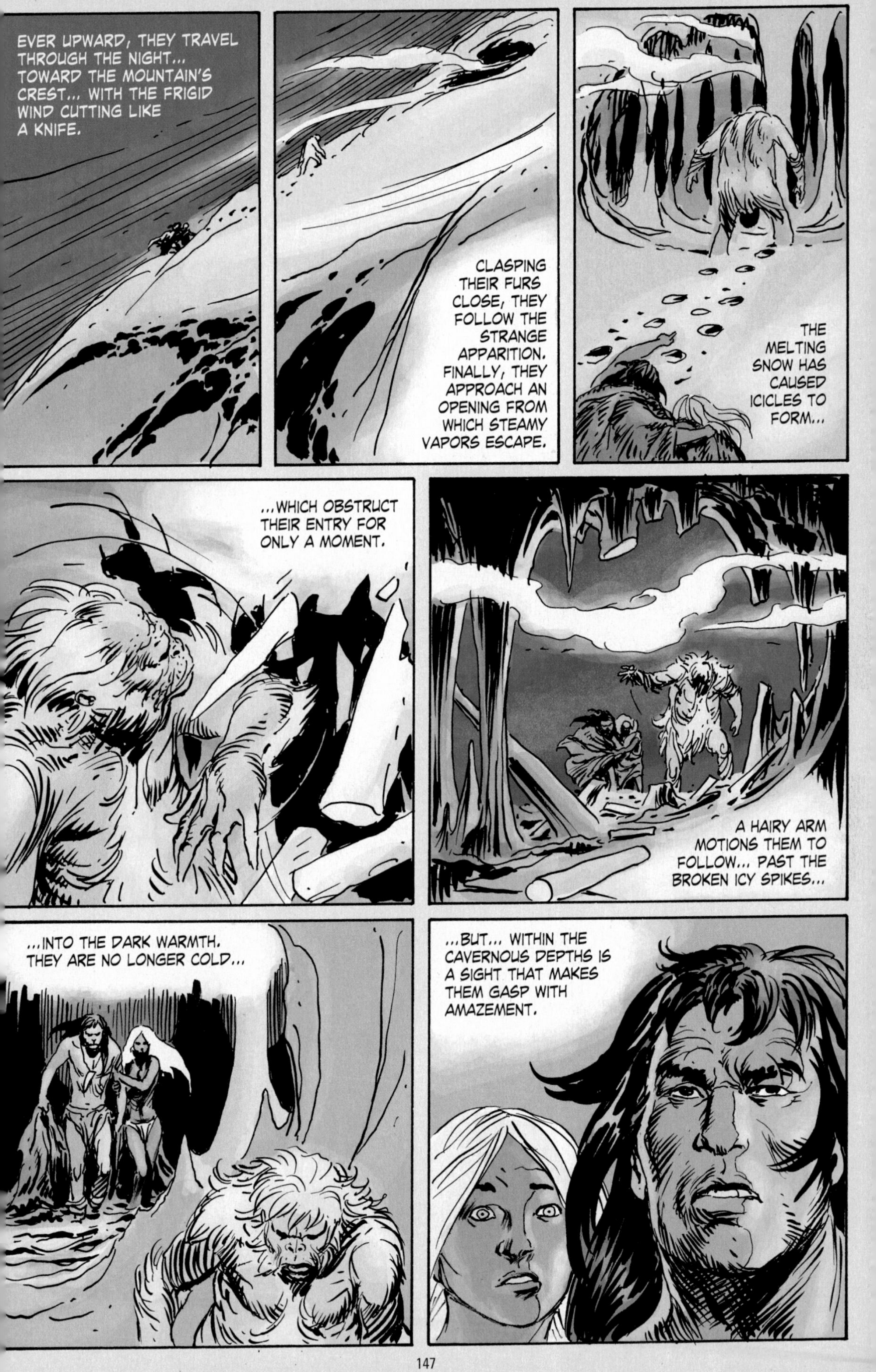
EVER UPWARD, THEY TRAVEL THROUGH THE NIGHT... TOWARD THE MOUNTAIN'S CREST... WITH THE FRIGID WIND CUTTING LIKE A KNIFE.
CLASPING THEIR FURS CLOSE, THEY FOLLOW THE STRANGE APPARITION. FINALLY, THEY APPROACH AN OPENING FROM WHICH STEAMY VAPORS ESCAPE.
THE MELTING SNOW HAS CAUSED ICICLES TO FORM...
...WHICH OBSTRUCT THEIR ENTRY FOR ONLY A MOMENT.
A HAIRY ARM MOTIONS THEM TO FOLLOW... PAST THE BROKEN ICY SPIKES...
...INTO THE DARK WARMTH. THEY ARE NO LONGER COLD...
...BUT... WITHIN THE CAVERNOUS DEPTHS IS A SIGHT THAT MAKES THEM GASP WITH AMAZEMENT.

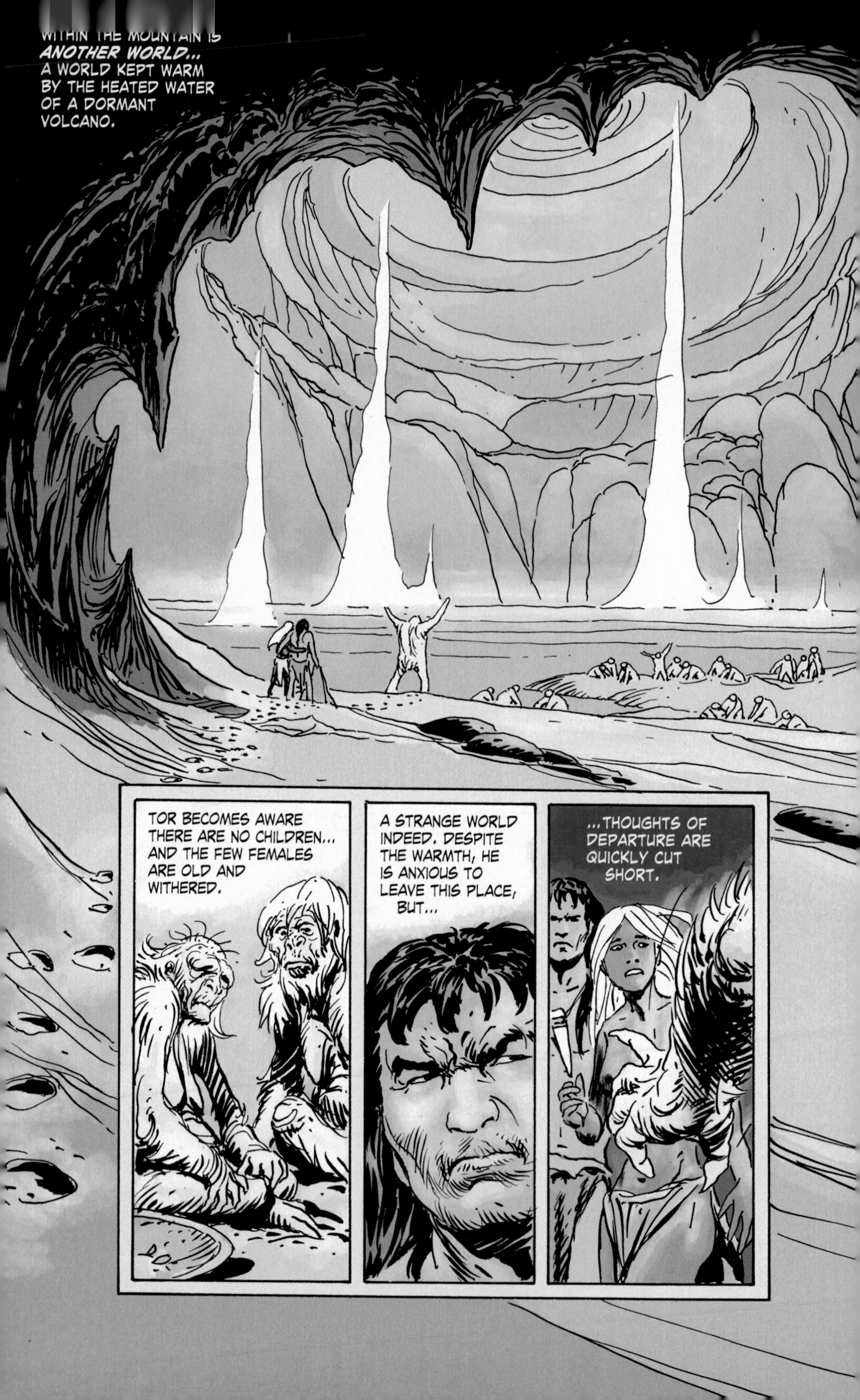
WITHIN THE MOUNTAIN IS ANOTHER WORLD... A WORLD KEPT WARM BY THE HEATED WATER OF A DORMANT VOLCANO.
TOR BECOMES AWARE THERE ARE NO CHILDREN... AND THE FEW FEMALES ARE OLD AND WITHERED.
A STRANGE WORLD INDEED. DESPITE THE WARMTH, HE IS ANXIOUS TO LEAVE THIS PLACE, BUT...
...THOUGHTS OF DEPARTURE ARE QUICKLY CUT SHORT.

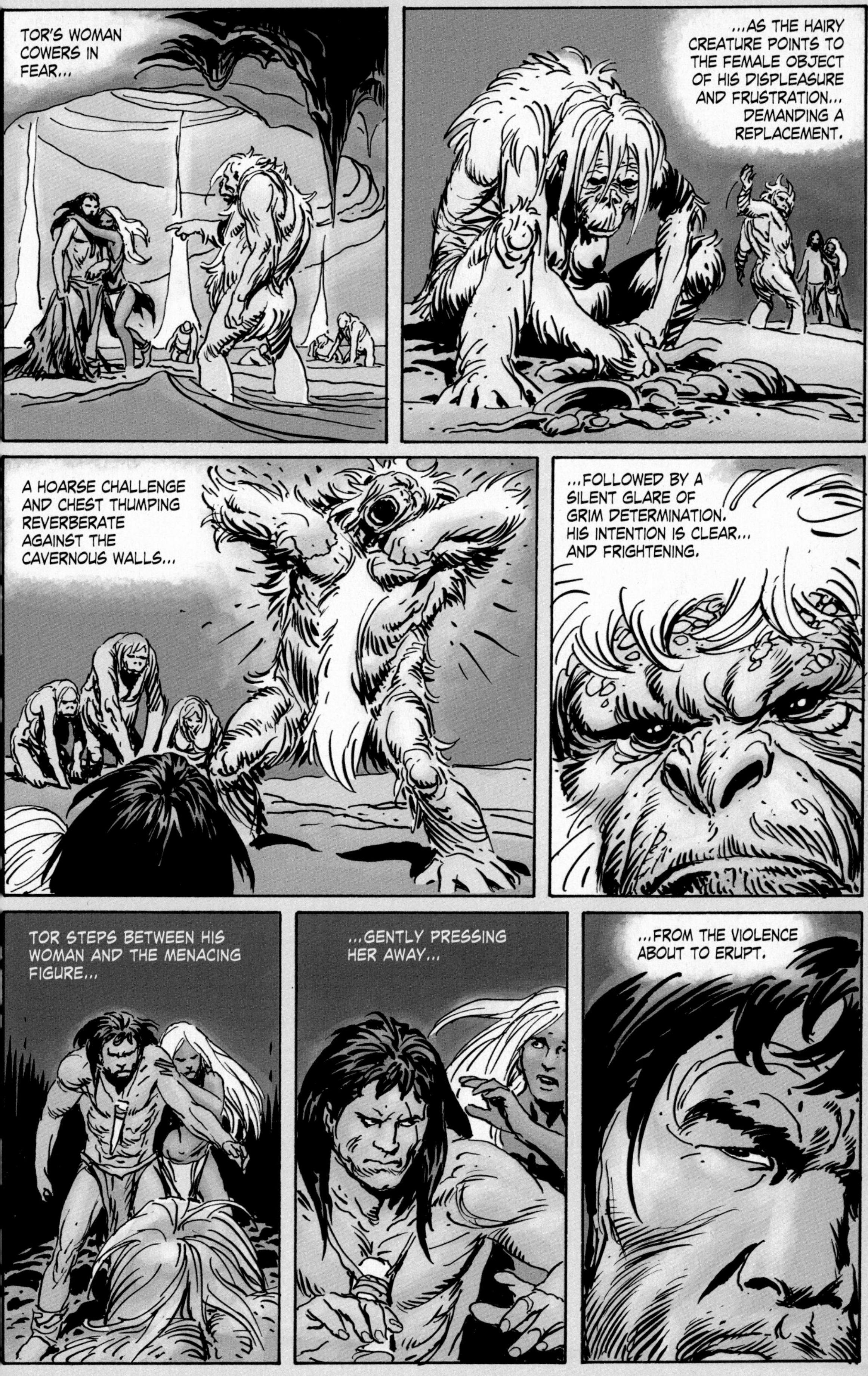
TOR'S WOMAN COWERS IN FEAR...
...AS THE HAIRY CREATURE POINTS TO THE FEMALE OBJECT OF HIS DISPLEASURE AND FRUSTRATION... DEMANDING A REPLACEMENT.
A HOARSE CHALLENGE AND CHEST THUMPING REVERBERATE AGAINST THE CAVERNOUS WALLS...
...FOLLOWED BY A SILENT GLARE OF GRIM DETERMINATION. HIS INTENTION IS CLEAR... AND FRIGHTENING.
TOR STEPS BETWEEN HIS WOMAN AND THE MENACING FIGURE...
...GENTLY PRESSING HER AWAY...
...FROM THE VIOLENCE ABOUT TO ERUPT.

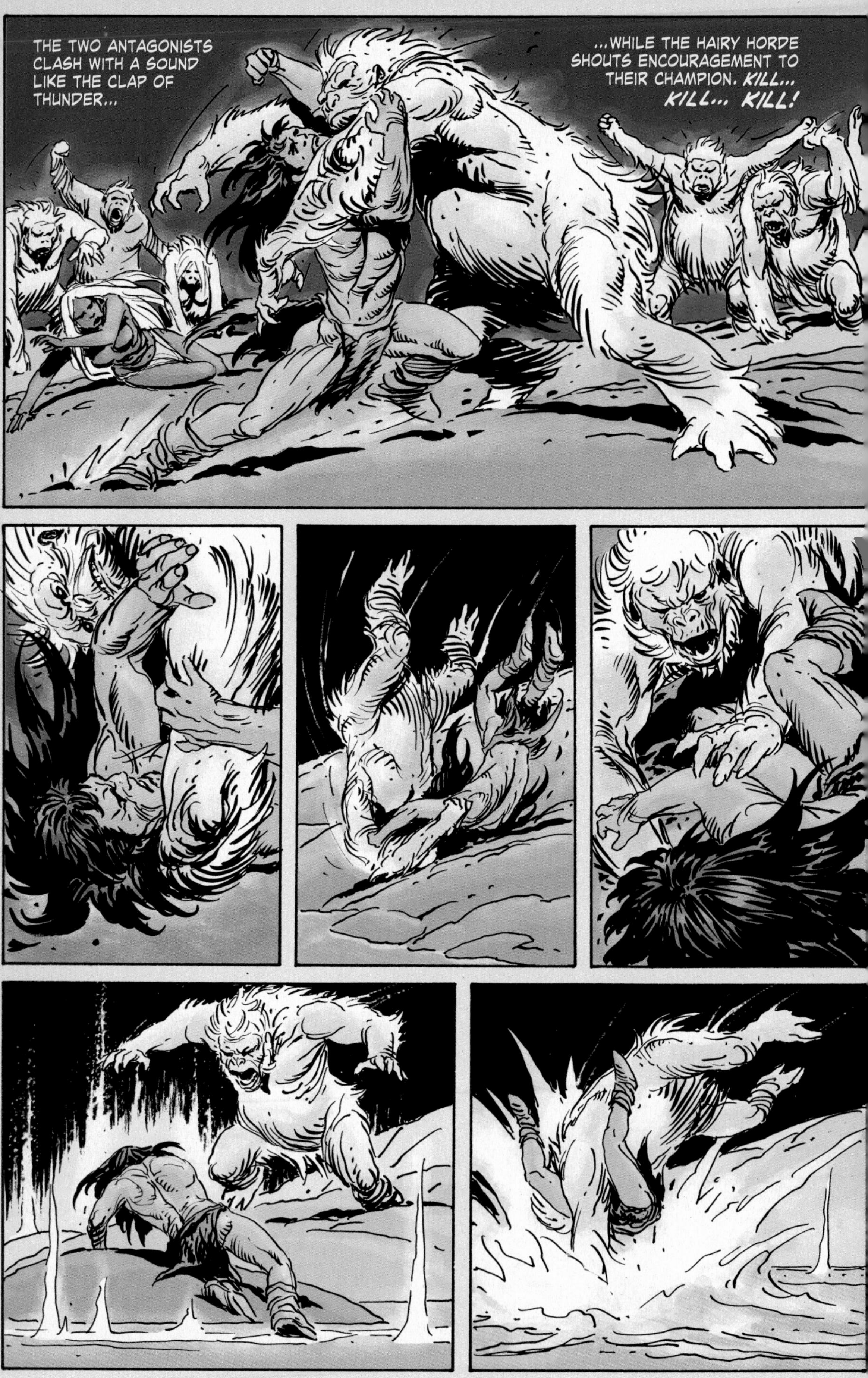
THE TWO ANTAGONISTS CLASH WITH A SOUND LIKE THE CLAP OF THUNDER...
...WHILE THE HAIRY HORDE SHOUTS ENCOURAGEMENT TO THEIR CHAMPION. KILL... KILL... KILL!

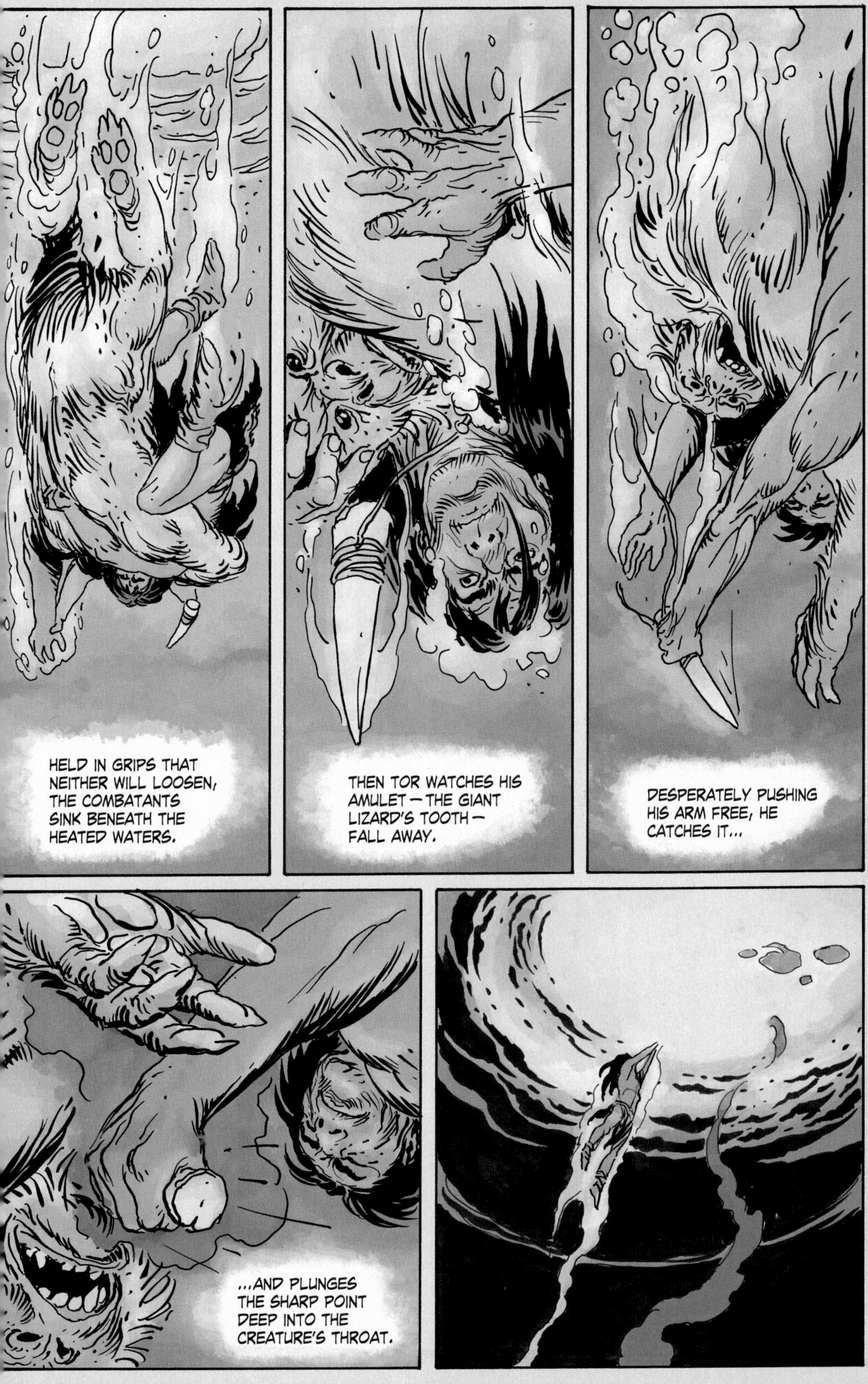
HELD IN GRIPS THAT NEITHER WILL LOOSEN, THE COMBATANTS SINK BENEATH THE HEATED WATERS.
THEN TOR WATCHES HIS AMULET — THE GIANT LIZARD'S TOOTH — FALL AWAY.
DESPERATELY PUSHING HIS ARM FREE, HE CATCHES IT...
...AND PLUNGES THE SHARP POINT DEEP INTO THE CREATURE'S THROAT.

GASPING FOR AIR, TOR SURFACES FROM THE BLOOD-TINTED WATERS.

HIS AUDIENCE IS SILENT AS HIS WOMAN RUNS TO JOIN HIM. STOLIDLY, HE REGARDS THE HAIRY ONES.

THE TWO DON THEIR CAST-OFF FURS AND WALK UNCHALLENGED FROM THE MOUNTAIN CAVE.

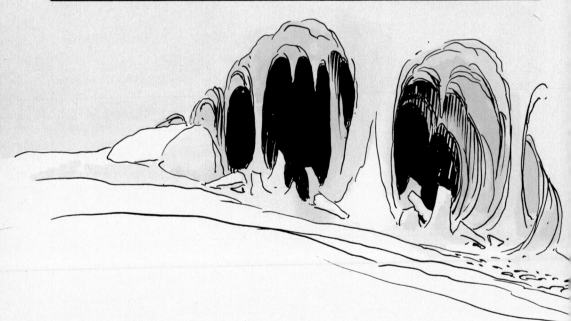

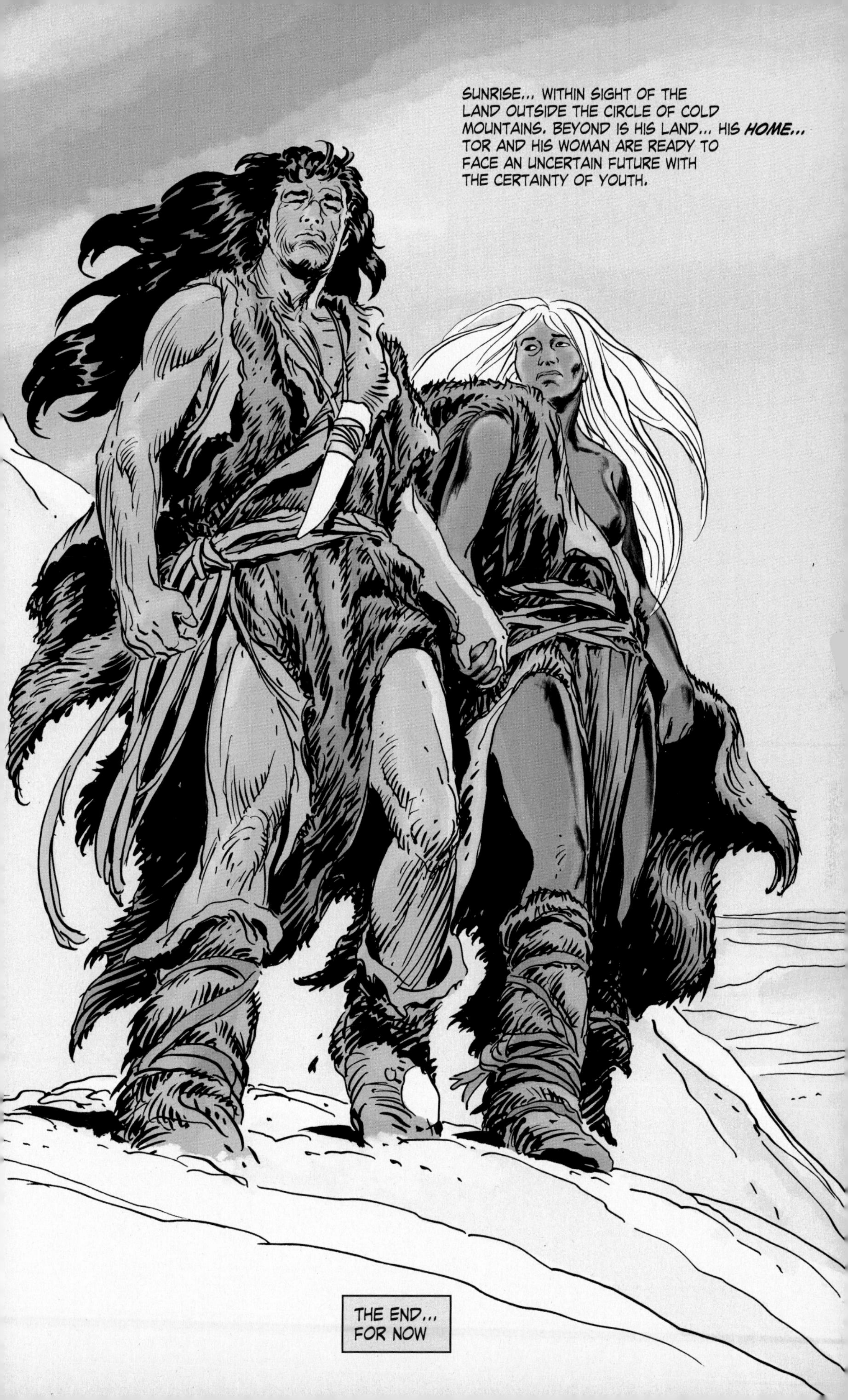
SUNRISE... WITHIN SIGHT OF THE LAND OUTSIDE THE CIRCLE OF COLD MOUNTAINS. BEYOND IS HIS LAND... HIS *HOME...* TOR AND HIS WOMAN ARE READY TO FACE AN UNCERTAIN FUTURE WITH THE CERTAINTY OF YOUTH.
THE END... FOR NOW

1.24.00

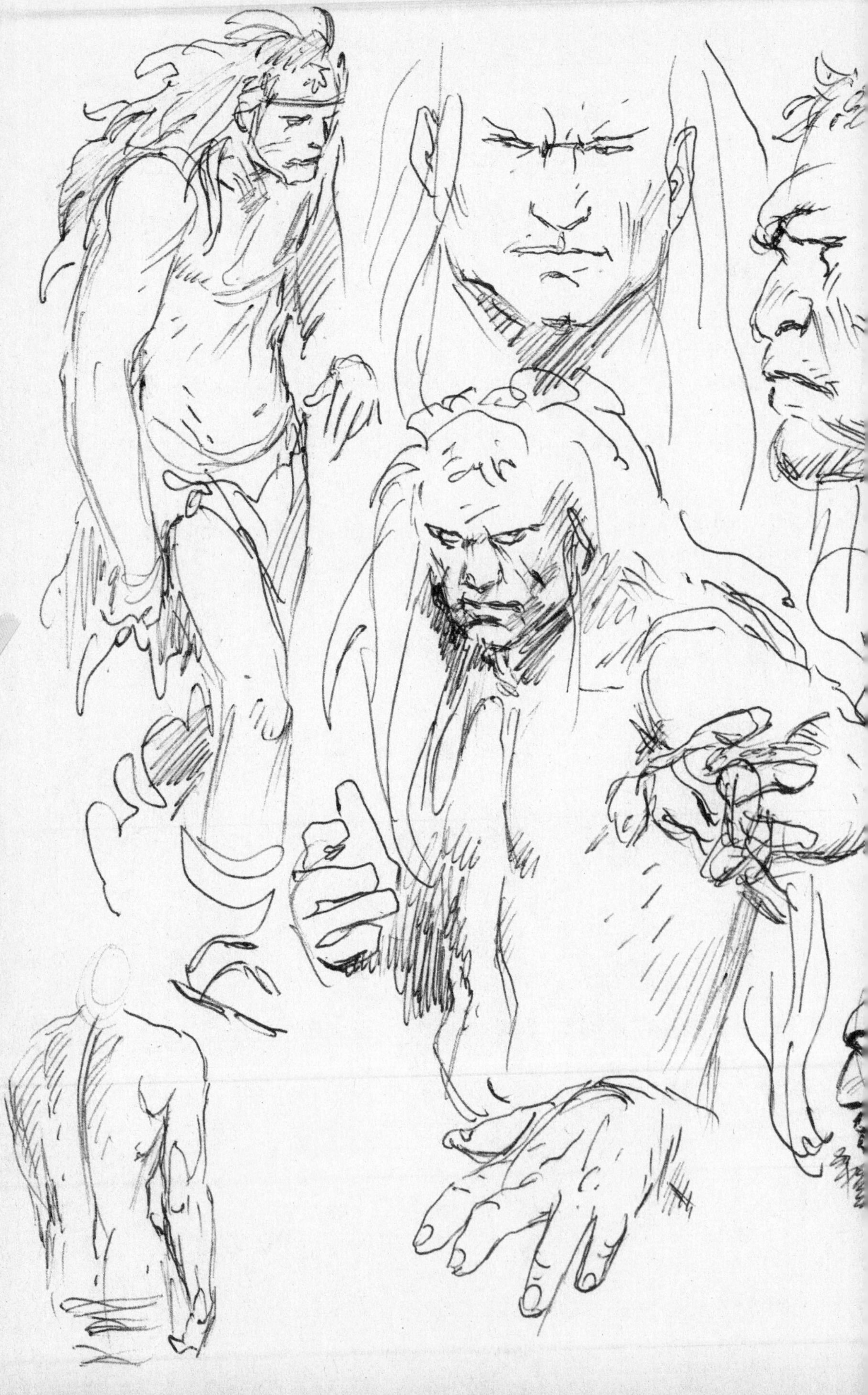

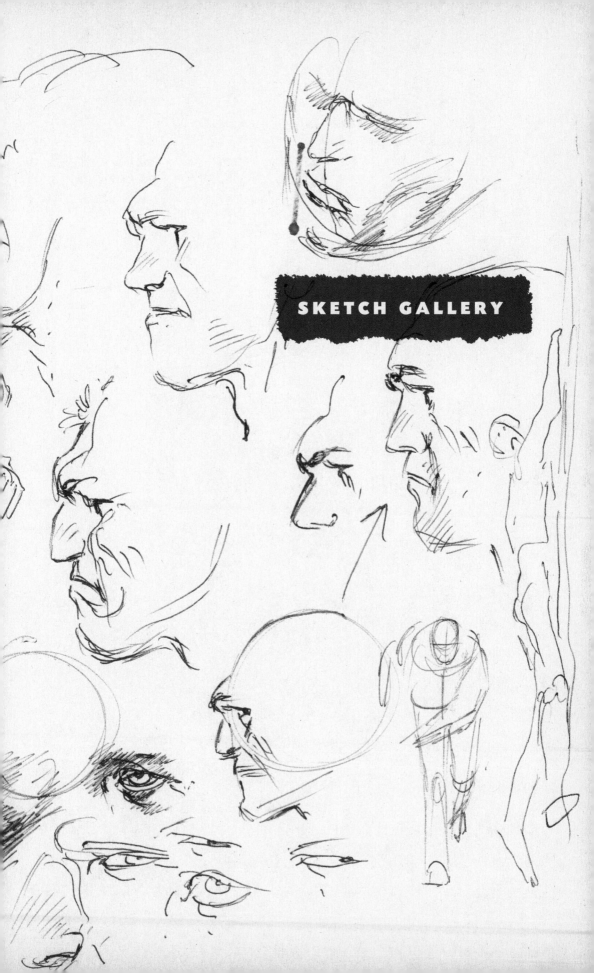

SKETCH GALLERY

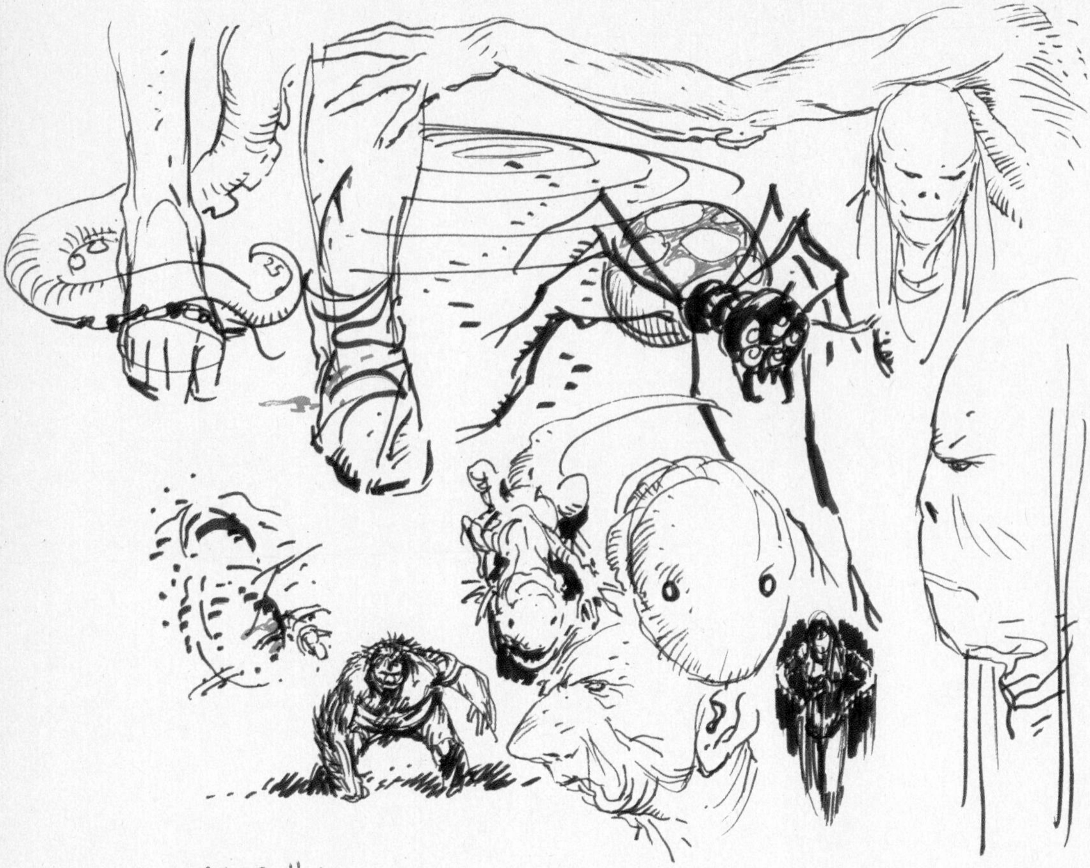

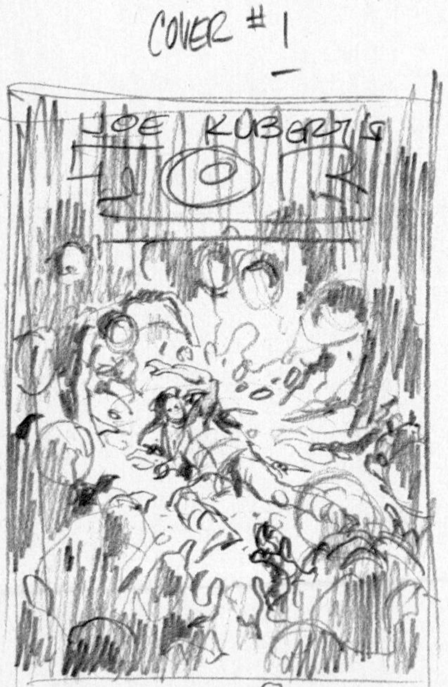
COVER # 1
JOE KUBERT'S
TOR

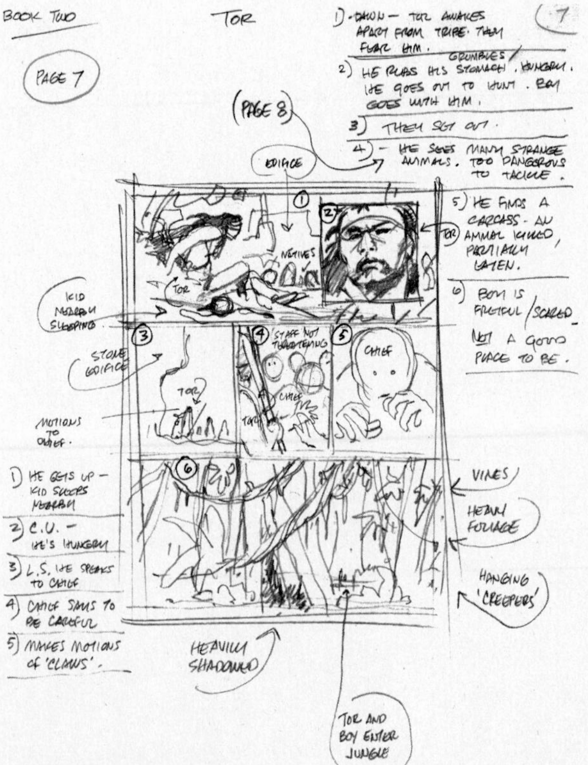
BOOK TWO
TOR
PAGE 7
7
1) DAWN – TOR AWAKES APART FROM TRIBE. THEY FEAR HIM.
2) HE RUBS HIS STOMACH. GRUMBLES / HUNGRY. HE GOES OUT TO HUNT. BOY GOES WITH HIM.
3) THEY SET OUT.
4) – HE SEES MANY STRANGE ANIMALS. TOO DANGEROUS TO TACKLE.
5) HE FINDS A CARCASS – AN ANIMAL KILLED, PARTIALLY EATEN.
6) BOY IS FRETFUL / SCARED – NOT A GOOD PLACE TO BE.
(PAGE 8)
EDIFICE
NATIVES
TOR
KID NEARBY SLEEPING
STONE EDIFICE
STAFF NOT THREATENING
CHIEF
MOTIONS TO CHIEF.
1) HE GETS UP – KID SLEEPS NEARBY
2) C.U. – HE'S HUNGRY
3) L.S. HE SPEAKS TO CHIEF
4) CHIEF SAYS TO BE CAREFUL
5) MAKES MOTIONS OF 'CLAWS'.
VINES
HEAVY FOLIAGE
HANGING 'CREEPERS'
HEAVILY SHADOWED
TOR AND BOY ENTER JUNGLE

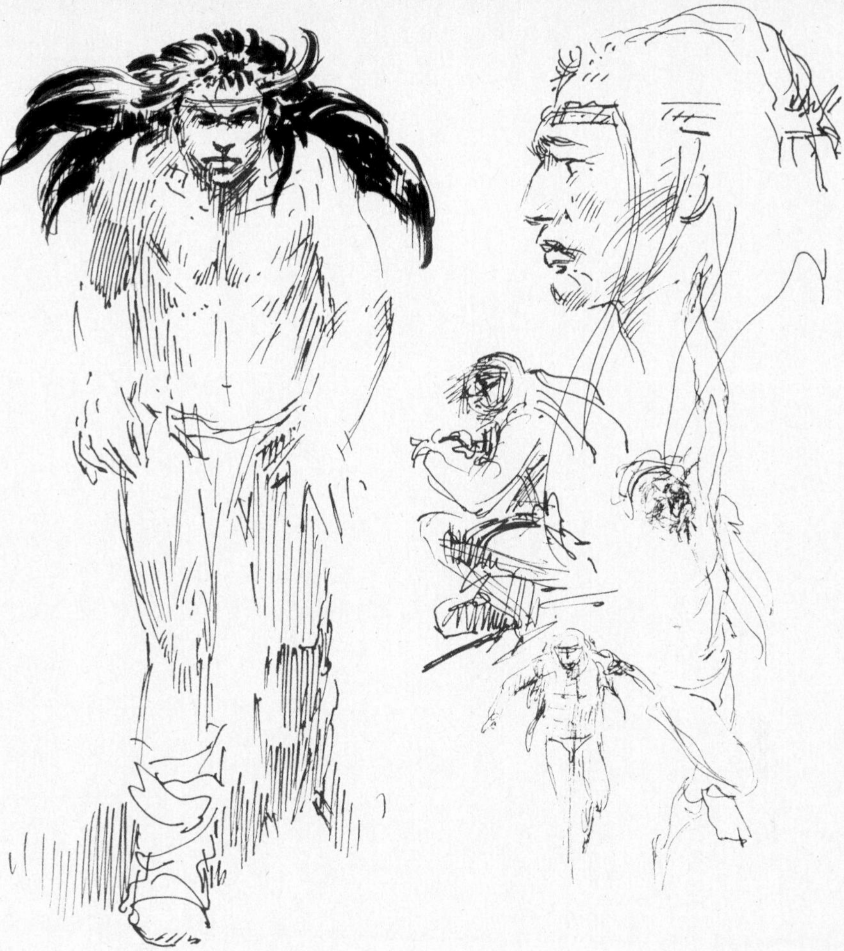

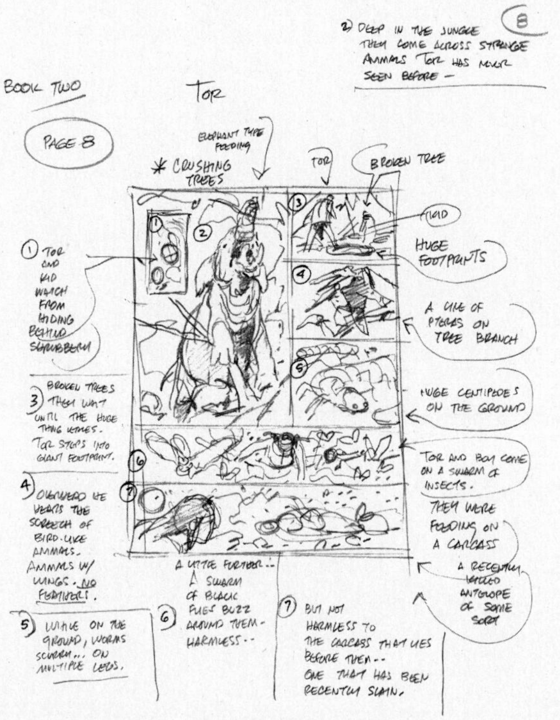
2) DEEP IN THE JUNGLE THEY COME ACROSS STRANGE ANIMALS TOR HAS NEVER SEEN BEFORE —
8
BOOK TWO
TOR
PAGE 8
ELEPHANT TYPE FEEDING
* CRUSHING TREES
TOR
BROKEN TREE
KID
HUGE FOOTPRINTS
A LINE OF PTERAS ON TREE BRANCH
HUGE CENTIPEDES ON THE GROUND
TOR AND BOY COME ON A SWARM OF INSECTS.
THEY WERE FEEDING ON A CARCASS
A RECENTLY KILLED ANTELOPE OF SOME SORT
1) TOR AND KID WATCH FROM HIDING BEHIND SHRUBBERY
3) BROKEN TREES THEY WAIT UNTIL THE HUGE THING LEAVES. TOR STEPS INTO GIANT FOOTPRINT.
4) OVERHEAD HE HEARS THE SCREECH OF BIRD-LIKE ANIMALS. ANIMALS W/ WINGS. NO FEATHERS.
5) WHILE ON THE GROUND, WORMS SCURRY... ON MULTIPLE LEGS.
A LITTLE FURTHER...
6) A SWARM OF BLACK FLIES BUZZ AROUND THEM. HARMLESS...
7) BUT NOT HARMLESS TO THE CARCASS THAT LIES BEFORE THEM... ONE THAT HAS BEEN RECENTLY SLAIN.

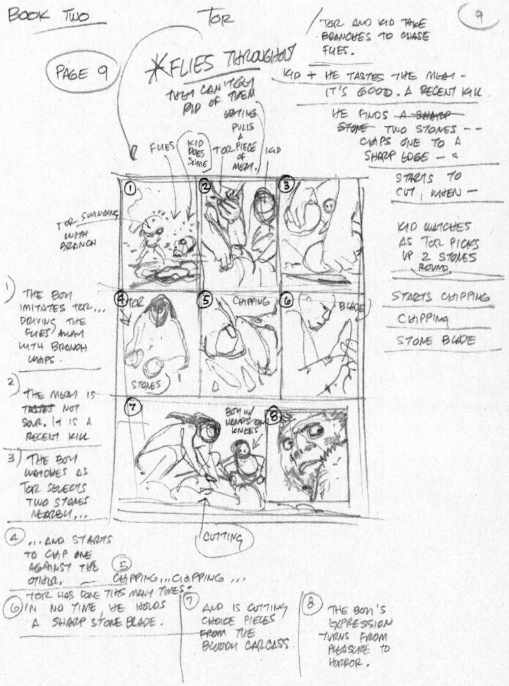
BOOK TWO
TOR
9
TOR AND KID TAKE BRANCHES TO CHASE FLIES.
PAGE 9
*FLIES THROUGHOUT
THEY CAN'T GET RID OF THEM
KID + HE TASTES THE MEAT — IT'S GOOD. A RECENT KILL
HE FINDS A SHARP STONE TWO STONES — CHIPS ONE TO A SHARP EDGE —
STARTS TO CUT, WHEN —
KID WATCHES AS TOR PICKS UP 2 STONES ROUND
STARTS CHIPPING
CHIPPING
STONE BLADE
FLIES
KID DOES SAME
TOR
EATING PULLS A PIECE OF MEAT.
KID
TOR SWINGING WITH BRANCH
TOR
STONES
CHIPPING
BLADE
BOY W/ HANDS ON KNEES
CUTTING
1) THE BOY IMITATES TOR... DRIVING THE FLIES AWAY WITH BRANCH WHIPS.
2) THE MEAT IS TASTES NOT SOUR. IT IS A RECENT KILL
3) THE BOY WATCHES AS TOR SELECTS TWO STONES NEARBY...
4) ...AND STARTS TO CHIP ONE AGAINST THE OTHER.
5) CHIPPING...CHIPPING...
TOR HAS DONE THIS MANY TIMES.
6) IN NO TIME HE HOLDS A SHARP STONE BLADE.
7) AND IS CUTTING CHOICE PIECES FROM THE BLOODY CARCASS.
8) THE BOY'S EXPRESSION TURNS FROM PLEASURE TO HORROR.

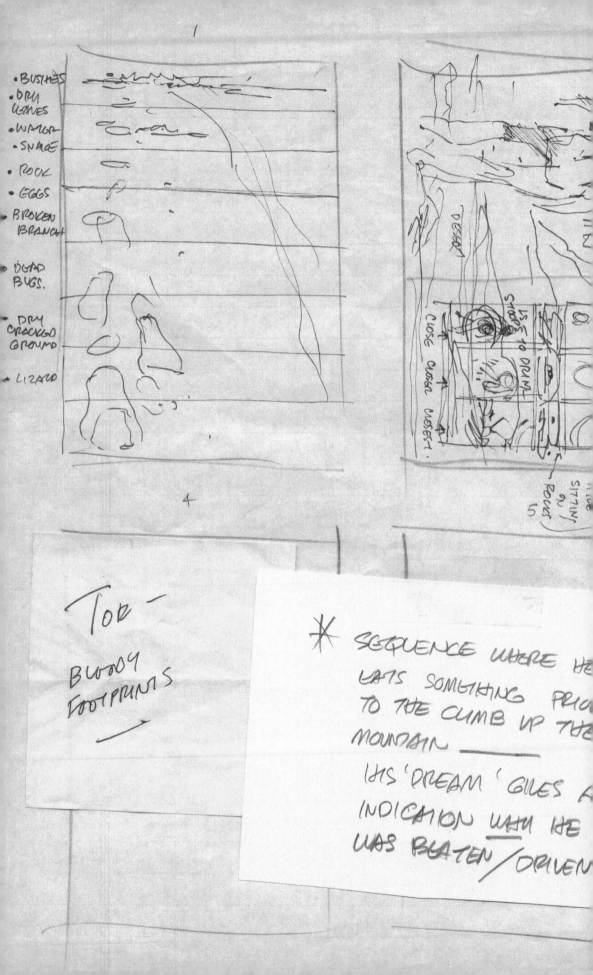

1

- BUSHES
- DRY LEAVES
- WATER
- SNAKE
- ROCK
- EGGS
- BROKEN BRANCH
- DEAD BUGS.
- DRY CRACKED GROUND
- LIZARD

DESERT

STARE TO DRINK

CLOSE CLOSER CLOSEST.

STILL SITTING (n ROCK)

4

5

TOP —

BLOODY FOOTPRINTS →

✳ SEQUENCE WHERE HE EATS SOMETHING PRIOR TO THE CLIMB UP THE MOUNTAIN ___

HIS 'DREAM' GIVES AN INDICATION WHY HE WAS BEATEN/DRIVEN

BOOK FIVE   TOR

PAGE ONE

TOR BEAT/SCARRED/EYES ALMOST CLOSED-

TOR'S ORIGINAL GROUP

HAIRY GUYS

4 ...AND HE IS STILL BEING STALKED BY THE TIGER HE HAD SLAIN.

TIGER

* TOR TO BE RENDERED — WASH ON GREY W/ FIGS HELD IN COLORS — OR

4 ARMS

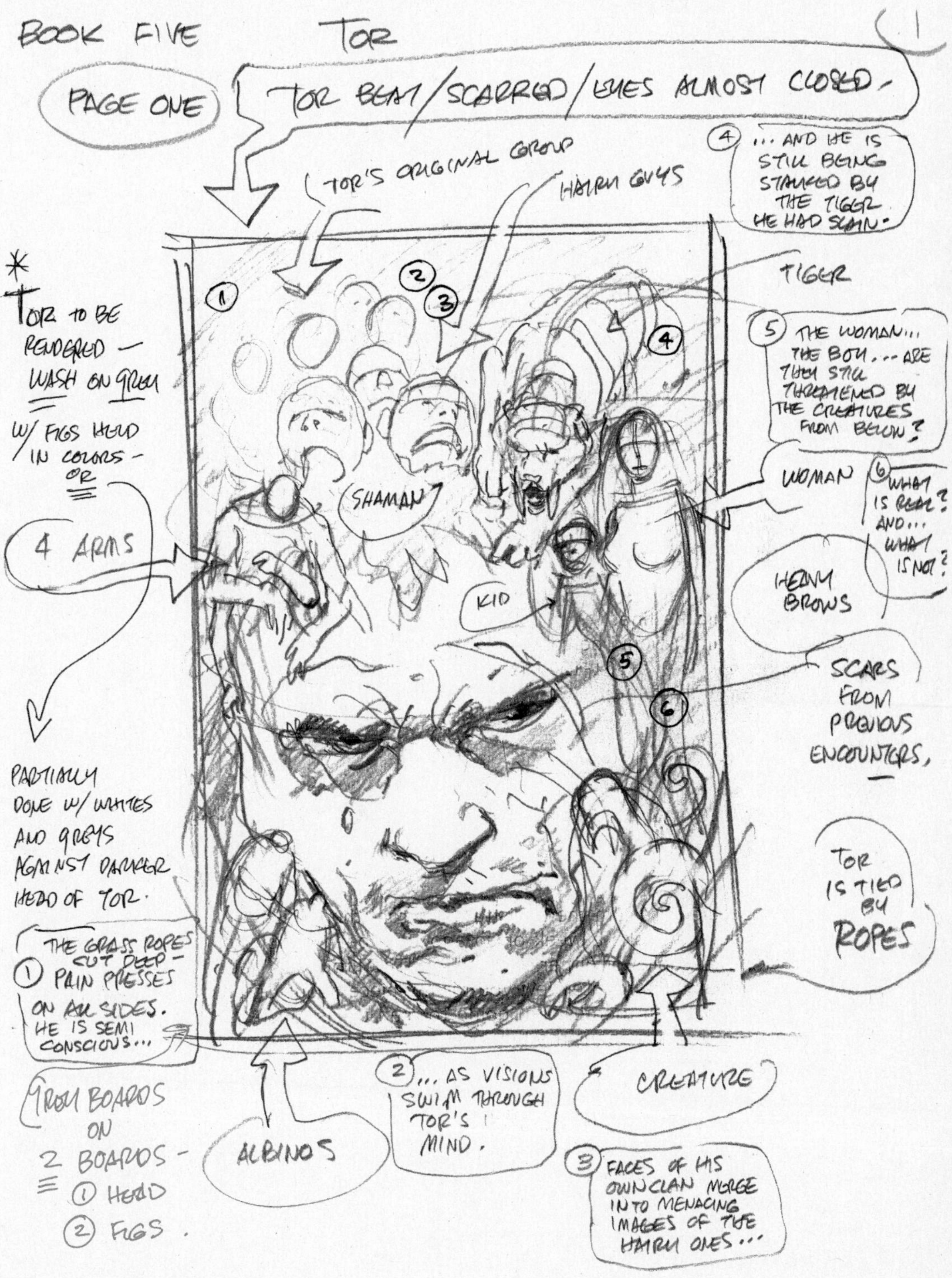

1
2
3
4
SHAMAN
KID
5
6

5 THE WOMAN... THE BOY... ARE THEY STILL THREATENED BY THE CREATURES FROM BELOW?

WOMAN

6 WHAT IS REAL? AND... WHAT IS NOT?

HEAVY BROWS

SCARS FROM PREVIOUS ENCOUNTERS.

PARTIALLY DONE W/ WHITES AND GREYS AGAINST DARKER HEAD OF TOR.

TOR IS TIED BY ROPES

1 THE GRASS ROPES CUT DEEP - PAIN PRESSES ON ALL SIDES. HE IS SEMI CONSCIOUS...

CREATURE

ALBINOS

2 ...AS VISIONS SWIM THROUGH TOR'S MIND.

3 FACES OF HIS OWN CLAN MERGE INTO MENACING IMAGES OF THE HAIRY ONES...

GREY BOARDS ON 2 BOARDS —
1 HEAD
2 FIGS.

J O E   K U B E R T

Born in 1926, Joe Kubert began his comics career at the age of eleven as an apprentice in Harry "A" Chesler's comic book production house. He has worked in the industry ever since, and in his more than sixty years in the field he has produced countless memorable stories for countless characters, including DC's Hawkman, Enemy Ace, Batman and the Flash. Kubert also edited, wrote and illustrated the DC title SGT. ROCK, which, beginning under its original title OUR ARMY AT WAR, he contributed to for thirty years.

In 1952, Kubert was a principal in the creation of the first 3-D comic book (*Three Dimension Comics* Vol. 1, No. 1), and his pioneering development of 3-D comics continued with the early appearances of what would become his best-known creation — a heroic caveman named Tor and his adventures "One Million Years Ago."

Kubert was also one of the first creators to embrace the long-form version of comics that became known as graphic novels, with his first two works in this medium being a graphic novel of Tor and the war adventure *Abraham Stone*. In 1996 he produced *Fax from Sarajevo*, a gripping graphic narrative that earned him accolades in the mainstream and trade press alike. He followed that success with two more historical graphic novels: *Yossel: April 19, 1943* (2003) and *Jew Gangster: A Father's Admonition* (2005).

Kubert has also been a pioneer in the realm of comics education. In 1976 he founded the first and only accredited school devoted solely to the art of cartoon graphics: The Joe Kubert School of Cartoon and Graphic Art in Dover, New Jersey, which has since produced many of today's leading cartoonists. Pursuing this educational path further, in 1998 he established a series of correspondence courses under the banner of Joe Kubert's World of Cartooning, and in 1999 his book *Superheroes: Joe Kubert's Wonderful World of Comics*, a guide to the art of creating powerful comic book characters, was published.

Kubert lives in New Jersey. Two of his five children, Adam and Andy, have also achieved great popularity as comic book artists.